Fountas & Pinnell

Leveled Literacy Intervention

Lesson Guide

VOLUME 2

LESSONS 31–70

Orange System

Irene C. Fountas

Gay Su Pinnell

Heinemann, Portsmouth, NH

Heinemann
361 Hanover Street
Portsmouth, NH 03801–3912
www.heinemann.com

Offices and agents throughout the world

ISBN-10: 0-325-01820-0
ISBN-13: 978-0-325-01820-1

Printed in Guangzhou, China
1109/11-81-09
16 15 14 13 12 11 10 09 NOR 3 4 5 6 7 8

LLI *Lesson Guide*, Orange System

SYSTEM **Orange**

NEW BOOK ***Playing Together***

GENRE **Narrative Nonfiction**

YOU WILL NEED

- Take-Home Book, *The Flower*
- *My Writing Book*
- Alphabet Linking Chart, enlarged version
- magnetic letter set

From the CD:
- Alphabet Linking Chart ✓
- Verbal Path ✓
- Letter Minibooks ✓
- Letters Made in Similar Ways document
- picture cards: *rock, rose, rug; goat, gum, girl; fox, four, fork*
- Lotto Game Board
- fold sheet
- Parent Letter

NEW BOOK
Playing Together, Level B

REREADING
Setting the Table, Level A

The Flower, Level A

Goals

- Connect words by the sound at the beginning.
- Use the Alphabet Linking Chart as a tool to connect to letters.
- Write the first letter of a word.
- Locate high-frequency words in continuous print.
- Use language structure as a source of information while reading.
- Use voice-print match and return sweep across two lines of text.
- Connect and talk about categories of words that indicate things children play with.
- Infer characters' feelings and motivations.
- Make personal connections with a text.

Analysis of New Book Characteristics

Playing Together, Level B

GENRE/FORM
- Narrative nonfiction

TEXT STRUCTURE
- Different kind of toy on each page
- No sequence
- Summary page labeled "toys" at the end

CONTENT
- Everyday activities
- Toys that will be familiar to most children

THEMES AND IDEAS
- Friendship
- Playing together

LANGUAGE AND LITERARY FEATURES
- NA

SENTENCE COMPLEXITY
- One seven-word simple sentence on every page
- Present tense
- Prepositional phrase
- Repeating pattern on every page with one variation (page 8—"play with *a*" rather than "play with *the*"

VOCABULARY
- Names of toys
- Pronoun: *we*

WORDS
- High-frequency words: *we, like, to, with, the, a*
- One-syllable words with one two-syllable word
- See the Word Analysis Charts in the *Program Guide* for specific words in each category.

ILLUSTRATIONS
- Photographs
- Close match between pictures and text

BOOK AND PRINT FEATURES
- Large font
- Ample space between words
- Two lines on each page of print
- Print on the left on a blank page; illustrations begin on the left page and spread over to the right, except for last page
- Periods

▸ Rereading Books

- *Setting the Table*, Level A
- *The Flower*, Level A

PROMPTING GUIDE 1
Refer to *Prompting Guide 1* as needed.

- Invite children to reread *Setting the Table* and *The Flower.*
- If needed, prompt for the use of language structure; e.g., "Try that again." and "Think what would sound right."

▸ Phonics/Word Work

- **PRINCIPLE** Hearing and saying beginning phonemes in words

"You can hear the first sound in a word."
"You can say a word to hear the first sound."

- Present children with picture cards in sets (one set at a time): (1) *rock, rose, rug;* (2) *goat, gum, girl;* (3) *fox, four, fork.*
- Demonstrate how to say the first sound of the pictured word, *rock,* and then the word: */r/ rock.*

My Writing Book

- Have the children choose one set of the picture cards you used to glue in *My Writing Book.* Tell children to write at the top of that page the first letter of the words pictured on the picture cards.
- Have children try writing a word they know that starts with the same letter as the first letter of the pictures that they glued into their writing books, for example, high-frequency words: *go, for.* Children may also attempt to write a CVC word. (Suggestions: *run, gum, get, fun.*) If children have difficulty with the vowel, just write it in and say its name.

Alphabet Linking Chart

- Have children say the first sound of each picture in the three-picture set. Then, have them find the first letter of the pictured item on the corresponding box on the enlarged Alphabet Linking Chart (or on their small versions).

▸ New Book

Playing Together, Level B

Introducing the Text

- Introduce children to the book by talking about how they play with their friends. Suggested language: "The name of this book is *Playing Together*. When you play together with your friends, what are some of the toys you like to play with? In this book, the children tell all the things they like to play with when they play together."
- "Turn to pages 2 and 3. On these pages what do the children like to play with? Yes, so they say, 'We like to play with the blocks.' Can you say that?"
- "Now turn to pages 4 and 5. Now, what do the children say they like to play with? Say the word *like*. What letter would come first in the word *like?* Find the word like and put your finger under it. Get a good look and say the word. Repeat for pages 10 and 11 and the last page. Have the children say and locate with.
- "Turn back to the beginning of the book and read about the toys the children say they like to play with when they play together."

PROMPTING GUIDE 1
Refer to *Prompting Guide 1* as needed.

Reading the Text

- As the children read, be sure they are returning to the left to start to read a new line of text.
- If needed, prompt for use of the language structure (searching for and using information), e.g., "What do the children say they want to play with now?"

Discussing and Revisiting the Text

Invite children to talk about the things the children liked to play with. Some key understandings children may express are:

- The children like to play with many different toys. [Extend by asking for examples. Have children turn to the pages that show their examples.]
- The children in the book are friends. [Extend by asking the children why they think this, e.g., they enjoy playing together.]
- This book makes me think of ________________. (Children can make connections to their personal experiences or other books that they have read.)

PROMPTING GUIDE 1
Refer to *Prompting Guide 1* as needed.

Teaching Points

- Based on your observations, use *Prompting Guide 1* to select a teaching point that will be most helpful to the readers.
- You may want to have the children locate a few easy high-frequency words quickly, e.g., *like, to, we, the.*

- Play Lotto with picture cards (see *Lesson Resources CD* for Lotto cards, picture cards, and directions).
- Present children with a Lotto card. Have each child read the names of objects pictured on his card.
- Then hold up a picture card and say its name. The player who has an object starting with the same sound gets the picture card and puts it over the picture on the Lotto card. The first player to cover all the boxes on his Lotto card wins.

Letter Minibooks

- If time allows, have children read some of the Letter Minibooks. Choose letters with which children need more practice. Have children run a finger over the letter on the cover, using the Verbal Path (see *Lesson Resources CD*). Then, have them read each page, thinking about the beginning sound.

Letter Sort

- Alternatively, have the children sort magnetic letters in two or three ways (see Instructional Routines, Ways to Sort and Match Letters, in the *Program Guide*).

Classroom Connection

- Give children the fold sheet with the three-way sort printed on it along with the sheet of picture cards for *bear, banana, bat, box, bird, hat, horse, heart, hook, helicopter, moon, mouse, mitten , motorcycle, monkey* (see *Lesson Resources CD*).
- Have children cut and sort pictures into three separate categories by beginning sounds and then glue the pictures onto their sort sheets.
- Give children the Take-Home Book *The Flower* to reread.

Home/School Connection

- Have the children take home their fold sheets to share with their families.
- Have children take home the Take-Home Book *The Flower* to read to their families.

Assessing Reading and Writing Behaviors

Observe to find evidence that children can:

- quickly connect words by the sound at the beginning.
- use the Alphabet Linking Chart as a tool.
- demonstrate voice-print match across two lines of text.
- return to the left margin to begin reading the second line of print.
- cross-check two different kinds of information.
- infer characters' feelings and emotions.
- understand the category of toys.

Supporting English Language Learners

To support English language learners, you can:

- **continue** to monitor for understanding of the concept of *first sound* and *first letter.*
- **use** picture cards for words that are in children's vocabularies or go over the pictures enough to help them understand the words.
- **provide** some extra explanation or demonstration to assure that children understand that the text is a sequence of actions.
- **use** the language of the text in a conversational way and have children repeat the language several times to help them remember the syntax.
- **go over** the labels to be sure they understand their meaning.
- **help** children in discussing the text by thinking aloud or making wondering statements about how the children have many toys to share together, how the children feel about playing together with the toys, and sharing their own experiences with playing together with friends.
- **help** children in constructing a syntactically correct sentence. Ask them to repeat the sentence with you several times.
- **demonstrate** saying words slowly.

Professional Development Links

When Readers Struggle: Teaching that Works
Chapter 13: Extending Reading Power: Writing to Read. Use this chapter to understand the role of writing in learning to read and building understanding.

Professional Development and Tutorial DVD, Orange System
View the Analysis section of the Tutorial DVD. Think about Searching for and Using Information as an important processing system. Reflect on evidence from your children in this area from your recent notes and Reading Record forms.

Guided Reading: Good First Teaching for All Children
Chapters 1 and 7 (pp. 5–6 and 92–93).
Teaching for Comprehending and Fluency: Thinking, Talking, and Writing About Reading, K–8
Chapter 2 (pp. 20–21). Use these chapters to explore the role of structure/syntax in reading.

LESSON 32 LEVEL B

SYSTEM **Orange**
NEW BOOK ***Polly***
GENRE **Fiction**

YOU WILL NEED

- Take-Home Book, *Playing Together*
- *My Writing Book*
- magnetic letter set

From the CD:

- Verbal Path ✓
- Letter Minibooks ✓
- Lotto cards
- picture card set for Lotto
- Recording Form for *Playing Together*
- fold sheet
- Parent Letter

NEW BOOK
Polly, Level A

REREADING
The Flower, Level A

Playing Together, Level B

Goals

- Make words by taking away the first letter and putting another letter in its place.
- Recognize and use simple phonograms with a VC pattern.
- Check words by looking at them from left to right.
- Match words by thinking about the beginning consonant sound.
- Read with voice-print match, self-monitoring, and self-correction behavior.
- Use language structure, meaning, and visual information while reading.
- Write left to right with good spacing between words.
- Start a sentence with an uppercase letter and write end punctuation.
- Write several high-frequency words quickly.
- Understand cause-and-effect in the story (Polly getting fatter from eating).
- Think about the story using the illustration on the cover.
- Understand that everything on the hat is disappearing because Polly likes to eat them.

Analysis of New Book Characteristics

Polly, Level A

GENRE/FORM

- Fiction

TEXT STRUCTURE

- Different kind of food or other object on each page
- Implied sequence as Polly eats each thing from the hat
- Concludes with everything on the hat being consumed

CONTENT

- Humorous situation
- Parrot eating all kinds of things
- Objects that will be familiar to most children

THEMES AND IDEAS

- Mischievous animal
- Silly situation

LANGUAGE AND LITERARY FEATURES

- Foreshadowing of problem on front cover
- Eight brief easy-to-understand episodes
- Surprise ending
- Character with a name

SENTENCE COMPLEXITY

- One four-word simple sentence on every page
- Present tense
- Repeating pattern on every page with no variation

VOCABULARY

- Names of food and other objects

WORDS

- High-frequency words: *likes, the, she*
- Pronouns
- One-syllable words with some two-syllable and three-syllable words
- See the Word Analysis Charts in the *Program Guide* for specific words in each category.

ILLUSTRATIONS

- Humorous drawings
- Close match between pictures and text
- Story line implied by illustrations

BOOK AND PRINT FEATURES

- Large font
- Ample space between words
- One line on each page of print
- Print on the left on a blank page; illustrations on the right page, except for last page
- Periods and exclamation point

▸ Rereading Books and Assessment

- *The Flower*, Level A
- *Playing Together*, Level B

PROMPTING GUIDE 1
Refer to *Prompting Guide 1* as needed.

- Listen to one child read *Playing Together* as you code the reading behavior on the Recording Form, have a brief comprehension conversation, and make a teaching point that you think will be most helpful to the reader. Score and analyze the Reading Record following the lesson.
- Have the other children reread *The Flower* and then *Playing Together.*
- If needed, prompt for the use of language structure and meaning; e.g., "Would ___make sense?" "Would ___sound right in the sentence?"

▸ Phonics/Word Work

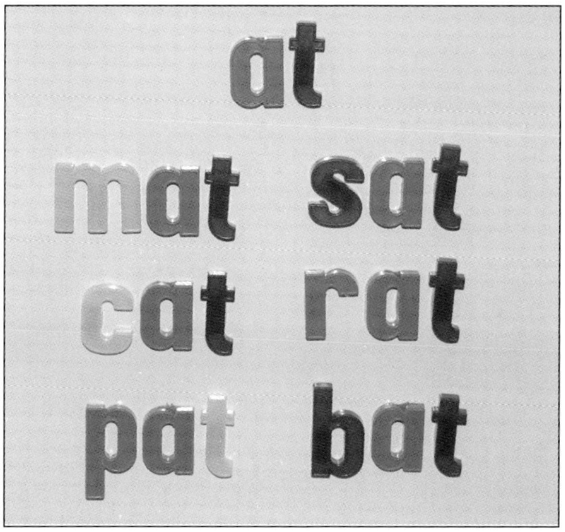

- **PRINCIPLE** Recognizing and using simple phonograms with a VC pattern (easiest): *-ad, -ag, -an, -am, -at, -ed, -en, -et, -ig, -in, -it, -og, -op, -ot, -ut*

"You can make new words by putting a letter before the word part or pattern."

- Place *-at* on the board with magnetic letters. Ask children what they know about these letters. They may say the letter names, say the word *at*, or say it is a pattern. [Suggested language: "Yes, all of those things are right. This is the word *at* but it is also a pattern that we can use to make a new word."]
- Place *b* at the beginning of the word and run your finger under it. Ask the children to say the first sound and then the sound of *at: b-at.* Ask them to read the word smoothly.
- Continue to have children make words by taking away the first letter and putting another letter in first place. Make *sat, mat, cat, rat,* and *pat.* Make *bat* again.
- Give the children magnetic letters: *a, t, s, m, c, r, p, b.* Have them make *at* and keep it still, but put new letters at the beginning to make a word as you say it. Then have children say the word and check it by running a finger under the word from left to right.

▸ Writing About Reading

Dictated Writing

- **MY WRITING BOOK**
- **PROMPTING GUIDE 1**

Refer to *Prompting Guide 1* as needed.

- If time allows, you may want to begin by having each child read recent pages from *My Writing Book*. Occasionally ask the child to locate a word in a sentence read.
- Dictate the following sentence and have children write it in their writing books:

    We like to play with blocks.

- The children should be able to write the easy high-frequency words such as *we, to, the*. Offer help as needed.
- Use sound boxes for the three sounds of *play* and *like* on a chart that all children can see (see Instructional Routines, Sound Boxes, in the *Program Guide*). After the children identify the three sounds in sequence, add the missing letters.
- Children should be able to start the last word (*blocks*), then you should write the rest of the word for children to copy from the whiteboard.

▸ New Book

Polly,
Level A

Introducing the Text

- Introduce children to the book by showing the cover. Suggested language: "Look at the big bird on the cover of this book. Do you know what kind of bird it is?"
- "Well, this bird is a parrot named Polly. Polly likes the things on this woman's big hat. What are some of those things that make her hat so pretty? Yes, Polly likes all of those beautiful things. The woman put her hat on the table and Polly sits on the hat. Polly likes all of the things on the big hat."
- "Turn to pages 2 and 3 to see what else Polly likes. Yes, she likes the banana. So what do you think Polly does with it?" Repeat for page 6 and have the children say and locate likes.
- "Now turn to pages 12 and 13 to see what Polly likes. Yes, she likes the corn. Find she and put your finger under it. Get a good look and say *she*. It has an uppercase *S* because it starts the sentence. Do you notice something about Polly? Yes, she is getting quite fat. I wonder why."
- "Well, you can read the story from the beginning to see what happens."

PROMPTING GUIDE 1
Refer to *Prompting Guide 1* as needed.

Reading the Text

- As the children read, notice their use of language structure, e.g., the use of the *s* on *likes*.
- Be sure children use picture information to support the processing of the print.

Discussing and Revisiting the Text

Invite the children to talk about what happens to the bird and the lady's hat. Some key understandings children may express are:

- Polly eats all the food on the lady's hat. [Extend by asking for examples from the story. Encourage children to use the pictures to show these examples.]
- The lady is surprised when she sees her hat without any food on it. [Extend by asking for supporting evidence from the pictures.]
- Next, the lady will __________. [Encourage any reasonable predictions such as scold the bird.]

PROMPTING GUIDE 1
Refer to *Prompting Guide 1* as needed.

Teaching Points

- Based on your observations, use *Prompting Guide 1* to select a teaching point that will be most helpful to the readers.
- You may want to have the children quickly locate a few easy high-frequency words, e.g., *like, to, we, the.*
- You may want children to quickly write these high-frequency words on a whiteboard a few times.
- Revisit the story to reinforce effective self-monitoring and the use of different kinds of information, e.g., "You noticed that wasn't right" or "Does it look right?"

▸ Optional Letter/ Word Work

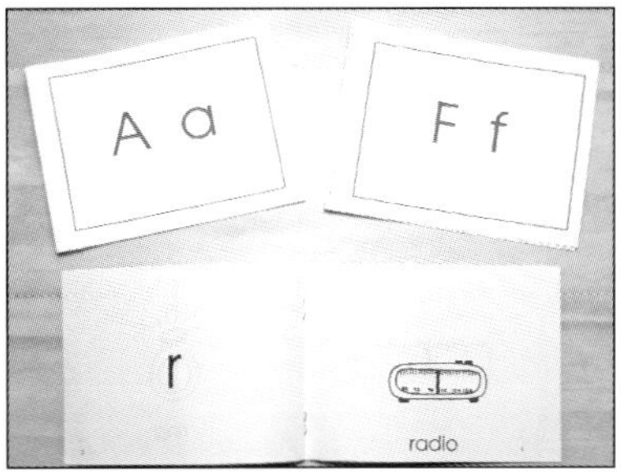

- Give children several Letter Minibooks to read. Choose letters with which children need more practice. Have them run a finger over the letter on the cover, using the Verbal Path. Then, have children read each page, thinking about the beginning sound of the letter. Have the children take home Letter Minibooks that are familiar to them.

Lotto

- Play Lotto with picture cards. Have each child first read the names of objects on his Lotto card.
- Then hold up a picture card and say its name. The player who has an object starting with the same sound gets the picture and puts it over the picture on the Lotto card. The first player to cover all the pictures on his Lotto card wins.

Classroom Connection

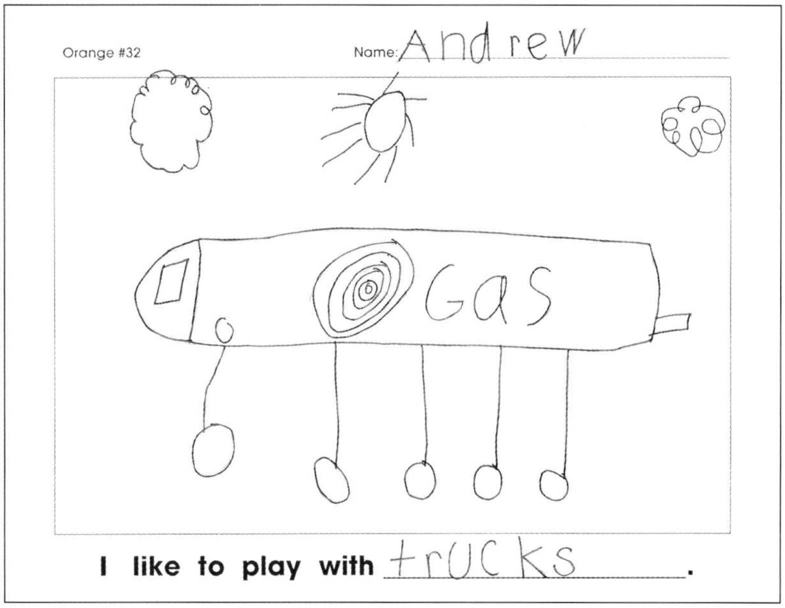

- Have the children take the Take-Home Book *Playing Together* and a fold sheet back to the classroom.
- Have children use *Playing Together* as a resource to write their own sentence about something they like to play with, e.g., "I like to play with ________" on the fold sheet.
- Children can illustrate their sentence.
- Give children Letter Minibooks of familiar letters to reread.

Home/School Connection

- Give children the Take-Home Book *Playing Together.*
- Have children take home their fold sheets to read to their families.
- Have children take home Letter Minibooks to read.

Assessing Reading and Writing Behaviors

Observe to find evidence that children can:

- quickly make words by taking away the first letter and putting another letter in first place, and then read the words.
- demonstrate voice-print match, self-monitoring, and self-correction behavior.
- use language structure, meaning, and visual information.
- write left to right with good spacing between words.
- start a sentence with an uppercase letter and write end punctuation.
- write several high-frequency words quickly.
- make predictions using the front cover.
- recognize cause-and-effect in the story (Polly getting fatter from eating).
- understand the sequence of action and events.

Supporting English Language Learners

To support English language learners, you can:

- **ask** children to repeat after you when building new words with the pattern *-at.*
- **make certain** children understand the meaning of the words being used in Phonics/Word Work.
- **monitor** for understanding of "starting with the same sound" when playing Lotto.
- **give** children some background about parrots (parrots talk, eat lots of things, etc.), but be sure children understand that this story is not real.
- **make sure** that children understand the objects in the story.
- **use** the language of the text in a conversational way and have children repeat the language several times to help them remember the syntax.
- **help** children understand that *she* means the same as *Polly*.
- **help** children attend to the *s* at the end of *likes*.
- **support** children in discussing what happens with Polly and how the woman is feeling at the end of the story.
- **confirm** that children understand the directions for the Classroom Connection by having them practice saying the sentence that they will write.

Professional Development Links

When Readers Struggle: Teaching that Works
Chapter 13: Extending Reading Power: Writing to Read. Use this chapter to understand the role of writing in overcoming reading difficulties.

Professional Development and Tutorial DVD, Orange System
View the Analysis section of your Tutorial DVD. Focus on Monitoring and Correcting Errors in *Prompting Guide 1* and think about what aspects of this your children control.

Interactive Writing: How Language and Literacy Come Together, Chapter 8 (pp. 17–19) and *Word Matters: Teaching Phonics and Spelling in the Reading/Writing Classroom*, Chapter 8 (pp. 80–82). Use these chapters to explore supporting children in using known words to write new words.

Teaching for Comprehending and Fluency: Thinking, Talking, and Writing About Reading, K–8
Chapter 5 (pp. 52–56). Use this chapter to explore supporting children in building systems of strategic actions for predicting, making connections, and inferring. Figures 5-3, 5-4, and 5-5 are particularly helpful.

YOU WILL NEED

- Take-Home Book, *Polly*
- magnetic letters
- word bags

From the CD:
- Letter Minibooks ✓
- Verbal Path ✓
- word cards: *to, too*
- fold sheet
- Parent Letter

SYSTEM **Orange**

NEW BOOK ***At the Farm***

GENRE **Nonfiction**

NEW BOOK
At the Farm, Level B

REREADING
Playing Together, Level B
Polly, Level A

Goals

- Recognize and use simple phonograms with a VC pattern.
- Make new words by substituting the first letter with another.
- Become aware of homonyms, *to, too.*
- Become aware of vowels.
- Recognize a category of animals.
- Read with voice-print match across two lines of print.
- Use return sweep to go back to the left margin to read the second line.
- Locate high-frequency words in continuous print.
- Connect names of adult and baby animals.
- Recognize the contrast of big and little.
- Discuss the farm setting (which may be unfamiliar to many children).

Analysis of New Book Characteristics

At the Farm, Level B

GENRE/FORM
- Narrative Nonfiction

TEXT STRUCTURE
- Different kind of animal on each page
- Adult animal always followed by baby animal of the same species
- No sequence other than pairing of adult and baby

CONTENT
- Familiar animals
- Concept of a farm

THEMES AND IDEAS
- Adult and baby animals

LANGUAGE AND LITERARY FEATURES
- NA

SENTENCE COMPLEXITY
- Alternating six- and nine-word simple sentences
- Present tense
- Prepositional phrases
- *Too,* set off by commas, to mean *also*
- Repeating pattern over every two pages

VOCABULARY
- Names of adult and baby animals: e.g., *pig, piglet*

WORDS
- High-frequency words: *a, is, at, the, and, little, too*
- One-syllable words with some two-syllable words
- See the Word Analysis Charts in the *Program Guide* for specific words in each category.

ILLUSTRATIONS
- Photographs
- Close match between pictures and text
- Contrasting adult and baby animals shown in illustrations

BOOK AND PRINT FEATURES
- Large font
- Ample space between words
- Two lines on each page of print
- Print on the left on a blank page; illustrations on the right page, except for last page
- Periods and commas

▸ Rereading Books

- *Playing Together*, Level B
- *Polly* Level A

PROMPTING GUIDE 1
Refer to *Prompting Guide 1* as needed.

- Invite children to reread *Playing Together* and *Polly.*
- If needed, prompt for self-monitoring using language structure; e.g., "You said ______. Does that sound right?"

▸ Phonics/Word Work

- **PRINCIPLE** Recognizing and using simple phonograms with a VC pattern (easiest): *-ad, -ag, -an, -am, -at, -ed, -en, -et, -ig, -in, -it, -og, -op, -ot, -ut*

"You can make new words by putting a letter before the word part or pattern."

- Place *-an* on the whiteboard with magnetic letters. Ask the children what they know about these letters. They may say the letter names, say the word *an*, or say it is a pattern. Suggested language: "Yes, all of those things are right. This is the word *an* but it is also a pattern that we can use to make a new word."
- Place *p* at the beginning of the word and run your finger under it. Ask the children to say the first sound and then the sound of *an: p-an.* Ask them to read the word smoothly.
- Have children continue to make words by taking away the first letter and putting another letter in first place. Make *can, tan, ran, fan,* and *man.* Make *pan* again.
- Give children magnetic letters: *a, n, c, t, r, f, m, p.* Have them make *an* and keep it still, but put new letters at the beginning to make a word as you say it. Have them say the word and check it by running a finger under the word from left to right.

▸ New Book

At the Farm, Level B

Introducing the Text

- Introduce children to the book by talking about any baby animals with which children are familiar. Suggested language: "There are lots of different animals at the farm. Some are adult animals and some are baby animals. What are some of the animals you might see at the farm?" Children respond.
- "Turn to pages 2 and 3. What animal is at the farm? Yes, a cat is at the farm. Say *at*. What letter would you expect to see first in *at*? Find at and put your finger under it. Say *at*."
- "Now turn to pages 4 and 5. If there is a cat at the farm, what baby animal might there be? Yes, and a little kitten is at the farm, too. Say the word *and*. What letter would you see first in *and*? Yes, it's an *A*. It's an uppercase *A*. Find And. Run your finger under it and say *and*."
- "Turn to pages 10 and 11. What animal do you see at the farm? Yes, a duck is at the farm. Find is on page 10. It has two letters and starts with *i*. Say *is* and run your finger under it. If a duck is on the farm, what baby animal will be at the farm? Yes, turn the page and you can see the little duckling. Clap *duckling*." Repeat for page 14.
- "Turn back to the beginning. Point and read softly about all of the adult animals and all of the baby animals at the farm."

PROMPTING GUIDE 1
Refer to *Prompting Guide 1* as needed.

Reading the Text

- As the children read, reinforce effective use of high-frequency words to check voice-print match.
- If the child is not in full control of early reading behaviors, you may want to prompt with "Were you right?" or "Did it match?"

Discussing and Revisiting the Text

Invite children to talk about the farm in the book. Some key understandings children may express are:

- There are lots of animals at the farm. [Extend by asking for examples. Have children show the pages with their examples.]
- There are pairs of big animals and little animals such as a dog and a puppy, a cat and a kitten. [Extend by asking how one pair of big and little animals might be related, e.g., they are mother and baby.]

PROMPTING GUIDE 1
Refer to *Prompting Guide 1* as needed.

Teaching Points

- Based on your observations, use *Prompting Guide 1* to select a teaching point that will be most helpful to the readers.
- If needed, demonstrate or reinforce checking the picture, e.g., *cat* with the first letter, *c*, in *cat*.

▸ Letter/Word Work

- Add the word cards *to* and *too* to children's word cards. Place word cards *to* and *too* in the pocket chart and read them to the children. Suggested language: "Both of these words sound the same but they mean different things. Listen while I use them in a sentence. *To:* We go *to* school. *Too:* I want to go, *too.* You might want to write the sentences on the board and underline *to* and *too.* Give children the word cards *to* and *too* and ask them to notice the difference.
- Have children put the word card *too* into their word bags.
- If time allows, have the children sort magnetic letters two or three different ways.

Letter Minibooks

- Give children several Letter Minibooks to read. Choose letters with which children need more practice. Have them run a finger over the letter on the cover, using the Verbal Path. Then, have children read each page, thinking about the beginning sound. Let children take home Letter Minibooks that are very familiar.

Classroom Connection

- Give children the fold sheet with the word *big* on one side and *little* on the other.
- Have children take the fold sheet back to the classroom and draw a picture of a big and little animal of their choice.
- Children can label their pictures by saying words and writing the letter sounds they can hear.
- Give children the Take-Home Book *Polly* and known Letter Minibooks to reread.

Home/School Connection

- Have children take home their pictures to share.
- Children can draw additional animals for *big* and *little* on the fold sheet.
- Give children the Take-Home Book *Polly* and Letter Minibooks to read to families.

Assessing Reading and Writing Behaviors

Observe to find evidence that children can:

- quickly make and check words using phonograms with a VC pattern.
- start to notice vowels.
- read with voice-print match across two lines of print.
- self-monitor and self-correct.
- understand the contrast of *big* and *little* (grown-up and baby) animals.

Supporting English Language Learners

To support English language learners, you can:

- **ask** children to repeat after you when building new words with the pattern *-an*.
- **check** that children understand the meaning of the words being used in Phonics/Word Work.
- **give** children some background about farms and baby animals, if necessary.
- **go over** the labels for animals, both baby and adult, to be sure children hear and say all of the animal names.
- **use** the language of the text in a conversational way and have children repeat the language several times to help them remember the syntax.
- **check** to be sure that children understand and can say the language structure because it is different from what the children have seen before.
- **support** children in discussing the adult and the baby animals, and think aloud about what this story reminds them of or what other animals could have been in the book.
- **check** for understanding of the words *big* and *little* in preparation for Classroom Connection.
- **have** children discuss what they might draw.
- **remind** children to say words slowly and record what they hear when labeling animals.

Professional Development Links

When Readers Struggle: Teaching that Works
Chapter 6: Text Matters: A Ladder to Success. Use this chapter to understand how the demands of texts affect readers.

Professional Development and Tutorial DVD, Orange System
View the sample lessons to notice the different opportunities children have for developing a core of high-frequency words.

Word Matters: Teaching Phonics and Spelling in the Reading/Writing Classroom
Chapter 9 (pp. 94–95). Use this chapter to explore vowels and phonograms. Appendix 15 contains an extensive list of phonograms.

Guided Reading: Good First Teaching for All Children
Pp. 16, 94, 95, 152, 158, 159. Use these pages to explore self-monitoring and self-correcting.

LESSON 34 LEVEL B

SYSTEM **Orange**

NEW BOOK ***The Sidewalk***

GENRE **Fiction**

YOU WILL NEED

- Take-Home Book, *At the Farm*
- *My Writing Book*
- magnetic letters
- word bags

From the CD:

- Letter Minibooks ✓
- Verbal Path ✓
- Letters Made in Similar Ways document
- Recording Form for *At the Farm*
- Parent Letter

NEW BOOK

The Sidewalk, Level A

REREADING

Polly, Level A

At the Farm, Level B

Goals

- Make words by taking away the first letter and putting another letter in first place.
- Recognize and use simple phonograms with a VC pattern.
- Check words by looking at them from left to right.
- Recognize easier high-frequency words quickly.
- Read with voice-print match, self-monitoring, and self-correction behavior.
- Use language structure, meaning, and visual information while reading.
- Say words slowly, listen for the easy-to-hear sounds, and write the letters.
- Write with good spacing between words.
- Start a sentence with an uppercase letter and write end punctuation.
- Understand and talk about the idea of drawing on the sidewalk with chalk.
- Understand and talk about ways movement and sound can be shown in illustrations.
- Understand cause-and-effect in the story (rain washing away the chalk).

Analysis of New Book Characteristics

The Sidewalk, Level A

GENRE/FORM

- Fiction

TEXT STRUCTURE

- Different kind of chalk drawing on every page
- Cumulative sidewalk drawing
- Surprise ending

CONTENT

- Everyday objects
- Concept of drawing on a sidewalk with chalk
- Concept that rain washes off chalk drawings
- Connection between rainbow and rain

THEMES AND IDEAS

- Art and creativity
- Temporariness of chalk drawings

LANGUAGE AND LITERARY FEATURES

- Foreshadowing of ending on page 15
- Eight brief easy-to-understand episodes
- Surprise ending

SENTENCE COMPLEXITY

- One four-word simple sentence on every page
- Present tense
- Imperative sentence

VOCABULARY

- Names of objects: *bus, bird, flower, dog, car, tree, rainbow, rain*

WORDS

- High-frequency words: *look, at, the*
- One-syllable words with some two-syllable words
- See the Word Analysis Charts in the *Program Guide* for specific words in each category.

ILLUSTRATIONS

- Childlike drawings
- Close match between pictures and text
- Story line implied by illustrations
- Interpretation of child's drawings required
- Colored chalk on each print page with illustration showing drawing in the same color on the right page

BOOK AND PRINT FEATURES

- Large font
- Ample space between words
- One line on each page of print
- Print on the left on a blank page; illustrations on the right page, except for last page
- Periods and exclamation point

▸ Rereading Books and Assessment

- *Polly,* Level A
- *At the Farm,* Level B

PROMPTING GUIDE 1
Refer to *Prompting Guide 1* as needed.

- Listen to one child read *At the Farm* as you code the reading behavior on the Recording Form, have a brief comprehension conversation, and make a teaching point that you think will be most helpful to the reader. Score and analyze the Reading Record following the lesson.
- Reread *Polly* and then *At the Farm.*
- If needed, prompt children to solve words; e.g., "Do you know a word like that?"

Take a Reading Record

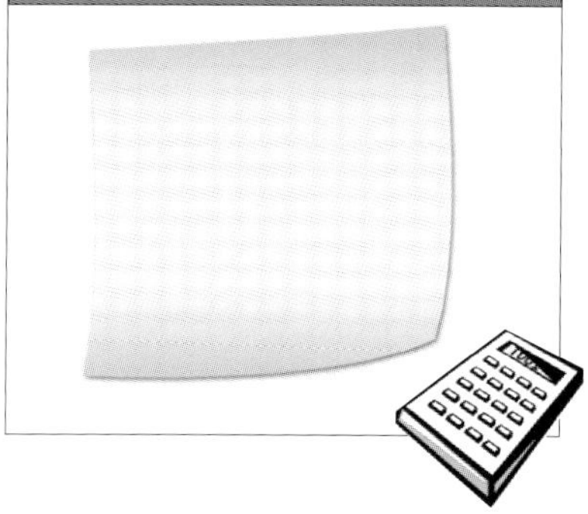

▸ Phonics/Word Work

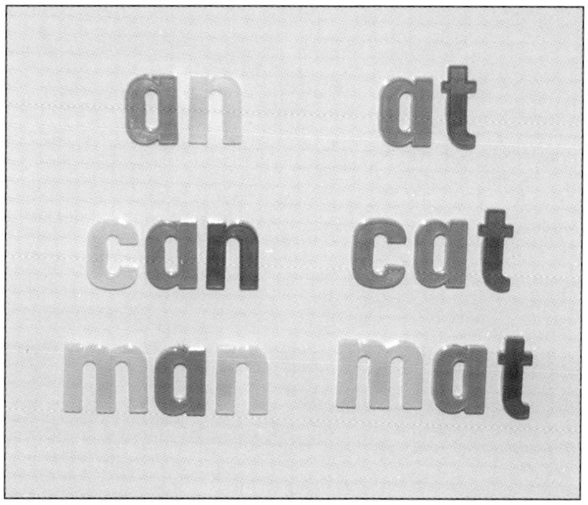

- **PRINCIPLE** Recognizing and using simple phonograms with a VC pattern (easiest): *-ad, -ag, -an, -am, -at, -ed, -en, -et, -ig, -in, -it, -og, -op, -ot, -ut*

"You can make new words by putting a letter before the word part or pattern."

- Place *-an* and *-at* on the whiteboard with magnetic letters. Suggested language: "You know that you can make words with these patterns. Can anyone think of a word you can make?"
- Children will respond with a word that uses one of the two patterns. Ask: "What pattern do you use to make ______?" Make the word and check by asking all children to read the word while you run your finger under it.
- Ask: "Can anyone use the other pattern to make a new word?" Children will respond with another word that fits the pattern. Repeat the process.
- Give the children magnetic letters *a, n, t, s, c, m.*
- Ask them to make *can, cat, man, mat, sat.*
- Go back to the whiteboard with phonograms for *-at* and *-an.* Make words quickly and have children read the words with the patterns.

▸ Writing About Reading

Independent Writing

- **MY WRITING BOOK**
- **PROMPTING GUIDE 1**

Refer to *Prompting Guide 1* as needed.

- Talk with the children about all the different animals that they can see at the farm. Make a list on the whiteboard or on chart paper. Then have the children read the list with you.
- Work with the children to make a list in *My Writing Book* of the variety of animals that are on the farm. Then have them write about two or three of the animals that are at the farm. For example:

  A cat is at the farm.
  A duck is at the farm.
  A pig is at the farm.
- Prompt children to write *at* and *the* quickly. Have children say *farm* and think about how it starts and ends. You can show children the middle letters on the whiteboard. Use sound boxes for words like *cat*, *pig*, and *duck*.
- Finally, have the children illustrate their writing. If time allows, you may want to write one or two of the sentences on sentence strips for children to cut apart and put back together again.

▸ New Book

The Sidewalk,
Level A

Introducing the Text

- Introduce children to the book by talking about drawing with chalk. Suggested language: "Did you ever use chalk to draw on the sidewalk? What things did you draw? This little girl is drawing on the sidewalk. She says to look at all of the things she draws."
- "Turn to pages 2 and 3. What drawing does the girl say to look at? Yes, she says, 'Look at the bus.' Can you say that?"
- "Turn to pages 4 and 5. Now what does she say to look at? Say the word *at*. What letter comes first in *at*? Find the word at. Put your finger under it and say *at*."
- "Turn to page 9. Look at the picture. The girl has made lines to show that the dog is making noise by barking and to show the wagging of the dog's tail."
- "Turn to page 11. What do the lines in this picture mean?"
- "Turn to pages 12 and 13. What does the girl say to look at now? Yes, she says to look at the tree. Say the word *look*. What letter comes first in *look?* Yes, and it is an uppercase *L* because the word *Look* starts a sentence."
- "Turn back to the beginning of the book and point and read about all the things the girl draws on the sidewalk."

PROMPTING GUIDE 1
Refer to *Prompting Guide 1* as needed.

Reading the Text

- As the children read, prompt for checking the picture; e.g., bus with the first letter of the word *bus*, if needed. Help children learn that they need to check on themselves.

Discussing and Revisiting the Text

Invite children to talk about the fun the girl had drawing on the sidewalk. Some key understandings children may express are:

- The girl drew lots of things on the sidewalk. [Extend by asking for children to show examples on the page.]
- You can show in a picture that something is moving. [Extend by asking children for an example.]
- The rain washed the girl's drawings away. [Encourage children to provide more detail.]
- The girl doesn't mind that the rain washed away her drawings. [Extend by asking for evidence, e.g., she's smiling, she drew a rainbow and likes rain.]

PROMPTING GUIDE 1
Refer to *Prompting Guide 1* as needed.

Teaching Points

- Based on your observations, use *Prompting Guide 1* to select a teaching point that will be most helpful to the readers.
- You may want to have children locate *at* and *the*, or have them write these words quickly on a whiteboard.

▸ Optional Letter/ Word Work

- Have the children read several Letter Minibooks. Choose letters with which children need more practice. Have children run a finger over the letter on the cover, using the Verbal Path. Then, have them read each page, thinking about the beginning sound. Let children take home Letter Minibooks that are very familiar. (If all letter books have been read several times, there will be no need to use Letter Minibooks again.)

Word Bags

- Have the children read through the word cards in their word bags. "Retire" words that are very well known and let children take them home. Keep the more complex words like, *look, come, and, he, has, here, likes, this, she, said, have, am, too* and any words that children still find difficult or do not recognize quickly and easily.

Letter Sort

- If time allows, have the children sort magnetic letters in two or three different ways (see Instructional Routines, Ways to Sort and Match Letters, in the *Program Guide*).

Classroom Connection

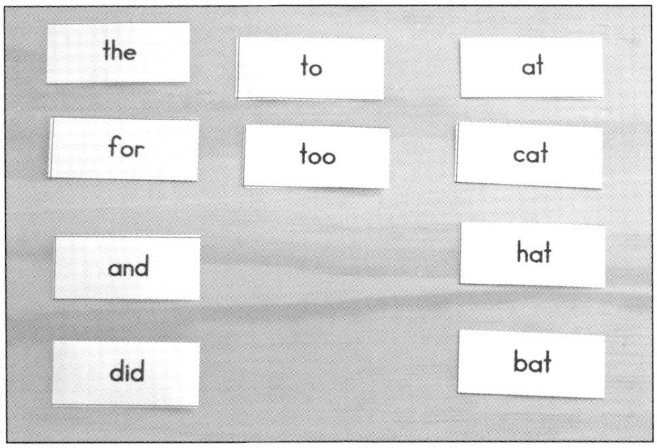

- Have children take their "retired" high-frequency word cards back to the classroom. Invite children to read and sort the word cards in various ways; e.g., number of letters, first letter, pattern.
- Have children take the Take-Home Book *At the Farm.*
- If needed, have children read Letter Minibooks

Home/School Connection

- Have the children take home their "retired" high-frequency word cards.
- Give the children the Take-Home Book *At the Farm* to read to family members.
- If needed, give children Letter Minibooks to read at home.

Assessing Reading and Writing Behaviors

Observe to find evidence that children can:

- quickly make and read words using VC phonograms.
- quickly recognize known high-frequency words.
- demonstrate voice-print match, self-monitoring, and self-correction behavior.
- use language structure, meaning, and visual information while reading.
- say words slowly, listen to, and write the letters for easy-to-hear sounds.
- write with good spacing between words.
- start a sentence with an uppercase letter and write end punctuation.
- understand the cause-and-effect in the story (rain washing away the chalk).

Supporting English Language Learners

To support English language learners, you can:

- **have** children say words aloud as they make them with magnetic letters during Phonics/Word Work and check that they are words that children understand.
- **check** that children know the meaning of all the words they recognize before word cards are "retired."
- **make sure** that children understand that the girl is drawing with chalk, which washes away with rainwater.
- **use** the language of the text in a conversational way and have children repeat the language several times to help them remember the syntax.
- **check** to see if children understand the labels for what the girl is drawing.
- **make certain** children understand the concept of *first* when prompting for checking the picture with the first letter of the word.
- **support** children in discussing how the girl feels about the rain washing away her drawings and ask for evidence from the book.
- **think aloud**/discuss with the children what this story reminds them of; e.g., "This story reminds me of when we had a picnic but it rained" or "The girl likes to draw and so do I."

Professional Development Links

When Readers Struggle: Teaching that Works
Chapter 7: Language Matters: Talking, Reading, and Writing. Use this chapter to understand teaching as conversation and how to increase meaningful talk in lessons.

Professional Development and Tutorial DVD, Orange System
View the Practice section on the Tutorial DVD. Use the Recording Forms to think about evidence of word-solving. How is the child recognizing or taking apart words?

Interactive Writing: How Language and Literacy Come Together
Chapter 8. Use this chapter to explore using writing to support children in learning about print.

YOU WILL NEED

- Take-Home Book, *The Sidewalk*
- *My Writing Book*
- magnetic letters: *i, t, b, s, f, h, p, w ,e, n, t*
- word bags

From the CD:

- Verbal Path ✓
- Letter Minibooks ✓
- Lotto Game Board
- word card: *went*
- fold sheet
- Parent Letter

SYSTEM **Orange**

NEW BOOK ***The Hat***

GENRE **Fiction**

NEW BOOK
The Hat, Level B

REREADING
At the Farm, Level B
The Sidewalk, Level A

Goals

- Recognize and use simple phonograms with a VC pattern.
- Change words by substituting a new letter for the first letter.
- Look closely at a word to learn it.
- Locate easy high-frequency words in a text.
- Read with voice-print match across two lines of text.
- Read with self-monitoring and self-correction behavior.
- Understand and discuss a cumulative story (through the pictures).
- Notice the exciting part of a story.
- Notice the sequence of size in the animals and think about what it means.
- Understand the cause-and-effect relationship.

Analysis of New Book Characteristics

The Hat, Level B

GENRE/FORM

- Fiction
- Animal Fantasy
- Classic Tales Series
- Play

TEXT STRUCTURE

- Different kind of animal on each page
- Animals in order from largest to smallest
- Sequence of events building to the ending

CONTENT

- Familiar animals
- Concept of squeezing into a hat, with the hat stretching to the breaking point

THEMES AND IDEAS

- Too much pressure leading to a pop
- Even a tiny addition causing the final pop
- Hilarious conclusion

LANGUAGE AND LITERARY FEATURES

- Events leading to conclusions
- Story line inferred from illustrations
- Illustrations supporting prediction

SENTENCE COMPLEXITY

- Simple six-word sentence on every page
- Past tense
- Prepositional phrases
- Repeating pattern on every page until the last

VOCABULARY

- Names of animals

WORDS

- High-frequency words: *the, went, in, a*
- One-syllable words and some two-syllable words
- See the Word Analysis Charts in the *Program Guide* for specific words in each category.

ILLUSTRATIONS

- Full color paintings
- Illustrations over two-page spreads
- Close match between pictures and text
- Illustrations that carry the plot and conclusion

BOOK AND PRINT FEATURES

- Large font
- Ample space between words
- Two lines on each page of print, except the last page.
- Print on the left page within the illustration but with a white circle around print
- Periods and exclamation point
- Play indicating three narrators

▸ Rereading Books

- *At the Farm*, Level B
- *The Sidewalk*, Level A

PROMPTING GUIDE 1
Refer to *Prompting Guide 1* as needed.

- Invite children to reread *At the Farm* and *The Sidewalk.*
- If needed, prompt for word solving as appropriate; e.g., "Read that again and start the word."

▸ Phonics/Word Work

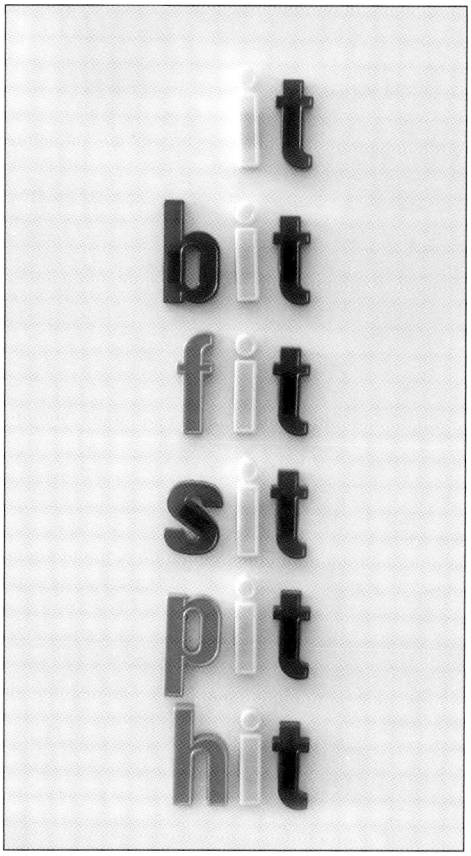

- **PRINCIPLE** Recognizing and using simple phonograms with a VC pattern (easiest): *-ad, -ag, -an, -am, -at, -ed, -en, -et, -ig, -in, -it, -og, -op, -ot, -ut*

"You can make new words by putting a letter before the word part or pattern."

- Place *-it* on the whiteboard with magnetic letters. Suggested language: "You can make words with this part. The part is *it.* Watch while I make a word."
- Make *bit* with magnetic letters and run your finger under the word from left to right. "Say the first sound of this word and think what it is."
- Children may respond with the word *bit.* If not, tell them the word and ask them to read it. They may notice that the word is like *but* except the middle letter is different. If so, contrast *but* and *bit.*
- Make *fit, sit, pit,* and *hit* and have the children read each word.

My Writing Book

- Have the children write two words with the pattern *it* in *My Writing Book.* Have children draw a line down the middle of the page of their writing books to create two columns and then write the words under *-it* down the left column.

▸ New Book

***The Hat*,**
Level B

Introducing the Text

- Introduce children to the book by showing the cover. Suggested language: "This book is called *The Hat.* A hat was lost in the woods and different animals are trying to get into it."
- "Turn to pages 2 and 3. What do you notice? Yes, the bear is trying to get in the hat. Why do you think the bear went in the hat? Yes, the bear went in the hat to try to get warm."
- "Now turn to the next page and what do you notice? Yes, the fox went in the hat. Say *went.* What letter would you see first in *went?* Run your finger under the word and say *went.* Lots of other animals were cold so they went in the hat, too." Repeat for pages 10 and 11.
- "What are you noticing about the hat? And what are you noticing about the animals that went in? Turn back to the beginning of the story. Point and read *The Hat* to find out what animals went in and what happened to the hat."

PROMPTING GUIDE 1
Refer to *Prompting Guide 1* as needed.

Reading the Text

- As the children read, support the use of picture information to solve new words.
- If the children have difficulty with the word *went,* repeat your phrase "and now who went in" once or twice as children turn the pages.

Discussing and Revisiting the Text

Invite the children to talk about what happened in the story. Some key understandings children may express are:

- Many animals go inside a hat until it pops. [Extend by asking for examples. Encourage children to show the pages with their examples.]
- The animals went inside the hat because they wanted to stay warm. [Extend by asking them why they think that.]
- The animals probably felt _______when the hat popped. [Encourage any reasonable responses.]
- This story reminds me of ________ [Encourage children to think of other stories they have heard like this one. Accept any reasonable response.]

PROMPTING GUIDE 1
Refer to *Prompting Guide 1* as needed.

Teaching Points

- Based on your observations, use *Prompting Guide 1* to select a teaching point that will be most helpful to the readers.
- You may want to have children locate easy high-frequency words such as *the, went,* and *in.*

▸ Letter/Word Work

LOTTO

at	it	the	and
my	like	up	me
see	went	to	do
can	come	in	is

- Have children play a new Lotto game with selected high-frequency words. Notice how quickly they can recognize *went.*
- Write *went* on the whiteboard and demonstrate reading it slowly while running a finger under the word from left to right. Ask the children to say the first sound of the word and then the word, as you demonstrate first: *w-went.*

Word Bags

- Give children the word card for *went* and ask them to look at the word on the card closely, run their finger under the word, and say *went.* Then have children read the word and put the word card into their word bags. You may want children to make *went* with magnetic letters one or two times.

Letter Minibooks

- Read several Letter Minibooks. Choose letters with which children need more practice. Have children run a finger over the letter on the cover, using the Verbal Path. Then, have children read each page, thinking about the beginning sound. Let children take home Letter Minibooks that are very familiar.

YOU WILL NEED

- Take-Home Book, *The Pet Store*
- *My Writing Book*
- magnetic letters: *p, u, t*
- word bags

From the CD:

- Letter Minibooks ✓
- Verbal Path ✓
- word card: *put*
- fold sheet
- Parent Letter

SYSTEM **Orange**

NEW BOOK ***Going on Vacation***

GENRE **Fiction**

NEW BOOK
Going on Vacation, Level B

REREADING
The Hat, Level B

The Pet Store, Level A

Goals

- Recognize and use beginning consonant sounds to write a word.
- Say words slowly to think about the individual sounds and write the letters.
- Locate easy high-frequency words in a text.
- Read with voice-print match across two lines of text.
- Return to the left margin to read the second line of print.
- Read with self-monitoring and self-correction behavior, checking the pictures with the first letters of words.
- Read high-frequency words quickly in isolation.
- Connect the events in the story to everyday life.
- Understand and discuss the idea of going on a trip or on vacation.

Analysis of New Book Characteristics

Going on Vacation, Level B

GENRE/FORM
- Fiction

TEXT STRUCTURE
- Narrative
- Seven brief episodes and the ending

CONTENT
- Most objects familiar to children
- Concept of packing a van to go on vacation

THEMES AND IDEAS
- Family
- Vacations
- Preparing

LANGUAGE AND LITERARY FEATURES
- NA

SENTENCE COMPLEXITY
- One seven-word simple sentence on every page except the last
- Past tense
- Repeating pattern on each page with no variation until the last page

VOCABULARY
- Names of objects: *bags, toys, car, balls, bears, food, dogs*

WORDS
- High-frequency words: *we, put, the, in, car*
- One-syllable words with one two-syllable word
- Hyphenated word *good-bye* on last page
- See the Word Analysis Charts in the *Program Guide* for specific words in each category.

ILLUSTRATIONS
- Full-page drawing on every right page
- Close match between pictures and text

BOOK AND PRINT FEATURES
- Large font
- Ample space between words
- Two lines on each page of print except final page
- Print on the left on a blank page; illustrations on the right page, except for last page
- Periods and exclamation point

▸ Rereading Books

- *The Hat* Level B
- *The Pet Store*, Level A

PROMPTING GUIDE 1
Refer to *Prompting Guide 1* as needed.

- Invite children to reread the play for *The Hat* and the story *The Pet Store*, if needed.
- Prompt readers to solve words using the language structure and first letter, e.g., "Read that again, and start the word."

▸ Phonics/Word Work

- **PRINCIPLE** Recognizing and using beginning consonant sounds and the letters that represent them: *s, m, t, b, f, r, n, p, d, h, c, g, j, l, k, v, w, z, qu, y, x*

"You can say a word slowly to help you write it."
"You can hear the sound at the beginning of a word."
"You can write a word by thinking about the beginning sound."

- Have children say words slowly and think about the sounds they hear. Start with *bag*. Say *bag*. Ask the children to say it slowly and think what they hear at the beginning of the word.
- Write the *b* on the whiteboard, and have children say the word again to hear more sounds and think of the letters. If children find it difficult to think of the vowel, just write it in. The goal of this exercise is to help children realize that saying a word slowly and thinking about the sounds will help them to write the word. Tell children that they can use the first sound and letter of a word to help start the word. If children can only come up with the first letter, just write the rest of the word. Have them write the word in *My Writing Book*.
- Repeat the process with *sun, cat, hit, but, he, we*, and have the children write the word each time.

▸ New Book

Going on Vacation,
Level B

Introducing the Text

- Introduce the children to the book by talking about what it means to go on vacation. Suggested language: "Did you ever go on a vacation? What does that mean? Yes, it means you go someplace away from home to have a nice time. Well, this family is getting ready to go on a vacation and they are putting things into their car. What are some things they might put into the car?"
- "Turn to pages 2 and 3. What are the boy and his dad putting in the car? Yes, so they say, 'We put the bags in the car.' Can you say that?"
- "Turn to pages 4 and 5 and you can see the toys. So what will the boy and girl say now? Yes, they say, 'We put the toys in the car.' Say the word *put*. What letter would you see first? Yes, the letter is *p*. Put your finger under the word, get a good look and say *put*." Repeat for pages 10 and 11 and locate in.
- "Turn back to the beginning of *Going on Vacation*. Point under each word and read softly to find out all the things that the family puts in the car."

PROMPTING GUIDE 1
Refer to *Prompting Guide 1* as needed.

Reading the Text

- As the children read about things that were put in the car, demonstrate or reinforce using the picture information and checking with the first letter of a word, as appropriate.

Discussing and Revisiting the Text

Invite the children to talk about all the things the family packed to go on vacation. Some key understandings children may express are:

- The family is packing the car to go on vacation. [Extend by asking children to name items they are putting in the car.]
- Then the family drives away.
- This story reminds me of when I went on vacation with my family. [Encourage children to talk about family trips they have taken.]
- It seems that the family is going to the beach. [Extend by asking children to find evidence in the story to support that conclusion.]
- The family is excited to go on vacation. [Extend by asking children why they think so.]

PROMPTING GUIDE 1
Refer to *Prompting Guide 1* as needed.

Teaching Points

- Based on your observations, use *Prompting Guide 1* to select a teaching point that will be most helpful to the readers.
- You may want the children to quickly locate *put, we, in,* or *the* on two or three pages of the book.

▸ Letter/Word Work

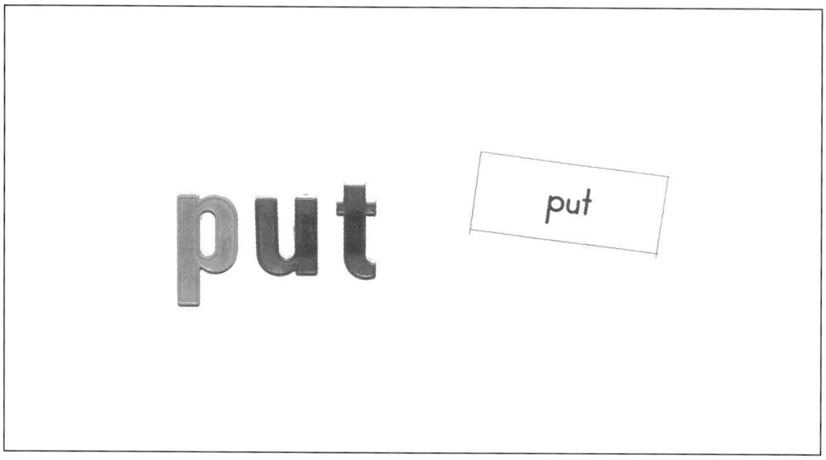

- Make *put* with the magnetic letters on the board and demonstrate reading it slowly while running a finger under it left to right. Ask the children to say the first sound of the word and then the whole word after you demonstrate first: *p-put.*
- Give children the word card for *put* and ask them to look at the word closely, run a finger under it, and say the word. Then have children read the word card and put it into their word bags. You may also want children to make *put* one or two times with magnetic letters.
- Have children take word cards from their word bags and lay the cards out on a flat surface. Tell children to pick up one word card at a time, say the word, and put the word card back into the bag.

Letter Minibooks

- Read several Letter Minibooks. Choose letters with which children need more practice. Have children run a finger over the letter on the cover, using the Verbal Path. Then, have children read each page, thinking about the beginning sound. Let children take home Letter Minibooks that are very familiar.

Classroom Connection

Orange #37 Name: Nicole

bag	fun	cat	but	sit	dog
bag	fun	cat	but	sit	dog

- Have children take the fold sheet with six columns and the words at the top of each column: *bag, fun, cat, but, sit, dog.*
- Show children how to fold down the top flap to cover the words while they try them below.
- Have children say one word slowly and then write it. Then, have children open the flap to check the printed word with the word that they wrote.
- Tell children that they can write more words on the back.

Home/School Connection

- Have children take home the fold sheets with the words they have written.
- Give children the Take-Home Book *The Pet Store* to read to their families.

Assessing Reading and Writing Behaviors

Observe to find evidence that children can:

- represent many sounds when saying words slowly and writing the letters.
- read with voice-print match across two lines of text.
- self-monitor and self-correct.
- make inferences about where the family is going and what they might do when they get there.

Supporting English Language Learners

To support English language learners, you can:

- **demonstrate** saying words slowly. If pronunciation is difficult, allow children to repeat the word after you. Be sure you are not the only one saying the word slowly.
- **monitor** for understanding of *beginning sound.*
- **have** children repeat the beginning sound of the word, the ending sound, and then the whole word. Do this several times.
- **check** to be sure that children understand the names of the objects the family members are packing.
- **use** the language of the text in a conversational way, and have children repeat the language several times to help them remember the syntax. Try to help children understand the prepositional phrase as a meaningful unit.
- **monitor** for understanding of *good-bye.*
- **help** children in discussing how the family gets ready for the vacation. Make wondering statements to assist children in making predictions about where they think the family might be going, and what will happen when they get there. "I wonder where they are going. I think they might be going to_________." (Use evidence to support this statement.)

Professional Development Links

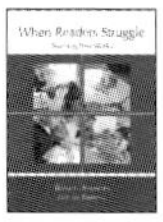

When Readers Struggle: Teaching that Works
Chapter 9: Learning to Read and Write: the Phonological Base. Use this chapter to understand how children learn to hear sounds in words.

Professional Development and Tutorial DVD, Orange System
Review the Sample LLI lessons to think about pacing across the lesson to complete it in thirty minutes.

Word Matters: Teaching Phonics and Spelling in the Reading/Writing Classroom
Chapter 8 (pp. 76–77, 78–80). Use this chapter to understand the role of phonology (understanding and using the sounds of language) in literacy.

Interactive Writing: How Language and Literacy Come Together
Chapter 8 (pp.116–120). Use this chapter to explore how interactive writing supports children in learning about spelling.

YOU WILL NEED

- Take-Home Book, *Going on Vacation*
- *My Writing Book*

From the CD:

- Letter Minibooks ✓
- Verbal Path ✓
- Lotto Game Board
- Recording Form for *Going on Vacation*
- fold sheet
- Parent Letter

SYSTEM **Orange**

NEW BOOK ***Wheels***

GENRE **Nonfiction**

NEW BOOK
Wheels, Level A

REREADING
The Pet Store, Level A

Going on Vacation, Level B

Goals

- Recognize and use simple phonograms with a VC pattern to write words.
- Recognize easy high-frequency words quickly.
- Read with voice-print match, self-monitoring, and self-correction behavior.
- Use language structure, meaning, and visual information while reading.
- Write easy high-frequency words quickly.
- Write with good spacing.
- Start a sentence with an uppercase letter and write end punctuation.
- Say words slowly to listen for and identify easy-to-hear initial sounds.
- Understand and talk about the fact that some machines have wheels.
- Use compare and contrast to see how machines are alike or different.

Analysis of New Book Characteristics

Wheels, Level A

GENRE/FORM
- Narrative Nonfiction

TEXT STRUCTURE
- Different kind of vehicle on every page
- No sequence

CONTENT
- Most vehicles familiar to children but some needing explanation
- Concept of wheels and movement

THEMES AND IDEAS
- Function of wheels
- Machines having moving parts

LANGUAGE AND LITERARY FEATURES
- NA

SENTENCE COMPLEXITY
- One four-word simple sentence on every page
- Present tense
- Repeating pattern on each page with no variation

VOCABULARY
- Names of vehicles: *bike, car, truck, bus, van, plane, train, wheelchair*

WORDS
- High-frequency words: *a, has*
- One-syllable words with one two-syllable word
- See the Word Analysis Charts in the *Program Guide* for specific words in each category.

ILLUSTRATIONS
- Photographs
- Close match between pictures and text

BOOK AND PRINT FEATURES
- Large font
- Ample space between words
- One line on each page of print
- Print on the left on a blank page; illustrations on the right page, except for last page
- Periods and exclamation point

▸ Rereading Books and Assessment

- *The Pet Store*, Level A
- *Going on Vacation*, Level B

PROMPTING GUIDE 1
Refer to *Prompting Guide 1* as needed.

- Listen to one child read *Going on Vacation* as you code the reading behavior on the Recording Form, have a brief comprehension conversation, and make a teaching point that you think will be most helpful to the reader. Score and analyze the Reading Record following the lesson.
- Have the other children reread *The Pet Store* and then *Going on Vacation.*
- Prompt children to notice ending marks if needed, e.g., "Look at the period at the end of the sentence. Make your voice go down."

Take a Reading Record

▸ Phonics/Word Work

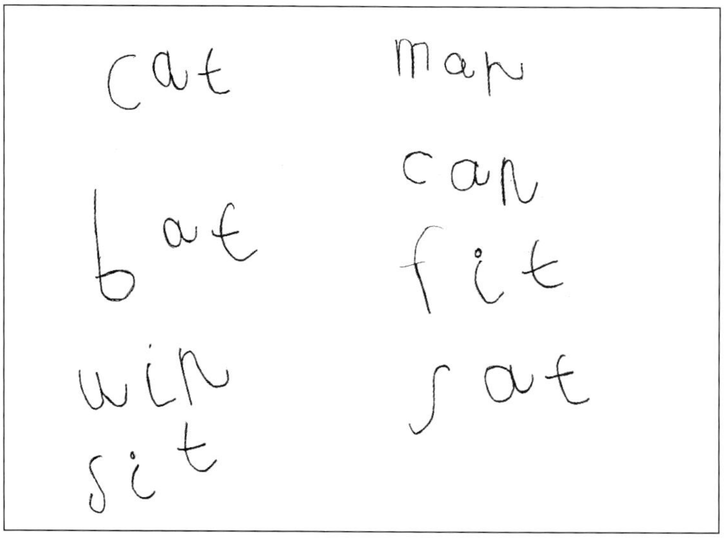

- **PRINCIPLE** Recognizing and using simple phonograms with a VC pattern (easiest): *-ad, -ag, -an, -am, -at, -ed, -en, -et, -ig, -in, -it, -og, -op, -ot, -ut*

"You can use the pattern (part) you know to help you write a word."

- Have the children write some new CVC words by thinking about some of the patterns they know. Have them watch and listen while you slowly say a word. Have them say the word slowly and think about the first sound and letter and then think about the pattern *(but, bug, hit, mat, hot, pet).*
- Demonstrate by writing *cat* on the whiteboard. Ask children to say it and notice the first letter and the pattern they hear when you say *c-at.*

My Writing Book

- Then have children use *My Writing Book* to write some words with simple phonograms, such as *-at, -an, -in,* and *-it.* Have children check their writing with the word you wrote on the whiteboard. Children can use the phonogram charts from Lessons 25, 26, 35, and 36 for help. If needed, use white correction tape to help them fix words.
- Have children choose two more three-letter words to write.

▸ Writing About Reading

Dictated Writing

- **MY WRITING BOOK**
- **PROMPTING GUIDE 1**

Refer to *Prompting Guide 1* as needed.

- If time allows, you may want to begin by having each child read recent pages from *My Writing Book.* Occasionally ask the child to locate a word in a sentence read.
- Dictate the following sentences for children to write in their writing books.

  We put the bags in the car.
  We put the balls in the car.

- Help the children say words slowly to listen for and write the letters for the easy-to-hear initial sounds.
- Emphasize good spacing and quick writing of the easy high-frequency words, *we, put, in, the.*
- When children are done writing, have them reread their sentences and then illustrate them.

▸ New Book

Wheels, Level A

Introducing the Text

- Introduce the children to the book by talking about common machines that have wheels. Suggested language: "This book is called *Wheels*. In this book you will read about lots of machines that have wheels. What are some machines that have wheels?"
- "Turn to pages 2 and 3. What has wheels? Yes, a bike has wheels."
- "Turn to page 6. What else has wheels? Yes, a truck has wheels. Can you say that? Say *has*. What letter comes first in *has?* Find has and put your finger under it."
- "Now, turn to the last page to see something else that has wheels. Yes, a wheelchair has wheels, too! Find has and put your finger under that word."
- "Now, turn back to the beginning of the story. Point and read softly about all the machines that have wheels."

PROMPTING GUIDE 1
Refer to *Prompting Guide 1* as needed.

Reading the Text

- As children read, support their identification of the different things that have wheels.
- You may need to tell some children the label for an item and then teach them to check it with the first letter of the word (see *Prompting Guide 1*, Self-Monitoring and Searching for and Using Information).

Discussing and Revisiting the Text

Invite children to talk about the different things that have wheels. Some key understandings children may express are:

- A lot of different things have wheels. [Extend by asking for examples. Have children show the pages that illustrate the examples they name.]
- Everything in this book has wheels but they are different. [Encourage children to talk about how the machines in the book are alike and different.]
- The word *wheelchair* has *wheel* in it.
- The car in *Going on Vacation* has wheels.

PROMPTING GUIDE 1
Refer to *Prompting Guide 1* as needed.

Teaching Points

- Based on your observations, use *Prompting Guide 1* to select a teaching point that will be most helpful to the readers.
- You might need to demonstrate or reinforce using one source of information to check another, e.g., the first letter of a word with the picture that illustrates the word.
- You may want to turn to page 16 and help children notice the chair with wheels and clap the compound word, *wheelchair*.

▸ Optional Letter/ Word Work

- Play Lotto with easy high-frequency words.

Letter Minibooks

- Read several Letter Minibooks. Choose letters with which children need more practice. Have them run a finger over the letter on the cover, using the Verbal Path. Then, have children read each page, thinking about the beginning sound. Have children take home Letter Minibooks that are very familiar to them.

Classroom Connection

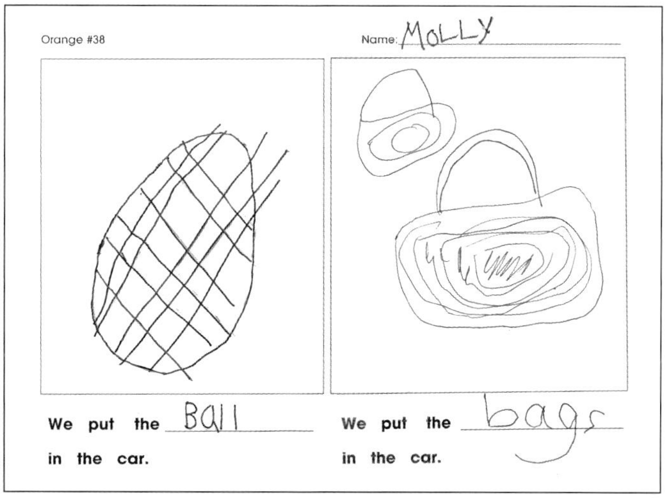

- Give children the fold sheet with the sentence, *We put the ______ in the car,* printed on each half (see *Lesson Resources CD*).
- Have students take the fold sheets back to the classroom and read the sentences. Then have them write and draw about what the children put in the car to take on vacation.
- Give them the Take-Home Book *Going on Vacation* to reread.
- If needed, have them reread Letter Minibooks with vowels.

Home/School Connection

- Give the children the Take-Home Book *Going on Vacation.*
- Have children take home fold sheets to read and share.
- Have them take home vowel Letter Minibooks as needed.

Assessing Reading and Writing Behaviors

Observe to find evidence that children can:

- use a variety of VC phonogram patterns as they participate in Phonics/Word Work and write in *My Writing Book.*
- quickly recognize known high-frequency words.
- demonstrate voice-print match.
- self-monitor and self-correct reading.
- use language structure, meaning, and visual information while reading.
- cross check one source of information with another.
- write easy high-frequency words quickly.
- write with good spacing, an uppercase letter, and end punctuation.
- understand what a wheel is and that wheels appear on all of the machines in the book.
- see how all the machines in the book are alike and some ways in which they are different.

Supporting English Language Learners

To support English language learners, you can:

- **model** how to say the beginning sound of a word, the ending phonogram, and finally the whole word. Ask children to repeat the word after you.
- **demonstrate** saying words slowly. If pronunciation is difficult, allow children to repeat after you. Be sure you are not the only one saying the word slowly.
- **have** children repeat the language of the text several times to help them remember the syntax.
- **check** for understanding of the objects in the book.
- **help** children in discussing what has wheels. Think aloud stating how two objects in the book are alike (or different). Assist students in making similar statements. Remember, their sentences do not need to be as detailed as yours. Use the pictures as support.
- **remind** children to read *Going on Vacation* at home. Ask them to discuss a trip with someone in their family. They can discuss a trip to the grocery store or the laundromat. Remind them to speak in their home language.

Professional Development Links

When Readers Struggle: Teaching that Works
Chapter 7: Language Matters: Talking, Reading, and Writing. Use this chapter to understand how to help children who have trouble using language structure.

Professional Development and Tutorial DVD, Orange System
View the Sample Lessons to see examples of teachers helping children say words slowly to write them.

Interactive Writing: How Language and Literacy Come Together, K–2
Chapter 8 (pp. 114–115). Use this chapter to explore saying, listening for, and recording sounds in words.

Teaching for Comprehending and Fluency: Thinking, Talking, and Writing About Reading, K–8.
Chapter 24 (pp. 378–380). Use this chapter to explore the teaching, prompting, and reinforcing of strategic actions.

LESSON 39 LEVEL B

SYSTEM **Orange**

NEW BOOK ***Hiding***

GENRE **Fiction**

YOU WILL NEED

- Take-Home Book, *Wheels*
- "Quack, Quack, Quack," enlarged poem
- highlighter tape
- stick-on notes

From the CD:

- *My Poetry Book*✓
- Letter Minibooks✓
- Verbal Path✓
- fold sheet
- Parent Letter

NEW BOOK
Hiding, Level B

REREADING
Going on Vacation, Level B

Wheels, Level A

Goals

- Use the first letter of a word and the language structure to read a word.
- Read known high-frequency words quickly.
- Locate words in a text by thinking about their sounds and letters.
- Read with voice-print match across two lines of text.
- Return to the left margin to read the second line of print.
- Read with self-monitoring and self-correction behavior, checking the pictures with the first letters of words.
- Use meaning, language structure, and visual information to solve words.
- Understand prepositional phrases that indicate where something is; e.g., *in the box; behind the chair.*
- Search for clues in the pictures.
- Talk about a cat's typical behavior.

Analysis of New Book Characteristics

Hiding, Level B

GENRE/FORM
- Fiction

TEXT STRUCTURE
- Narrative
- Seven brief episodes and an ending

CONTENT
- Familiar places around the house
- Concept of hiding
- Typical cat behavior

THEMES AND IDEAS
- Home
- Pets

LANGUAGE AND LITERARY FEATURES
- Simple story with surprise at the end
- Character with name

SENTENCE COMPLEXITY
- One seven-word simple sentence on every page except the last
- Present tense
- Repeating pattern on each page with variation in the preposition starting the phrase on each page
- Use of *too*, set off by commas, to mean *also*

VOCABULARY
- Names of places to hide: *box, bag, closet, chair, basket, rug, bed*
- Prepositions: *in, behind, under*

WORDS
- High-frequency words: *likes, to, in, the, too*
- One-syllable words with some two-syllable words
- See the Word Analysis Charts in the *Program Guide* for specific words in each category.

ILLUSTRATIONS
- Drawing on every right page
- Close match between pictures and text

BOOK AND PRINT FEATURES
- Large font
- Ample space between words
- Two lines on each page of print
- Print on the left on a blank page; illustrations on the right page, except for last page
- Periods and exclamation point
- Word *in* in bold to signal word stress

▸ Rereading Books

- *Going on Vacation*, Level B
- *Wheels*, Level A

PROMPTING GUIDE 1
Refer to *Prompting Guide 1* as needed.

- Invite children to reread *Going on Vacation* and *Wheels*.
- If needed, prompt readers for word-solving using information from the pictures and the first letter of words; e.g., "Think what would make sense and look right" or "Read that again and start the word."

▸ Phonics/Word Work

Quack, Quack, Quack
One day I saw a little duck
With feathers on his back.
I said, "Good morning, little duck."
And he said, "Quack, quack, quack."

- **PRINCIPLE** Recognizing and using beginning consonant sounds and the letters that represent them: *s, m, t, b, f, r, n, p, d, h, c, g, j, l, k, v, w, z, qu, y, x*

"You can hear the sound at the beginning of a word."
"You can read a word by thinking about the first letter and the sound."

- Read "Quack, Quack, Quack" (poem 7) to children once and talk about the meaning.
- Tell children that this poem has some words in it that they know. Ask, "Can you find a word you know?" Children may locate words such as: *said, I, little, he, and, on* with a masking card or highlighter tape.
- Have children find words that are new to them. Share with them that it will help them to read up to the new word and get their mouths ready to say the sound of the first letter.
- Cover the word *his* with a stick-on note. Demonstrate by reading the first two lines up to the word *his* and making the sound. Uncover *his* and have children read it while you run a finger under it left to right.
- Repeat and invite children to read *his* with you. Cover *morning* and *duck* in the third line and repeat the process.
- Have the children read the reproduced version of the poem in *My Poetry Book* and do a quick illustration.

▸ New Book

Hiding, Level B

Introducing the Text

- Introduce the children to the book by showing the cover. Suggested language: "Meet Puff, the fluffy cat. This book is called *Hiding* and it tells about all of the places where Puff likes to hide. Do you know places where cats like to hide?" Children respond.
- "Turn to page 3. Where does Puff like to hide? Yes, Puff likes to hide in the box. Say the word *likes*. What letter would you see first in *likes?* Find l and put your finger under it. Get a good look and say it."
- "Turn to page 7. What do you see? Yes, you notice Puff's tail sticking out of the closet. Say the word *in*. It has two letters."
- "Turn to page 13. Where is Puff now? Yes, he is under the rug. Clap *under*. *Under* starts with a *u*, just like *up*. Can you find under and put your finger under it? Say *under*." Repeat for page 15.
- "Turn back to the beginning of the story. Point and read softly about all of the places where Puff likes to hide."

PROMPTING GUIDE 1
Refer to *Prompting Guide 1* as needed.

Reading the Text

- The children should have strong control of voice-print match by now.
- You may want to help children check on their use of picture information to check the first letter of a word (e.g., *bed*) and their use of the pictures for the prepositions *in* and *under*.

Discussing and Revisiting the Text

Invite the children to talk about Puff and all of the places he likes to hide. Some key understandings children may express are:

- Puff, the cat, likes to hide in many different places. [Extend by asking for examples. Encourage children to show the pages that illustrate the examples they name.]
- At the end, Puff hides in the bed. [Extend by asking children how they know this.]
- Cats like to hide in lots of different places. [Encourage children to share their own knowledge of cats.]
- This story reminds me of ______________________________.

PROMPTING GUIDE 1
Refer to *Prompting Guide 1* as needed.

Teaching Points

- Based on your observations, use *Prompting Guide 1* to select a teaching point that will be most helpful to the readers.
- You may want the children to quickly locate the words *in* or *under* on one or two pages.
- You may need to demonstrate ways that children can check on their reading.

Poem #7

Quack, Quack, Quack

One day I saw a little duck
With feathers on his back.
I said, "Good morning, little duck."
And he said, "Quack, quack, quack."

- If time allows, have children draw a quick picture to illustrate the poem.
- Have children reread the poem, "Quack, Quack, Quack," which they have just read in *My Poetry Book*. Say several words, both known and unknown, that appear in the poem. Have children say the first sound and the letter. Then have them locate and read the word. Suggestions: *day, saw, little, quack* (six times in the poem), *said, feathers, with, back, duck*.

Letter Minibooks

- Read several Letter Minibooks. Choose letters with which children need more practice. Have them run a finger over the letter on the cover, using the Verbal Path. Then, have children read each page, thinking about the beginning sound. Let children take home Letter Minibooks that are well known.

Classroom Connection

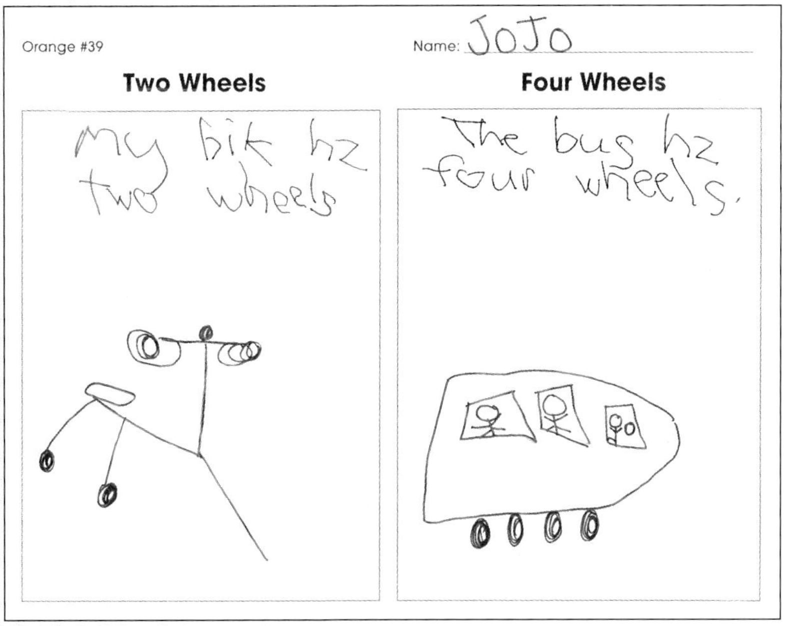

- Give children the fold sheet folded in half. On one half is written "Two Wheels" and on the other side is written "Four Wheels."
- Children can draw and write about something that they know that has two wheels and something that has four wheels.
- Have children read the Take-Home Book *Wheels*.
- If needed, have students read the vowel Letter Minibooks.

Home/School Connection

- Children can take home Letter Minibooks for the vowels.
- Have them take home *Wheels* to read to family members.
- Have them take home their fold sheets to share.

Assessing Reading and Writing Behaviors

Observe to find evidence that children can:

- represent several sounds by saying words slowly and writing them.
- read with voice-print match across two lines of text.
- self-monitor and self-correct.
- make inferences about the personality of the cat.

Supporting English Language Learners

To support English language learners, you can:

- **monitor** for understanding of "Think what would make sense and look right."
- **monitor** for understanding of, "You can read a word by thinking about the first letter and the sound."
- **reread** the poem several times and act it out to reinforce its meaning.
- **demonstrate** reading up to a word and getting your mouth ready to say the sound of the letter.
- **check** that children know the meaning of all the words being located in the poem.
- **check** for understanding of the concept of hiding.
- **use** the language of the text in a conversational way.
- **have** children repeat the language several times to help them remember the syntax and the labels for objects and places mentioned in the story.
- **check** to be sure that children understand the meaning of *in* and *under*.
- **support** children's discussion of where Puff likes to hide, what kind of cat Puff is, and model how you would think to figure out where Puff was hiding. "I noticed in this picture that Puff likes to hide in__________. He makes me laugh."

Professional Development Links

When Readers Struggle: Teaching that Works
Chapter 8: Words Matter: Building Power in Vocabulary. Use this chapter to help in understanding how children come to understand the meaning of abstract words such as *behind*.

Professional Development and Tutorial DVD, Orange System
You may want to view the LLI Sample Lessons to notice how children are developing phonological awareness.

Word Matters: Teaching Phonics and Spelling in the Reading/Writing Classroom
Chapter 8 (pp. 76–77, 78–80). Use this chapter to understand the role of phonology (understanding and using the sounds of language) in literacy.

Guided Reading: Good First Teaching for All
Chapter 12 (pp. 154–155). Use this chapter to explore using the first letter of a new word and language structure to solve new words.

YOU WILL NEED

- Take-Home Book, *Hiding*
- *My Writing Book*
- "Little Frog," enlarged poem
- stick-on notes
- highlighter tape
- magnetic letters

From the CD:

- *My Poetry Book*✓
- Letters Made in Similar Ways document
- Recording Form for *Hiding*
- fold sheet
- Parent Letter

SYSTEM **Orange**

NEW BOOK ***The Show***

GENRE **Fiction**

NEW BOOK
The Show, Level A

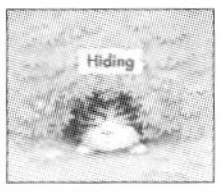

REREADING
Wheels, Level A

Hiding, Level B

Goals

- Recognize and use beginning consonant sounds and the letters that represent them.
- Use language structure and meaning in combination with the first letter of a word.
- Recognize easier high-frequency words quickly.
- Read with voice-print match across two lines of text.
- Read with consistent self-monitoring and self-correction behavior.
- Use language structure, meaning, and visual information while reading.
- Write easy high-frequency words quickly.
- Say words slowly to listen for and identify sounds and the letters that represent them.
- Reread writing to know what to write next.
- Understand and discuss the central idea of the book (concept of a show, performers, and an audience.)
- Understand a show as entertainment that people enjoy.

Analysis of New Book Characteristics

The Show, Level A

GENRE/FORM
- Fiction

TEXT STRUCTURE
- Different kind of circus performer on every page
- No sequence
- Part-to-whole with combined act of three performers plus audience on last page

CONTENT
- Most performers familiar to children, but some needing explanation
- Concept of a show with clown and animals doing tricks

THEMES AND IDEAS
- Entertaining a crowd
- Enjoyment

LANGUAGE AND LITERARY FEATURES
- NA

SENTENCE COMPLEXITY
- One five-word simple sentence on every page
- Imperative sentence
- Repeating pattern on each page with no variation except alternating *the* and *a*

VOCABULARY
- Names of performers: *clown, horse, dog, bear, lion, elephant, tiger*
- Content words: *show*

WORDS
- High-frequency words: *come, and, see, the, a, an*
- One-syllable words with some two-syllable words and one three-syllable word
- See the Word Analysis Charts in the *Program Guide* for specific words in each category.

ILLUSTRATIONS
- Colorful and amusing drawings
- Close match between pictures and text
- Illustrations that convey the feeling of an ongoing show

BOOK AND PRINT FEATURES
- Large font
- Ample space between words
- One line on each page of print
- Print on the left on a blank page; illustrations on the right page, except for last page
- Periods and exclamation point

▸ Rereading Books and Assessment

- *Wheels*, Level A
- *Hiding* Level B

PROMPTING GUIDE 1
Refer to *Prompting Guide 1* as needed.

- Listen to one child read *Hiding* as you code the reading behavior on the Recording Form, have a brief comprehension conversation, and make a teaching point that you think will be most helpful to the reader. Score and analyze the Reading Record following the lesson.
- Have the other children reread *Wheels* and then *Hiding*.
- Prompt for word solving using more than one source of information; e.g., "Try that again and think what would make sense and look right."

Take a Reading Record

▸ Phonics/Word Work

Little Frog

One day I saw a little frog
Going hop, hop, hop.
I said, "Hello, little frog
Can you stop, stop, stop?"

- **PRINCIPLE** Recognizing and using beginning consonant sounds and the letters that represent them: *s, m, t, b, f, r, n, p, d, h, c, g, j, l, k, v, w, z, qu, y, x*

"You can hear the sound at the beginning of a word."
"You can read a word by thinking about the first letter and the sound."

- Read "Little Frog" (poem 8) to children once and talk about the meaning.
- Tell children that this poem has some words that they know. Have the children locate words like *I, little, said,* and put highlighter tape on the words.
- Tell children that when they are reading, they will find words that are new to them. Share with children that it will help them to read up to the word and get their mouths ready to say the sound of the first letter.
- To demonstrate, cover the *rog* in *frog* with a stick-on note, then read the first two lines up to the word *frog* and make the *f* sound. Uncover the rest of the word *frog* and have children read it while you run a finger under it left to right.
- Repeat the process and invite children to read the word with you. Repeat the process with *hop* and *stop* in the second line. If children seem to understand this easily, you can point out that *stop* has an *s* and then a *t,* and that both letters help you to read the word.

▸ Writing About Reading

Independent Writing

- **MY WRITING BOOK**
- **PROMPTING GUIDE 1**

Refer to *Prompting Guide 1* as needed.

- If time allows, you may want to begin by having each child read recent pages from *My Writing Book*. Occasionally ask the child to locate a word in a sentence read.
- Talk with the children about Puff and the places he likes to hide.
- Have children write about two places that Puff likes to hide. When you talk with the children to help them compose, you help them go from their ideas to spoken language and then to written language.
- You may want to support children's writing of words like *hide* by displaying three sound boxes containing the letters *h, i,* and *d* respectively. Then show children the silent *e* in the third box (see Instructional Routines, Sound Boxes, in the *Program Guide*).
- Finally, have the children reread and illustrate their sentences.

▸ New Book

The Show, Level A

Introducing the Text

- Introduce children to the book by showing the cover. Suggested language: "Have you ever seen the show at the circus? Today you are going to read about the show that all the animals and clowns put on at the circus. The writer of this story tells about all the things that you can see at the circus show."
- "Turn to pages 2 and 3. What does the writer tell you to come and see? Yes, so the writer says 'Come and see the clown.' Say *come*. What letter do you expect to see first? Yes, it's an uppercase *C* because the word *Come* starts the sentence. Put your finger under the word and say *come*."
- "Turn to pages 10 and 11. "What should you come and see now? Yes, so the writer says, 'Come and see the lion.' Say *and*. What letter would come first in *and*? Yes, *and* starts with the letter *a*. Put your finger under the word and say it."
- "Turn back to the beginning of the story. Point and read softly about all the things you can come and see at the show."

PROMPTING GUIDE 1
Refer to *Prompting Guide 1* as needed.

Reading the Text

- As the children read, reinforce any self-correction behaviors, e.g., "You fixed that" (see *Prompting Guide* 1).
- Notice how children use the picture information and check it with the first letter of the word that they are trying to figure out.

Discussing and Revisiting the Text

Invite children to talk about all the different things they would see at the circus. Some key understandings children may express are:

- People see a lot of different and fun things at a show. [Extend by asking for examples, showing pages. You may want to use the word *acts* if they understand this easily.]
- This show is like a circus. [Encourage children to talk about the similarities they see.]
- People like going to shows like this one. [Extend by asking why they think that.]

PROMPTING GUIDE 1
Refer to *Prompting Guide 1* as needed.

Teaching Points

- Based on your observations, use *Prompting Guide 1* to select a teaching point that will be most helpful to the readers.
- You may want the children to locate *come, see,* and *and* on one or two pages and quickly write these words a few times on the whiteboard.
- Reinforce effective problem solving, or demonstrate a way to problem solve if needed.

▸ Optional Letter/ Word Work

Little Frog

One day I saw a little rabbit

Going hop, hop, hop

I said, "Hello little rabbit

Can you stop, stop, stop?"

- Using shared reading, have children reread the poem substituting *rabbit* (on a stick-on note) for the word *frog*. Repeat with the word *bunny*.
- Have children shut their eyes while you make the substitutions. They can then take turns reading the poem, checking the first letter closely to determine the key word.
- If they understand this easily, you can add a verse with the word *bunny*.

Letter Sort

- If looking at print and distinguishing the features of letters in words is not smooth and quick, spend a minute or two having the children sort magnetic letters *b*, *f*, and *r* along with the other letters a few different ways.

Classroom Connection

- Give children the fold sheet that is divided into four squares with the title, *Hiding*, in the first square. In the other three squares is written, *Puff likes to hide* ________.
- Have children take the fold sheet to the classroom, cut the squares apart, and staple the pages into a booklet. Then they finish the sentences with where Puff likes to hide (using the Take-Home Book as a model) and illustrate their sentences.
- Have children read the Take-Home Book *Hiding*.

Home/School Connection

- Give children the Take-Home Book *Hiding*.
- Have children take home their fold sheets to read to family members. They may finish their illustrations if not completed in the classroom.

Assessing Reading and Writing Behaviors

Observe to find evidence that children can:

- use beginning consonant sounds and the letters that represent them while reading words in connected text.
- quickly recognize high-frequency words.
- demonstrate voice-print match, self-monitoring, and self-correction behavior.
- write easy high-frequency words quickly.
- say words slowly to listen for and identify sounds.
- understand what a show is.

Supporting English Language Learners

To support English language learners, you can:

- **teach** for understanding of "Try that again and think what would make sense and look right."
- **reread** the poem, "Little Frog," several times and act it out to reinforce its meaning.
- **demonstrate** reading up to a word and getting your mouth ready to say the sound of the letter.
- **check** that children know the meaning of all the words being located in "Little Frog."
- **check** to be sure that children understand the concept of a show.
- **use** the language of the text in a conversational way. Have children repeat the language several times to help them remember the syntax and the labels for all of the people/animals in the show.
- **encourage** children's discussion of what happens at the show, what the show is like, what the show reminds them of, and how people at the show might be feeling by modeling your thinking out loud.
- **model** saying a word slowly and moving your finger across the sound boxes. Ask children to repeat the process after you.

Professional Development Links

When Readers Struggle: Teaching that Works
Chapter 7: Language Matters: Talking, Reading, and Writing. Use this chapter to understand how to help children who have trouble using language structure.

Professional Development and Tutorial DVD, Orange System
View the Instructional Routine, Sound Boxes, in Teaching Within the LLI Lesson to notice the precision of the teacher's language.

Interactive Writing: How Language and Literacy Come Together
Chapter 8 (pp.109–120). Use this chapter to explore how constructing a text supports children in learning how words work.

Teaching for Comprehending and Fluency: Thinking, Talking, and Writing About Reading, K–8
Chapter 8 (pp. 96–Figure 8-6, 97–98). Use this chapter to explore a discussion of the role of self-correction in early reading.

YOU WILL NEED

- Take-Home Book, *The Show*
- magnetic letters: *o, p, t, m, h, s*
- highlighter tape

From the CD:

- *My Poetry Book* ✓
- *My ABC Book* ✓
- Go Fish cards
- fold sheet
- Parent Letter

SYSTEM **Orange**

NEW BOOK ***Hop, Hop, Hop***

GENRE **Fiction**

NEW BOOK
Hop, Hop, Hop, Level B

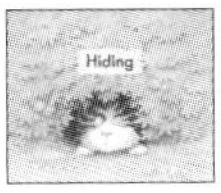

REREADING
Hiding, Level B

The Show, Level A

Goals

- Recognize and use simple phonogram patterns with a VC structure.
- Begin to notice consonant clusters.
- Begin to gain control of the entire alphabet–letter names and sounds.
- Read verbs from a list, separated by commas.
- Locate known high-frequency words in a text.
- Understand a simple sequence of actions.
- Read with control of voice-print match across one or two lines of text.
- Begin to pause at natural breaks (indicated by line breaks).
- Read with close attention to print, self-monitoring, and self-correction behavior.
- Notice what makes the ending funny.
- Understand that there will be other books to read about the character Bunny and the Rabbit family.

Analysis of New Book Characteristics

Hop, Hop, Hop, Level B

GENRE/FORM

- Fiction
- Simple Animal Fantasy
- Series (second book in *Bunny* Series)

TEXT STRUCTURE

- Narrative
- Seven brief episodes that could be in any order except for the last two pages

CONTENT

- Familiar places around the house
- Concept of hopping
- Bunny behavior

THEMES AND IDEAS

- Bunny as a small child
- Home and fun

LANGUAGE AND LITERARY FEATURES

- Simple story
- Character narrating story

SENTENCE COMPLEXITY

- One six-word simple sentence on every page except the last two pages which respectively have an eight- and a seven-word sentence
- Repeating pattern with slight changes (*in* and *on;* repetition of *hop;* addition of *and* on the last page
- Present tense
- Prepositional phrases

VOCABULARY

- Names of places to hop: *grass, leaves, wall, rocks, puddle, stairs, bed, tub*
- Prepositions: *in, on, up*

WORDS

- High-frequency words: *I, can, in, the, on, a, up, and*
- One-syllable words with one two-syllable word
- Onomatopoetic word in illustration
- See the Word Analysis Charts in the *Program Guide* for specific words in each category.

ILLUSTRATIONS

- Soft pastel painting on every right page
- Close match between pictures and text

BOOK AND PRINT FEATURES

- Large font
- Ample space between words
- Two lines on each page of print
- Print on the left on a blank page; illustrations on the right page, except for last page
- Periods and exclamation point

▸ Rereading Books

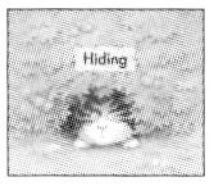

- *Hiding*, Level B
- *The Show*, Level A

PROMPTING GUIDE 1
Refer to *Prompting Guide 1* as needed.

- Invite children to reread *Hiding* and *The Show*.
- Prompt children to use language structure and give close attention to visual information in the prepositional phrases; e.g., "Does it look right and sound right?"

▸ Phonics/Word Work

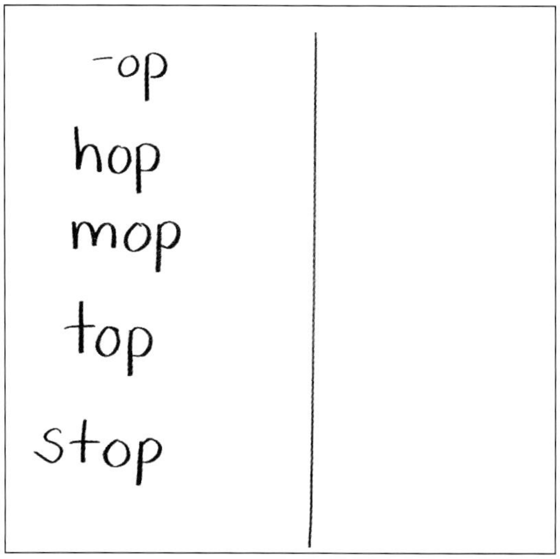

- **PRINCIPLE** Recognizing and using simple phonograms with a VC pattern (easiest): *-ad, -ag, -an, -am, -at, -ed, -en, -et, -ig, -in, -it, -og, -op, -ot, -ut*

"You can look at the pattern [part] you know to help you read a word."

"You can make new words by putting a letter or a letter cluster before the word part or pattern."

- Make a two-column chart on chart paper. Write *-op* at the top of the first column. Invite children to name the letters and say the word part. Suggested language: "What letter do you put first to make *hop?*" Children will respond with an *h*. Write *hop* on the chart. Repeat the process for *mop* and *top*.
- "Sometimes you see two letters that go together in a word. If I write *st* and then write *-op*, I make the word *stop*. Write *stop* on the chart. Then have children read the whole list of words on the chart.
- Have children locate and highlight the *-op* words in the poem "Little Frog" (poem 8) with highlighter tape or a masking card.
- Save the chart for use in subsequent lessons. You will be adding columns for more phonogram lists.

▸ New Book

***Hop, Hop, Hop*,**
Level B

Introducing the Text

- Introduce children to the book by first showing the cover of *My Family* from Getting Started, Lesson 8. Quickly read through it. Then show the new book and ask children what they notice (the same bunny).
- Suggested language: "This is Bunny Rabbit. She is going to tell about the places where she can hop. Turn to page 2. Bunny Rabbit says she can hop in the grass."
- "Turn to page 5. What do you see? So Bunny Rabbit will say, 'I can hop in the leaves.' Say the word *can*. What letter comes first? Find can and get a good look. Put your finger under it and say *can*.
- "Turn to page 7 and see where Bunny Rabbit can hop. Now, what will she say? Say the word *on*. What letter would you see first? Yes, find the word on and put your finger under it. Get a good look and say *on*."
- Look at several more pages and use the language.
- "And turn to the end of the story to see Bunny Rabbit's favorite place to hop." Have children say and locate and.
- Now turn back to the beginning. Point and read softly about all of the places where Little Bunny says she can hop. Remember to point under each word.

PROMPTING GUIDE 1
Refer to *Prompting Guide 1* as needed.

Reading the Text

- As children read, prompt for self-monitoring as needed.
- You may need to teach, prompt for, or reinforce a child's search for, and use of, meaning; e.g., "What would make sense?" or use of language structure; e.g., "Think what would sound right."

Discussing and Revisiting the Text

Invite children to talk about what Bunny Rabbit likes to do. Some key understandings children may express are:

- Bunny Rabbit likes to hop on lots of different things. [Extend by asking for examples, show pictures.]
- At the end of the story, she hops into the bath tub and makes a big splash. [Extend by asking if they think this ending was funny and why.]
- This story reminds me of __________. [Accept any reasonable response such as jumping on my own bed.]
- The bunny seems to like hopping on her bed best of all. [Extend by asking why they think that.]
- Tell children that this story is part of a Bunny Rabbit series and they will be reading more books about Bunny and her family.

PROMPTING GUIDE 1
Refer to *Prompting Guide 1* as needed.

Teaching Points

- Based on your observations, use *Prompting Guide 1* to select a teaching point that will be most helpful to the readers.

▸ Letter/Word Work

- Introduce a personal alphabet book, *My ABC Book,* to children. (See Instructional Routines, *My ABC Book,* in the *Program Guide.*) The book has 26 pages, one for each letter. (Children have already had a great deal of work on letters and sounds. *My ABC Book* will help to "tidy up" letter knowledge.) You may take letters in any order indicated by assessment of children's knowledge, beginning with the most familiar letters. The book will already have the printed letter and the picture from the Alphabet Linking Chart.
- Have the children go to a page in their *My ABC Book,* read the letter and the word, and then color the picture. Finally, have them write a word that they know that begins with the letter. (This may not be necessary for very difficult letters such as *X.*)
- To start, go to pages for *Bb, Mm, Tt* and have children color in pictures of *bear, moon,* and *turtle.* After they color in a picture, have them write a word that begins with the letter on the page. You should follow this procedure each time children use *My ABC Book.*

Magnetic Letters

- Give children the letters: *o, p, t, m, h, s.* Let them make words with *-op.* Then add another *p* and show them how to make *pop.*

Classroom Connection

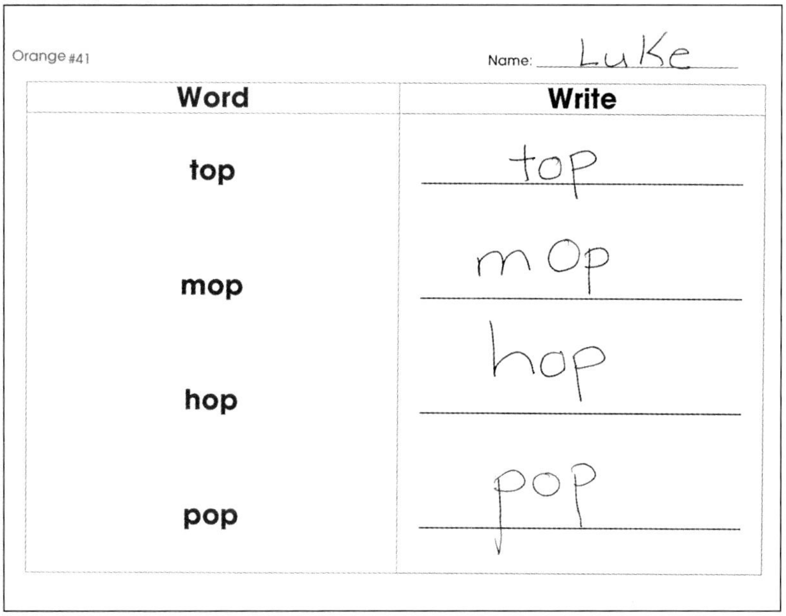
Orange #41 Name: Luke

Word	Write
top	top
mop	mOp
hop	hop
pop	pop

- Give children the fold sheet to practice writing words with the *-op* pattern.
- Give children the Take-Home Book *The Show.*

Home/School Connection

- Have children take home their fold sheets to read to family members.
- Give children the Take-Home Book *The Show* to read to family members.
- Children can play *Go Fish* with high-frequency words (see *Lesson Resources CD*).

Assessing Reading and Writing Behaviors

Observe to find evidence that children can:

- quickly use phonogram patterns to read and write words.
- be helped with letters of the alphabet that they still do not control.
- use commas to pause briefly while reading.
- quickly locate high-frequency words in a text.
- pause at natural breaks.
- self-monitor and self-correct reading.
- interpret Bunny's actions.
- understand the sequence of Bunny's actions.

Supporting English Language Learners

To support English language learners, you can:

- **monitor** for understanding of "It has to look right and sound right."
- **demonstrate** through writing and orally the meaning of "Sometimes you see two letters that go together in words." Ask children to repeat after you when you say */s/ /t/ – /st/ /op/ –stop*
- **check** for understanding of the pictures in *My ABC Book.*
- **model** the meaning of *hop* with actions or by using another word, such as *jump*.
- **use** the language of the text in a conversational way. Have children repeat the language several times to help them remember the syntax (especially on page 14).
- **discuss** each place the bunny hops, and ask children to repeat those places.
- **use** the prompts "What would make sense?" or "Think what would sound right" only if children have been taught the meaning of these prompts.
- **use** pictures to support children's discussion of where the bunny likes to hop and how she feels about hopping. Think aloud about what the story reminds you of.

Professional Development Links

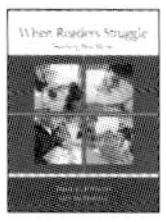

When Readers Struggle: Teaching that Works
Chapter 9: Learning to Read and Write: the Phonological Base. Use this chapter to understand the role of phonological awareness in using word patterns.

Professional Development and Tutorial DVD, Orange System
Spend some time viewing Teaching Within the LLI Lesson to be sure you know how to use the instructional routines effectively.

Voices on Word Matters: Learning About Phonics and Spelling in the Literacy Classroom
Chapter 6 (p. 63). Use this chapter to explore the important role of personal alphabet books to help in letter learning.

Guided Reading: Good First Teaching for All Children
Chapter 12 (pp. 14–162). Use this chapter to understand teaching for early reading strategies.

SYSTEM **Orange**

NEW BOOK ***The Puppet Show***

GENRE **Fiction**

YOU WILL NEED

- Take-Home Book, *Hop, Hop, Hop*
- *My Writing Book*
- "Rain on the Rooftops," enlarged poem
- phonogram chart from Lesson 41
- magnetic letter set
- highlighter tape

From the CD:

- *My Poetry Book* ✓
- *My ABC Book* ✓
- Letters Made in Similar Ways document
- Recording Form for *Hop, Hop, Hop*
- fold sheet
- Parent Letter

NEW BOOK
The Puppet Show, Level A

REREADING
The Show, Level A
Hop, Hop, Hop, Level B

Goals

- Self-monitor voice-print match.
- Self-correct most errors.
- Recognize and use beginning consonant sounds and the letters that represent them.
- Use language structure and meaning in combination with the first letter of a word to solve new words.
- Recognize and write easy high-frequency words quickly.
- Read with voice-print match, self-monitoring, and self-correction behavior.
- Use language structure, meaning, and visual information while reading.
- Write high-frequency words quickly.
- Say words slowly, listen for sounds, and write letters that represent them.
- Form letters efficiently.
- Understand and discuss the concept of a puppet show.
- Understand a show as entertainment that people enjoy.

Analysis of New Book Characteristics

The Puppet Show, Level A

GENRE/FORM

- Fiction

TEXT STRUCTURE

- Different activities and objects related to going to a puppet show
- Sequence of activities building to watching the show and the end of the show

CONTENT

- Most activities familiar to children, but some needing explanation
- Concept of puppets and a show

THEMES AND IDEAS

- Entertaining a crowd
- Enjoying a show

LANGUAGE AND LITERARY FEATURES

- Anticipation built through illustrations

SENTENCE COMPLEXITY

- One five-word simple sentence on every page, except the last
- Repeating pattern on each page with no variation

VOCABULARY

- Names of everything the narrator sees: *children, ticket, popcorn, seats, stage, puppets, show*

WORDS

- High-frequency words: *I, can, see, the*
- One-syllable words with some two-syllable words
- See the Word Analysis Charts in the *Program Guide* for specific words in each category.

ILLUSTRATIONS

- Colorful and amusing drawings
- Close match between pictures and text
- Illustrations that convey the excitement of going to a puppet show
- Illustration saying *The End* and no text as the last page

BOOK AND PRINT FEATURES

- Large font
- Ample space between words
- One line on each page of print
- Print on the left on a blank page; illustrations on the right page, except for last page
- Periods

Rereading Books and Assessment

- *The Show* Level A
- *Hop, Hop, Hop*, Level B

PROMPTING GUIDE 1
Refer to *Prompting Guide 1* as needed.

- Listen to one child read *Hop, Hop, Hop* as you code the reading behavior on the Recording Form, have a brief comprehension conversation, and make a teaching point that you think will be most helpful to the reader. Score and analyze the Reading Record following the lesson.
- Have the other children reread *The Show* and then *Hop, Hop, Hop.*
- Prompt for self-monitoring and self-correcting as needed; e.g., "Think of what would make sense and check with the letters."

Phonics/Word Work

- **PRINCIPLE** Recognizing and using simple phonograms with a VC pattern (easiest): *-ad, -ag, -an, -am, -at, -ed, -en, -et, -ig, -in, -it, -og, -op, -ot, -ut*

"You can look at the pattern [part] you know to help you read a word."

"You can make new words by putting a letter or a letter cluster before the word part or pattern."

- Using shared reading, have the children reread the poem "Little Frog" (poem 8) in *My Poetry Book* and identify words with the *-op* pattern.
- Read the poem, "Rain on the Rooftops" (poem 2) to the children, discuss it, and then have them join in a couple of times as you point under each word.
- Using the chart that you began in Lesson 41, write *-ot* at the top of the second column. Suggested language: "Some words have the part or pattern *ot* in them. Can you find a word in the new poem that has that part or pattern?" Have the children respond with the word *not* (or point it out) and highlight it with highlighter tape or highlighter marker.
- Point to *-ot* at the top of the column. Invite children to name the letters and say the word part. Ask: "What letter do you need to put first to make *not?*" Children will respond with an *n*. Write *not* on the chart. Repeat the process for *hot, pot,* and *lot.*
- If time allows, work with another pattern (e.g., *en, ed*).

Writing About Reading

Dictated Writing

- **MY WRITING BOOK**
- **PROMPTING GUIDE 1**

Refer to *Prompting Guide 1* as needed.

- If time allows, you may want to begin by having each child read recent pages from *My Writing Book*. Occasionally ask the child to locate a word in a sentence read.
- Dictate the following sentences for children to write in their writing books:

  I can hop in the grass.
  I can hop up the stairs.
- Use sound boxes on the whiteboard to support *hop* or *grass* if needed.
- Support quick writing of high-frequency words such as *up, in, can, the, I.*
- If time allows, write one sentence on a sentence strip, cut it up, and have the children put it together.

▸ New Book

***The Puppet Show*,**
Level A

Introducing the Text

- Introduce the children to the book by talking about what puppets are. Suggested language: "This little girl and her mother are going into the theater to see a puppet show. The little girl tells all the things that she can see."
- "Turn to pages 2 and 3. What does the little girl see first? Yes, she can see the children."
- "Now turn to pages 4 and 5. And what can she see? Yes, she can see the ticket. Find the word <u>can</u>. Run your finger under it and say *can*."
- "Turn to pages 10 and 11 to see what the little girl can see."
- "Now turn back to the beginning of the story to read about some of the things that the little girl can see at the show. Remember to point under each word."

PROMPTING GUIDE 1
Refer to *Prompting Guide 1* as needed.

Reading the Text

- Reinforce effective self-monitoring and the use of meaning or language to problem solve.
- Use prompts such as, "Were you right?" or "What would sound right?"

Discussing and Revisiting the Text

Talk about the things the little girl saw at the theater and help children notice the sequence. Invite children to talk about a similar experience. Some key understandings children may express are:

- The girl sees many things at the puppet show. [Extend by asking for examples. Have children show the pages that illustrate these examples.]
- The girl is probably excited about the puppet show. [Extend by asking why they think that.]
- This book reminds me of _________. [Encourage any reasonable response from the children's own experience.)
- The children enjoy the puppet show. [Extend by asking why they think that, e.g., they are clapping at the end.]

PROMPTING GUIDE 1
Refer to *Prompting Guide 1* as needed.

Teaching Points

- Based on your observations, use *Prompting Guide 1* to select a teaching point that will be most helpful to the readers.
- Reinforce effective monitoring, and the use of meaning or language information to solve new words.
- You may also want the children to quickly write a few of the high-frequency words such as *can* and *see.*

▸ Optional Letter/ Word Work

- Give the children the magnetic letters: *o, t, n, h, p,* and *l.* Have them make words with *-ot.* Then have them put away the letters and write two of the words in *My Writing Book.*

My ABC Book

- Have the children work on their personal alphabet books, *My ABC Book.* Invite them to go to the pages for *Cc, Hh,* and *Ll* and color the *cat, hat,* and *leaf.* Then have them write a word that begins with *c, h,* and *l* on the appropriate pages.

Letter Sort

- Finally, have the children sort their magnetic letters two or three ways letters that have tails, e.g., letters that have tall parts, and letters without tails. (See Instructional Routines, Ways to Sort and Match Letters, in the *Program Guide.*)

Classroom Connection

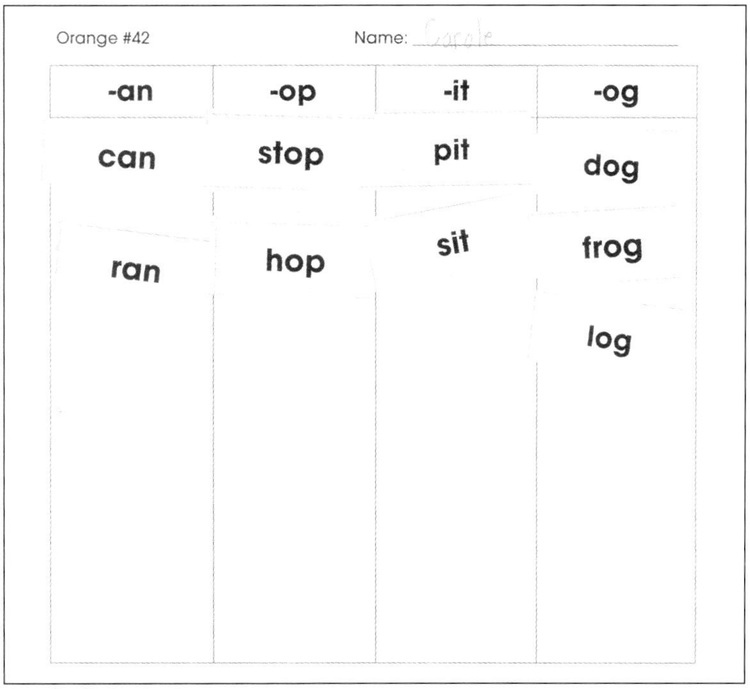

Orange #42 Name:

-an	-op	-it	-og
can	stop	pit	dog
ran	hop	sit	frog
			log

- Give the children the fold sheet with four columns labeled *-an, -op, -it, -og* and the words with VC patterns (*dog, log, pit, sit, ran, can, frog, hop, stop*).
- Have children take it back to the classroom to cut apart and sort.
- Let children glue their words on the fold sheet or take them home to sort again.
- Have the children reread the Take-Home Book *Hop, Hop, Hop.*

Home/School Connection

- Have the children take home their fold sheets and word cards to read to family members.
- Give children the Take-Home Book *Hop, Hop, Hop* to read to family members.

Assessing Reading and Writing Behaviors

Observe to find evidence that children can:

- use beginning consonant sounds, language structure, and meaning.
- self-monitor voice-print match.
- recognize high-frequency words quickly and use them to monitor reading.
- quickly write high-frequency words.
- say words slowly, listen for sounds, and write letters that represent the sounds.
- form letters efficiently.
- understand and discuss the concept of a puppet show.
- understand a show as entertainment that people enjoy.

Supporting English Language Learners

To support English language learners, you can:

- **help** children in understanding the concept of going to a puppet show in the theatre.
- **use** the language of the text in a conversational way. Have children repeat the language several times to help them remember the syntax.
- **monitor** for understanding of the prompts, "Were you right?" or "What would sound right?"
- **check** to be sure that children understand and can name all of the things that the little girl sees.
- **use** the pictures as support for talking about the things the little girl saw and the sequence of actions. Introduce terms like *first, next,* and *after that,* but don't expect children to use them consistently.
- **think** aloud about what this story makes you think of and encourage children to do the same.

Professional Development Links

When Readers Struggle: Teaching that Works
Chapter 7: Language Matters: Talking, Reading, and Writing. Use this chapter to understand how to help children who have trouble using language structure.

Professional Development and Tutorial DVD, Orange System
Notice the precise language used by the teacher in Sound Boxes, Instructional Routines.

Teaching for Comprehending and Fluency: Thinking, Talking, and Writing About Reading, K–8
Chapter 7 (pp. 74–78). Use this chapter to explore how fluency changes over time. Figure 7-3 provides important information about transitions in fluency in early reading.

Interactive Writing: How Language and Literacy Come Together
Chapter 8 (pp. 109–120). Use this chapter to explore how constructing a text supports children in learning how words work.

YOU WILL NEED

- Take-Home Book, *The Puppet Show*
- *My Writing Book*
- magnetic letter set
- "Little Frog," "Rain on the Rooftops," enlarged poems
- word bags

From the CD:

- *My Poetry Book*✓
- *My ABC Book*✓
- Letters Made in Similar Ways document
- fold sheet
- Parent Letter

SYSTEM **Orange**

NEW BOOK ***Rain***

GENRE **Nonfiction**

NEW BOOK
Rain, Level B

REREADING
Hop, Hop, Hop, Level B

The Puppet Show, Level A

Goals

- Recognize and use simple phonogram patterns with a VC structure.
- Begin to notice consonant clusters.
- Gain control of the entire alphabet, letter names, and sounds.
- Locate known high-frequency words in a text.
- Notice a sequence of events.
- Read with full control of voice-print match.
- Give close attention to print.
- Self-monitor and self-correct reading using meaning, language, structure, and visual information.
- Write high-frequency words quickly.

Analysis of New Book Characteristics

Rain, Level B

GENRE/FORM
- Nonfiction

TEXT STRUCTURE
- Series of scenarios, each showing rain falling on something
- Conclusion with rain falling on the narrator, shown on cover and last page

CONTENT
- Familiar places and animals
- Concept of rain falling

THEMES AND IDEAS
- Enjoyment of nature

LANGUAGE AND LITERARY FEATURES
- NA

SENTENCE COMPLEXITY
- One four-word sentence and one seven word sentence on every page except the last
- Repeating pattern with no changes except for alternation of *a* and *the*
- Present tense
- Prepositional phrases

VOCABULARY
- Names of places and animals on which rain is falling: *pig, grass, frog, flowers, bird, trees, dog*
- Content word: *rain*
- Prepositions: *in, on*
- Pronoun: *me*

WORDS
- High-frequency words: *look, at, the, is, on, a, me*
- One-syllable words with some two-syllable words
- See the Word Analysis Charts in the *Program Guide* for specific words in each category.

ILLUSTRATIONS
- Photographs on every right page
- Close match between pictures and text

BOOK AND PRINT FEATURES
- Large font
- Ample space between words
- Three lines of print on each page
- Print on the left on a blank page; illustrations on the right page, except for last page
- Periods and exclamation point

▸ Rereading Books

- *Hop, Hop, Hop*, Level B
- *The Puppet Show*, Level A

PROMPTING GUIDE 1
Refer to *Prompting Guide 1* as needed.

- Invite children to reread *Hop, Hop, Hop* and *The Puppet Show.*
- Prompt for word solving using known words; e.g., "Do you know a word that starts like that?"

▸ Phonics/Word Work

-op	-ot
hop	not
mop	hot
top	pot
stop	lot

- **PRINCIPLE** Recognizing and using simple phonograms with a VC pattern (easiest): *-ad, -ag, -an, -am, -at, -ed, -en, -et, -ig, -in, -it, -og, -op, -ot, -ut*

"You can look at the pattern [part] you know to help you read a word."
"You can write words by using the patterns and the sounds."

- Reread the poems "Little Frog" (poem 8) and "Rain on the Rooftops" (poem 3). Ask children to find a word with a pattern they know and read it.
- Suggested language: "When you think about the first sound and letter and the word part or pattern that you know, it helps you to write a new word." Using the whiteboard, demonstrate writing *hop* and have few other words the children suggest.
- If time allows, quickly write words using the VC phonogram *-ot* as the children suggest them.
- Have children work in *My Writing Book* to write *top, not, hat, bat, can, cat, man, hot,* and other words from the charts you have made. Remind children to think about the first part of the word and the part or pattern of the word they know. Encourage children to suggest words.

▸ New Book

***Rain*,**
Level B

Introducing the Text

- Introduce children to the book by talking about how they feel when it rains. Suggested language: "Look at the rain. Do you like how the rain feels when it falls on you? This girl is telling us to look at the rain. She tells all the things the rain is falling on."
- "Turn to pages 2 and 3. The girl says, 'Look at the rain.' Say *look*. What letter would you see first in *look?* Yes, it's an uppercase *L*. Find look. Run your finger under it and say *look*. What is the rain is falling on? Yes, so the girl says, 'The rain is falling on a pig.'"
- "Turn to pages 6 and 7. Look at the rain in this picture. What is the rain falling on? Yes, it is falling on a frog. Say *on*. What letter would come first in *on?* Put your finger under *on* and say it."
- "Turn to pages 10 and 11 to see what the rain is falling on now."
- "Turn back to the beginning of the book and read about the rain and all the things that it is falling on. Point under each word and read softly."

PROMPTING GUIDE 1
Refer to *Prompting Guide 1* as needed.

Reading the Text

- As children read, prompt for solving words using meaning from pictures and language structure, as appropriate (see *Prompting Guide 1,* Searching For and Using Information), e.g., "Try that again and think what would sound right."

Discussing and Revisiting the Text

Invite children to talk about what things the girl sees the rain fall on in the story. Some key understandings children may express are:

- The girl sees lots of things that get wet in the rain. [Extend by asking for examples. Have the children show the pictures that illustrate these examples.]
- At the end of the story, the rain falls on the girl.
- The girl likes the rain. [Extend by asking why they think that.]
- The grass, flowers, and trees like the rain, too. [Extend by asking why children think grass, flowers, and trees like the rain.]
- This story about the rain reminds me of ____________. [Encourage any reasonable response.]

PROMPTING GUIDE 1
Refer to *Prompting Guide 1* as needed.

Teaching Points

- Based on your observations, use *Prompting Guide 1* to select a teaching point that will be most helpful to the readers.
- If appropriate, reinforce effective problem-solving and independence.

▸ Letter/Word Work

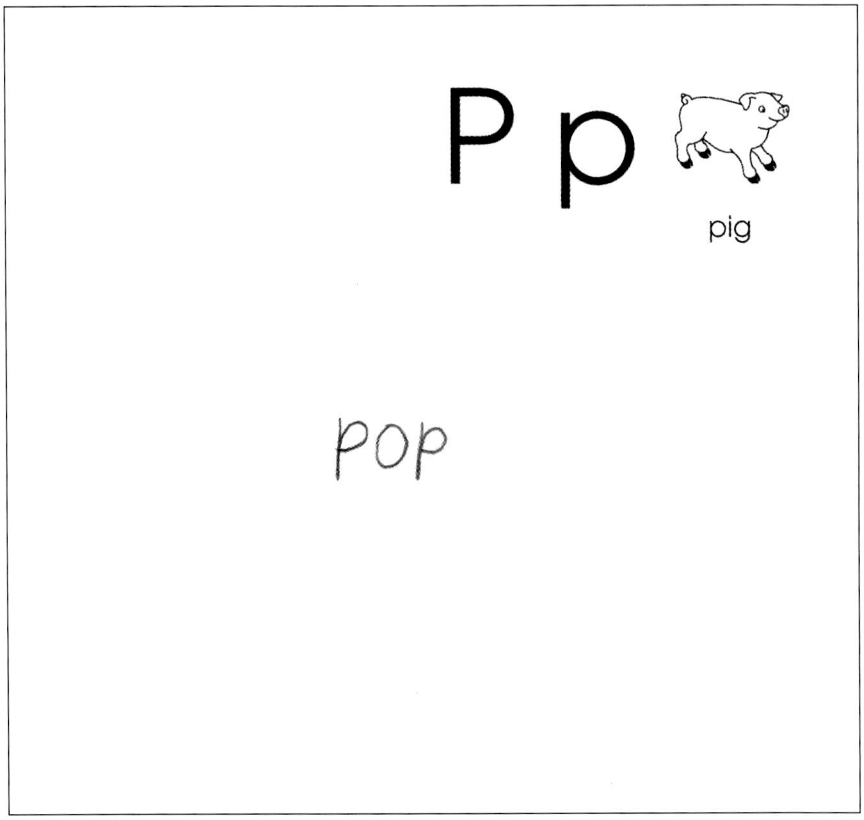

- Have children work in *My ABC Book.* Have them go to the pages for *Kk, Pp, Ss,* and color in *kite, pig,* and *sunflower.*

Word Bags

- Have the children take their word cards from their word bags, and lay the cards out face down. Have children turn over one card at a time, read it, and then put the card back into their word bags.

Letter Sort

- If time allows, and more letter work is needed to help the children distinguish the features of print, have the children sort magnetic letters in two or three different ways (see Instructional Routines, Ways to Sort and Match Letters, in the *Program Guide*).

Classroom Connection

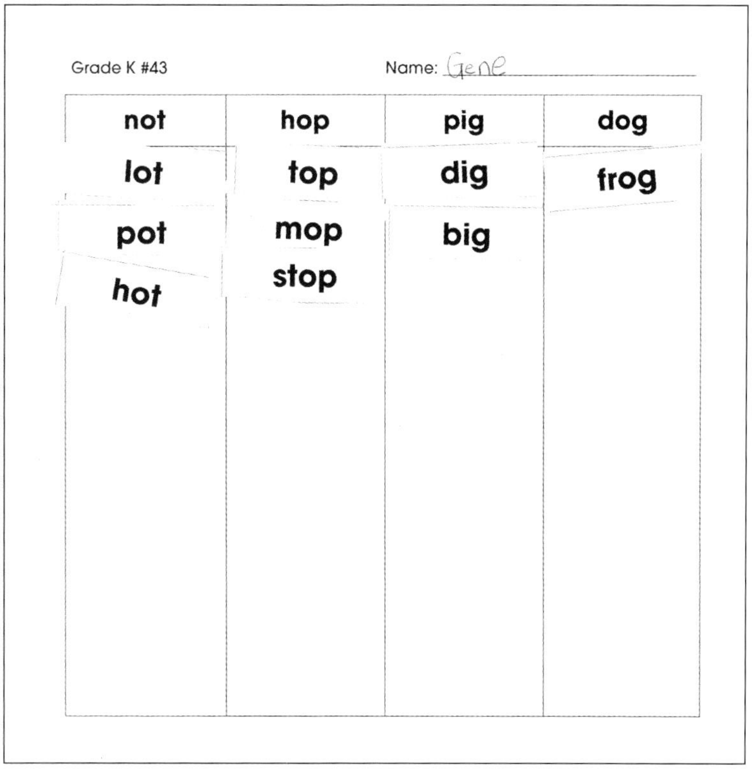
Grade K #43 Name: Gene

not	hop	pig	dog
lot	top	dig	frog
pot	mop	big	
hot	stop		

- Give children the four-column fold sheet with a word at the top of each column—*not, hop, pig, dog*—and the words *mop, top, stop, frog, hot, pot, lot, big, dig* to cut apart and sort into the columns.
- Children can glue their sorted words onto the fold sheet and read them. Alternatively, children can take the loose words home to sort again and then glue onto the fold sheet.
- Give children the Take-Home Book *The Puppet Show* to reread.

Home/School Connection

- Have children take home their fold sheets and sorting words.
- Give children the Take-Home Book *The Puppet Show* to read to family members.
- Have children take home letter cards to sort if they don't have access to magnetic letters.

Assessing Reading and Writing Behaviors

Observe to find evidence that children can:

- use simple phonogram patterns with a VC structure quickly and with flexibility.
- begin to notice consonant clusters in the poem and books.
- report a sequence of events when discussing a story.
- control voice-print match, pay close attention to print, self-monitor, and self-correct.
- quickly write high-frequency words.

Supporting English Language Learners

To support English language learners, you can:

- **teach** for understanding of "Do you know a word that starts like that?"
- **demonstrate** the Phonics/Word Work principle using clear, precise language and the whiteboard. "I want to write *hop*. I know */h/*. Write it." "I know */op/*. Write it." "Now my word says *hop*." Ask children to repeat the sounds and then the whole word.
- **check** to be sure children understand and can name the words and pictures being used in Letter/Word Work.
- **use** the language of the text in a conversational way. Have children repeat the language several times to help them remember the syntax.
- **check** for knowledge of the vocabulary in the book.
- **discuss** that some of the words have an */s/* at the end because it means there are more than one. Ask children to repeat those words.
- **use** the pictures to support children in discussing where the rain fell. Prompt children to talk about what the story makes them think about. "Tell about a time you were out in the rain."

Professional Development Links

When Readers Struggle: Teaching that Works
Chapter 9: Learning to Read and Write: the Phonological Base. Use this chapter to understand the role of phonological awareness in using word patterns.

Professional Development and Tutorial DVD, Orange System
Select an LLI Sample Lesson and use the Reflection Guide (*Lesson Resources CD*) for the odd-numbered lesson to analyze it.

Word Matters: Teaching Phonics and Spelling in the Reading/Writing Classroom
Chapter 9 (pp. 93–94). Use this chapter to explore the concept of consonant clusters. Appendix 7 provides lists of words with consonant clusters in the initial position.

Guided Reading: Good First Teaching for All Children
Chapter 12 (pp. 149–162). Use this chapter to understand teaching for early reading strategies.

SYSTEM **Orange**

NEW BOOK ***My Baby Sister***

GENRE **Fiction**

YOU WILL NEED

- Take-Home Book, *Rain*
- *My Writing Book*
- phonogram chart from Lesson 42
- word bags

From the CD:

- *My Poetry Book*✓
- *My ABC Book*✓
- Recording Form for *Rain*
- fold sheet
- Parent Letter

NEW BOOK

My Baby Sister, Level A

REREADING

The Puppet Show, Level A

Rain, Level B

Goals

- Write words using a wide range of VC phonogram patterns with flexibility.
- Recognize the entire alphabet, letter names, and sounds.
- Locate known words in continuous print.
- Read with voice-print match with self-monitoring, and self-correction behavior.
- Use language structure, meaning, and visual information while reading.
- Write easy high-frequency words quickly.
- Say words slowly, listen for and identify the easy-to-hear sounds, and write the letters that represent them.
- Start a sentence with an uppercase letter and write end punctuation.
- Understand the concept of taking care of a baby and getting her to stop crying.
- Understand why the baby stops crying.

Analysis of New Book Characteristics

My Baby Sister, Level A

GENRE/FORM

- Fiction

TEXT STRUCTURE

- Different activities and objects related to getting a baby to stop crying
- Sequence of activities building to the baby smiling

CONTENT

- Most objects familiar to children
- Concept of taking care of a baby

THEMES AND IDEAS

- Family
- Caring for younger children

LANGUAGE AND LITERARY FEATURES

- Anticipation built through illustrations
- Clear story problem
- Satisfying ending

SENTENCE COMPLEXITY

- One four-word simple sentence on every page
- Repeating pattern on each page with no variation

VOCABULARY

- Names of everything the boy tells the baby to look at: *ball, book, bear, rattle, duck, dog, baby, smile*

WORDS

- High-frequency words: *look, at, the*
- One-syllable words with some two-syllable words
- See the Word Analysis Charts in the *Program Guide* for specific words in each category.

ILLUSTRATIONS

- Soft pastel
- amusing drawings
- Close match between pictures and text
- Illustrations that convey the boy is caring for the baby
- Change in the baby showing on page 15, with another change (*to happy*) on the last page

BOOK AND PRINT FEATURES

- Large font
- Ample space between words
- One line on each page of print
- Print on the left on a blank page; illustrations on the right page, except for last page
- Periods and exclamation point

▸ Rereading Books and Assessment

- *The Puppet Show*, Level A
- *Rain*, Level B

PROMPTING GUIDE 1
Refer to *Prompting Guide 1* as needed.

- Listen to one child read *Rain* as you code the reading behavior on the Recording Form, have a brief comprehension conversation, and select a teaching point that will be most helpful to the reader. Score and analyze the Reading Record following the lesson.
- Have the other children reread *The Puppet Show* and then *Rain.*
- Prompt children to self-monitor and self-correct, if needed; e.g., "Try that again and think what would make sense and look right."

▸ Phonics/Word Work

-op	-ot	-it	-in	-an	-at
hop	not	sit	pin	can	sat
mop	hot	fit	fin	man	cat
top	pot	bit	win	fan	mat
stop	lot				bat
	got				

- **PRINCIPLE** Recognizing and using simple phonograms with a VC pattern (easiest): *-ad, -ag, -an, -am, -at, -ed, -en, -et, -ig, -in, -it, -og, -op, -ot, -ut*

"You can look at the pattern [part] you know to help you read a word."
"You can write words by using the patterns and the sounds."

- Suggested language: "When you think about the first sound and letter and the pattern you know, it helps you to write a new word." Using the chart begun in Lesson 42, demonstrate thinking about the first sound and letter and the word part as you write words with the phonogram patterns *-it, -in, -an, -at.*
- Have children work in *My Writing Book* to listen for the first and last part of words as they write words with the phonogram patterns *top, not, got, sit, win, can, cat, sat* and other words from the charts you have made. Encourage children to suggest words.

My Poetry Book

- Use shared reading to have children reread the poems "Little Frog" (poem 8) and "Rain on the Rooftops" (poem 3) in *My Poetry Book.* Ask children to find a word with a pattern they know and read it.

Writing About Reading

Independent Writing

- **MY WRITING BOOK**
- **PROMPTING GUIDE 1**

Refer to *Prompting Guide 1* as needed.

- If time allows, you may want to begin by having each child read recent pages from *My Writing Book*. Occasionally ask the child to locate a word in a sentence read.
- Talk with the children about some of the things that the rain is falling on. Then ask them to write about two of the things that rain is falling on, e.g.,

  Rain is falling a dog.
  Rain is falling on a pig.
- As the children write, have them say *rain* slowly to listen for the three sounds. On the opposite page in *My Writing Book,* make three sound boxes. The children say the word slowly and identify the sounds in sequence. Have them write the letters. Remind them to start with an uppercase *R*. Support the child's slow articulation of the word.
- Prompt for accurate writing of *is, me, on*. Have the children reread and illustrate their sentences.
- You may want children to locate a word or two in the text (*is, ou*).

▸ New Book

My Baby Sister,
Level A

PROMPTING GUIDE 1
Refer to *Prompting Guide 1* as needed.

Introducing the Text

- Introduce children to the book by showing the cover and reading the title of *My Baby Sister.* Suggested language: "This little boy has a baby sister who keeps crying. So he gets things to show her so she will stop crying and be happy."
- "Turn to pages 2 and 3. What does the boy tell his baby sister to look at? Yes, he tells her to look at a ball."
- "Now turn to pages 5 and 6 and what does he say? Say the word *look.* What letter will come first in *look?* It's an uppercase *L* because the word *look* starts the sentence."
- "Turn to page 8. What does he tell the baby to look at now? Yes, a rattle. Is she still crying? Yes, she is."
- "Go back to the beginning of the book, and read to find out how the boy makes his baby sister stop crying. Point under each word and read softly."

Reading the Text

- You will want to reinforce the children's ability to process the text with ease.
- Observe, notice, and reinforce children's self-monitoring or self-correction behavior.

Discussing and Revisiting the Text

Invite children to talk about all the things the boy used to try to stop the baby from crying and how he finally gets her to stop. Some key understandings children may express are:

- The boy tried to get his baby sister to stop crying. [Extend by asking for examples. Have children show the pages with their examples.]
- She wouldn't stop crying. [Extend by asking why they think she would not stop.]
- She stopped crying because she saw herself in the mirror.
- The baby felt happy at the end. [Extend by asking how they know.]

PROMPTING GUIDE 1
Refer to *Prompting Guide 1* as needed.

Teaching Points

- Based on your observations, use *Prompting Guide 1* to select a teaching point that will be most helpful to the readers.
- Prompt for effective problem solving and independence, e.g., "What can you try?" or "How can you help yourself?"

▸ Optional Letter/ Word Work

- Have children work in *My ABC Book*. Go to pages for *Dd, Ff, Gg* and color in pictures for *dog, fish,* and *gate.*

Word Bags

- Have the children take their word cards out of their word bags, and lay the cards face down on a flat surface. Have children turn over one card at a time, read it, and then put the card back into their word bags.

Classroom Connection

- Have the children take the fold sheet copy of the poem "Rain on the Rooftops" back to the classroom.
- Have children illustrate the poem and read it.
- Give children the Take-Home Book *Rain* to reread.

Home/School Connection

- Have children take home their fold sheet copies of the poem "Rain on the Rooftops" to read to family members.
- Give children the Take-Home Book *Rain* to read to family members.
- Invite children to play an alphabet game with family members (see the Parent Letter in the *Lesson Resources CD* for details).

Assessing Reading and Writing Behaviors

Observe to find evidence that children can:

- use a wide range of VC phonogram patterns with flexibility to write words.
- demonstrate alphabet knowledge of letter names and sounds.
- read with voice-print match and self-monitoring.
- demonstrate use of language structure, meaning, and visual information while reading.
- write easy high-frequency words quickly.
- say words slowly, listen for the easy-to-hear sounds, and write the letters that represent the sounds.
- start a sentence with an uppercase letter and write end punctuation
- understand the concept of taking care of a baby and getting her to stop crying.
- understand why the baby stops crying.

Supporting English Language Learners

To support English language learners, you can:

- **check** to be sure children understand and can name the words and pictures being used in Letter/Word Work.
- **use** the language of the text in a conversational way. Have children repeat the language several times to help them remember the syntax.
- **name** the items the boy has.
- **check** for understanding of why the boy keeps saying "Look at the_____."
- **use** the pictures to support children in discussing what the boy does to try to get the baby to stop crying. Assist children in using language to describe why the baby stopped crying.
- **think** aloud about how you think the boy might be feeling. Ask children how they think the boy is feeling at different points in the story.
- **support** children in constructing a syntactically correct sentence for writing.
- **ask** children to repeat words after you to work on articulation of the sounds in the word. Be sure the children say the words themselves even if they hear a sound from your articulation.

Professional Development Links

When Readers Struggle: Teaching that Works
Chapter 11: Learning to Solve Words: Effective and Efficient Phonics. Use this chapter to understand how to help children dig deeper into print.

Professional Development and Tutorial DVD, Orange System
View the LLI even-numbered Sample Lesson and use the Reflection Guide (*Lesson Resources CD*) to analyze it.

Voices on Word Matters: Learning About Phonics and Spelling in the Literacy Classroom
Chapter 11 (pp. 131–139). Use this chapter to explore the links in language and literacy.

SYSTEM **Orange**

NEW BOOK ***So Big!***

GENRE **Fiction**

YOU WILL NEED

- Take-Home Book, *My Baby Sister*
- *My Writing Book*
- phonogram chart from Lesson 44
- magnetic letters
- word bags

From the CD:

- *My ABC Book* ✓
- word cards: *not, got*
- fold sheet
- Parent Letter

NEW BOOK

So Big!, Level B

REREADING

Rain, Level B

My Baby Sister, Level A

Goals

- Recognize and use simple phonogram patterns with a VC structure.
- Write words by using the patterns and the sounds.
- Generate words that have a particular phonogram pattern.
- Begin to gain control of the entire alphabet, letter names, and sounds.
- Locate known words in continuous print.
- Read with control of voice-print match, close attention to print, self-monitoring, and self-correction behavior.
- Write high-frequency words quickly.
- Understand perspective (big and little).
- Notice a sequence of events.
- Understand why the ending of the story is surprising.
- Notice and understand story clues close to the end of the book.

Analysis of New Book Characteristics

So Big, Level B

GENRE/FORM

- Fiction
- Fantasy

TEXT STRUCTURE

- Series of objects belonging to a giant, who narrates the story
- Conclusion shows the narrator

CONTENT

- Comparison of sizes
- Perspective in terms of what is big
- Concept of a giant

THEMES AND IDEAS

- Make-believe character

LANGUAGE AND LITERARY FEATURES

- Foreshadowing of theme on title page (book called *Jack* with picture of beanstalk on its cover)
- Giant revealed on last page when full perspective is revealed through illustrations
- Fairy tale quality communicated through illustrations

SENTENCE COMPLEXITY

- Two four-word sentences on every page except the last
- Repeating pattern with no changes until the last page
- Present tense
- Prepositional phrases
- Use of *too*, set off by commas, to indicate *also*

VOCABULARY

- Names of objects the giant owns: *hat, coat, bag, bowl, spoon, book, chair*
- Prepositions: *in, on, at*
- Pronoun: *me, my, I*
- Content word: *rain*

WORDS

- High-frequency words: *look, at, my, is, big, me, I, am, too*
- All one-syllable words
- See the Word Analysis Charts in the *Program Guide* for specific words in each category.

ILLUSTRATIONS

- Full color paintings on each right page
- Close match between pictures and text

BOOK AND PRINT FEATURES

- Large font
- Ample space between words
- Two lines on each page of print except the last, which has three
- Print on the left on a blank page; illustrations on the right page, except for last page
- Periods and exclamation point
- The word *I* in bold to indicate stress on words

▶ Rereading Books

- *Rain*, Level B
- *My Baby Sister*, Level A

PROMPTING GUIDE 1
Refer to *Prompting Guide 1* as needed.

- Invite the children to reread *Rain* and *My Baby Sister.*
- Prompt children for word solving using known words; e.g.,, "Do you know a word that starts like that?"

▶ Phonics/Word Work

-op	-ot	-it	-in	-an	-at	-ig
hop	not	sit	pin	can	sat	pig
mop	hot	fit	fin	man	cat	big
top	pot	bit	win	fan	mat	wig
stop	lot				bat	dig
	got					jig

- **PRINCIPLE** Recognizing and using simple phonograms with a VC pattern (easiest): *-ad, -ag, -an, -am, -at, -ed, -en, -et, -ig, -in, -it, -og, -op, -ot, -ut*

"You can look at the pattern [part] you know to help you read a word."
"You can write words by using the patterns and the sounds."

- Write the word *pig* on the whiteboard and discuss with children. Suggested language: "You can notice a part or a pattern in the word *pig. Pig* starts with *p*. What is the part or pattern you see at the end?" Children may respond by saying the letters or the word part.
- "What are some other words with an end part like *pig* (*-ig*)?" Either have the children generate words, such as *big,* or write them yourself and ask children what they think each word is.
- Use the phonogram chart from Lesson 44. Have children read the words in the columns of the chart. Then add the column for the phonogram *-ig.*

My Writing Book

- Then have children write words in *My Writing Book: dig, big, pig.* You can vary this activity by having children write *win, pin,* or other words to help them notice that both the *-ig* and *-in* patterns have the vowel *i.*
- If time allows, have the children make words like *big* or *win* with magnetic letters and break them apart (*b-ig, w-in*).
- Save the phonogram chart for use in Lesson 46.

▸ New Book

So Big!, Level B

Introducing the Text

- Introduce children to the book by talking about all the big things that children see around them. Suggested language: "This book is called *So Big!*"
- "The character in this story tells us to look at all the big things he has. Turn to pages 2 and 3. What do you see? Yes, he is holding his hat and he says, 'Look at my hat.' His hat is big, isn't it?"
- "Now turn to pages 4 and 5. You can see his big coat. He says to look at his coat. Say the word *look*. What letter would come first? Yes, and it is an uppercase *L*. Find the word look and put your finger under it. Get a good look and say *look*."
- "Now, turn to pages 12 and 13 and you'll see something big. Yes, his book is big. He says, 'My book is big.' Say the word *my*. What letter would come first in *my?* Find my with an uppercase *M*. Get a good look and say *my*."
- "Turn the page to 14 and 15. What big thing do you see now? Yes, so he says, 'Look at my chair.' *At* begins with *a*. Can you find the word at?"
- "At the end of the story, you will meet the special character who has all of these big things."
- Turn back to the beginning. Read about big things in the story *So Big!* Point under each word and read softly.

PROMPTING GUIDE 1
Refer to *Prompting Guide 1* as needed.

Reading the Text

- Be sure to notice and reinforce how children are demonstrating control of early reading behaviors.

Discussing and Revisiting the Text

Invite children to talk about the big things in the story and the story's connection to *Jack and the Beanstalk*. Some key understandings children may express:

- The pictures in this story show a lot of big things. [Extend by asking children to show and name some of these big things, such as the hat, chair, coat, etc.]
- All of the big things belong to the giant at the end of the story. [Extend by asking why they think this.]
- This story makes me think of *Jack and the Beanstalk*. [Extend by asking the children why they think *So Big!* and *Jack and the Beanstalk* are alike.]

PROMPTING GUIDE 1
Refer to *Prompting Guide 1* as needed.

Teaching Points

- Based on your observations, use *Prompting Guide 1* to select a teaching point that will be most helpful to the readers.
- Reinforce effective problem solving such as self-correcting and rereading to solve new words, e.g., "You worked that out."

▸ Letter/Word Work

- Have children work in *My ABC Book* and go to pages for *Jj, Rr, Vv,* and color in pictures for *jack-in-the-box, ring,* and *vacuum* as they say them.

Word Bags

- Add the word cards *not* and *got* to children's word bags. Have them match the words to the charts on phonogram patterns.
- Have the children take their word cards out of their word bags, and lay the cards face down on a flat surface. Have children turn over one card at a time, read it, and then put the card back into their word bags.

Classroom Connection

- Give children the fold sheet with the cut-up sentence, *Look at the smile!*, printed on it (see *Lesson Resources CD*). It would be helpful to give them an envelope for the cut-up sentence.
- Have children cut up the sentence, mix it up, and then put it back in order.
- Next have them write the sentence at the top of the fold sheet and draw a picture of what the boy did to make the baby smile.
- Have children reread the Take-Home Book *My Baby Sister.*

Home/School Connection

- Have children take home their fold sheets and cut-up sentences. Have them remake the sentence, glue it onto the fold sheet under where they previously wrote the words, and read it to family members.
- Give them the Take-Home Book *My Baby Sister* to read to their families.

Observe to find evidence that children can:

- use simple phonogram patterns with a VC structure quickly and with flexibility.
- notice consonant clusters in their reading.
- control voice-print match, pay close attention to print, self-monitor, and self-correct.
- write high-frequency words quickly.
- pick up clues that the book is about a giant.
- understand the surprise ending and interpret the pictures.

Supporting English Language Learners

To support English language learners, you can:

- **demonstrate** the Phonics/Word Work principle again, if necessary.
- **be sure** children understand and can name the words and pictures being used in Letter/Word Work.
- **use** the language of the text in a conversational way. Have children repeat the language several times to help them remember the syntax.
- **name** the items the character has.
- **check** for understanding that the character is a giant. Think aloud about what the book makes you think of—*Jack and the Beanstalk.*
- **show** children the clue (if necessary) towards the end of the book, discussing that illustrations provide important information.
- **remind** children to read to someone at home even if they do not speak English. Encourage them to talk to someone at home about the book either in English or in their home language.

Professional Development Links

When Readers Struggle: Teaching that Works
Chapter 7: Language Matters: Talking, Reading, and Writing. Use this chapter to understand how to help children understand the language of texts.

Professional Development and Tutorial DVD, Orange System
Now that you are very familiar with the lesson structure, routines, and program components, you may want to spend some time briefly reviewing each section of the DVD.

Interactive Writing: How Language and Literacy Come Together, K–2
Chapter 8 (pp. 113–114, and 118–119). Use this chapter to explore more about the learning of high-frequency words.

Guided Reading: Good First Teaching for All Children
Chapter 12. Use this chapter to understand supporting early reading strategies.

SYSTEM **Orange**

NEW BOOK ***The Parade***

GENRE **Fiction**

YOU WILL NEED

- Take-Home Book, *So Big!*
- *My Writing Book*
- magnetic letters
- phonogram chart from Lesson 45
- word bags

From the CD:

- *My ABC Book* ✓
- Letters Made in Similar Ways document
- Recording Form for *So Big!*
- fold sheet
- Parent Letter

NEW BOOK

The Parade, Level A

REREADING

My Baby Sister, Level A

So Big!, Level B

Goals

- Use a wide range of VC phonogram patterns to write words.
- Recognize the entire alphabet, letter names, and sounds.
- Locate known words in continuous print.
- Read with voice-print match.
- Read with consistent self-monitoring and self-correction behavior.
- Use language structure, meaning, and visual information to monitor reading and solve words.
- Write easy high-frequency words quickly.
- Say words slowly to identify the first sound and letter.
- Reread writing to know what to write next.
- Understand and discuss the concept of a parade.
- Label items that will be seen in a parade.

Analysis of New Book Characteristics

The Parade, Level A

GENRE/FORM

- Fiction

TEXT STRUCTURE

- Different items related to a parade
- Sequence of items revealing the parade bit-by-bit
- Ends with view of the crowds and more of the parade

CONTENT

- Most objects familiar to children, with some that may need explanation
- Concept of a parade

THEMES AND IDEAS

- Neighborhood celebrations
- Holidays

LANGUAGE AND LITERARY FEATURES

- Anticipation built through illustrations

SENTENCE COMPLEXITY

- One four-word simple sentence on every page
- Repeating pattern on each page with no variation

VOCABULARY

- Names of everything related to the parade: *flags, clowns, band, truck, car, people, parade*

WORDS

- High-frequency words: *look, at, the*
- One-syllable words with some two-syllable words
- See the Word Analysis Charts in the *Program Guide* for specific words in each category.

ILLUSTRATIONS

- Colorful drawings
- Celebration communicated through illustration
- Close match between pictures and text

BOOK AND PRINT FEATURES

- Large font
- Ample space between words
- One line on each page of print
- Print on the left on a blank page; illustrations on the right page, except for last page
- Periods and exclamation point

▸ Rereading Books and Assessment

- *My Baby Sister*, Level A
- *So Big!*, Level B

PROMPTING GUIDE 1
Refer to *Prompting Guide 1* as needed.

- Listen to one child read *So Big!* as you code the reading behavior on the Recording Form, have a brief comprehension conversation, and make a teaching point that you think will be most helpful to the reader. Score and analyze the Reading Record following the lesson.
- Have the other children reread *My Baby Sister* and then *So Big!*
- Prompt for self-monitoring and self-correcting; e.g., "You are nearly right" or "Try that again and think what would look right (or sound right or make sense)."

▸ Phonics/Word Work

-ig	-og
pig	dog
big	log
wig	fog
dig	hog
jig	jog

- **PRINCIPLE** Recognizing and using simple phonograms with a VC pattern (easiest): *-ad, -ag, -an, -am, -at, -ed, -en, -et, -ig, -in, -it, -og, -op, -ot, -ut*

"You can look at the pattern [part] you know to help you read a word."
"You can write words by using the patterns and the sounds."

- Display the phonogram chart from Lesson 45. Have children read the words on the chart.
- Write the word *dog* on the whiteboard. Suggested language: "You can see a part or a pattern in the word *dog*. *Dog* starts with *d*. What is the pattern or part you see at the end of *dog*?" Children may respond by saying the letters or the word part.
- "What are some other words like *dog* with *-og* at the end?" Either have children generate words or write them yourself and ask children what they think each word is.

My Writing Book

- Then have children write words in *My Writing Book: dog, fog, jog.* You can vary this activity by having children write words with both the *-ig* and *-og* ending patterns. Help children notice that both parts, or patterns, have a vowel and a *g*.

Magnetic Letters

- If time allows, have children make three or four words with magnetic letters and break them apart *(b-ig, d-ig, l-og, d-og)*.

Writing About Reading

Interactive Writing

- **MY WRITING BOOK**
- **PROMPTING GUIDE 1**

Refer to *Prompting Guide 1* as needed.

- Talk with the children about all the big things the giant had.
- Compose two or three sentences that the giant would say about his big things, such as:

  Look at my hat.
  My hat is big.
  Look at my coat.
  My coat is big.
- Use interactive writing to construct a few sentences that the giant said.
- Prompt the children for quick writing of the easy high-frequency words (*at, is, my*).
- Encourage children to say words slowly so they can identify the first sound and letter to help them with unknown words (*coat, hat*).
- Have the children reread the sentences. If time allows, invite the children to make quick sketches to illustrate one of the sentences and glue them on the chart. Or, invite them to write the sentences in *My Writing Book.*

▸ New Book

The Parade,
Level A

Introducing the Text

- Introduce children to the book by talking about what they know about parades. Suggested language: "This book is about all the things you can look at when you are at a parade. What are some of the things you might see at the parade?"
- "You can see flags at a parade. Turn to page 2 and look at the flags."
- "Now turn to page 6 and what do you see? Yes, there's a band. Say *look*. Can you find look on page 6?"
- "Turn to page 12 and you can look at more things at the parade. Yes, look at all those balloons."
- "Now turn to page 16 and you can see everything at the parade."
- "Turn back to the beginning so you can look at each thing you see at the parade. Point under each word and read softly."

PROMPTING GUIDE 1
Refer to *Prompting Guide 1* as needed.

Reading the Text

- As children read, prompt them to solve words by using picture information and checking with the first letter in the word if needed, e.g., "That makes sense and does it look right?"
- Be sure to reinforce self-monitoring; e.g., "Was that okay?" and any self-correcting behavior; e.g., "You noticed that was wrong," if appropriate.

Discussing and Revisiting the Text

Invite children to talk about the parade. Some key understandings children may express are:

- A parade is a lot of people marching in a line. [Extend by asking for examples of some of the things the people saw in the parade. Have the children show the pictures that support their ideas.]
- People really like to look at parades. [Extend by asking why they think that.]
- The parade in this book reminds me of ________________. [Extend by asking children for details from their own experience with parades or other shows.]

PROMPTING GUIDE 1
Refer to *Prompting Guide 1* as needed.

Teaching Points

- Based on your observations, use *Prompting Guide 1* to select a teaching point that will be most helpful to the readers.
- You may want to turn to page 16, and have children name the things in the parade. Encourage them to think about the sequence.

▸ Optional Letter/ Word Work

- Have children work in *My ABC Book*. Go to pages for *Ww, Nn, Qq* and have them color in pictures for *window, nest,* and *queen.*

Word Bags

- Have the children take their word cards out of their word bags and lay the cards face down on a flat surface. Have children turn over one card at a time, read it, and then put the card back into their word bags.

Letter Sort

- If time allows, and more letter sorting is needed to strengthen the children's ability to distinguish letter features quickly, have the children sort magnetic letters two or three ways (see Instructional Routines, Ways to Sort and Match Letters, in the *Program Guide*).

Classroom Connection

- Have children read the Take-Home Book *So Big!*
- Give the children the fold sheet and have them think of things the Giant had that are big. Have them draw a picture and write, "My ________ is big."

Home/School Connection

- Give children the Take-Home Book *So Big!* to read to their families.
- Have children take home their fold sheets to share with family members.
- Have children review high-frequency words.

Assessing Reading and Writing Behaviors

Observe to find evidence that children can:

- use a wide range of VC phonogram patterns with flexibility.
- understand the entire alphabet, letter names and sounds.
- control voice-print match.
- demonstrate self-monitoring and self-correction behavior.
- demonstrate use of language structure, meaning, and visual information while reading.
- write easy high-frequency words quickly.
- say words slowly to identify the first sound and letter.
- reread writing to know what to write next.
- understand the concept of a parade and the idea of sequence.

Supporting English Language Learners

To support English language learners, you can:

- **teach** for understanding of "You are nearly right." "Try that again and think what would look right (or sound right or make sense)."
- **demonstrate** the Phonics/Word Work principle again, if necessary.
- **check** to be sure children understand and can name the words and pictures being used in Letter/Word Work.
- **introduce** the concept of a parade, if necessary.
- **use** the language of the text in a conversational way. Have children repeat the language several times to help them remember the syntax.
- **name** the things the children see at the parade.
- **support** for understanding and pronunciation of the plural nouns (e.g., *people*).
- **ask** children to repeat words after you to work on articulation of the sounds in the word. Be sure the children say the words themselves even if they hear a sound from your articulation.
- **remind** children to read to someone at home even if they do not speak English and to talk about the book in English or their home language.

Professional Development Links

When Readers Struggle: Teaching that Works
Chapter 13: Extending Reading Power: Writing to Read. Use this chapter to understand how writing can help children learn about print.

Word Matters: Teaching Phonics and Spelling in a Reading/Writing Classroom
Chapter 12 (pp. 138–139). Use this chapter to review the important role of letter sorting in the learning of letters and words.

Interactive Writing: How Language and Literacy Come Together, K–2
Chapter 7 (pp. 102–104, 106). Use this chapter to review how writing supports children in learning about letters.

YOU WILL NEED

- Take-Home Book, *The Parade*
- *My Writing Book*
- magnetic letters: *b, f, h, i, m, s, t*
- phonogram chart from Lesson 46
- magnetic letters

From the CD:

- *My ABC Book* ✓
- word cards: CVC words with phonograms *-op, -og*
- Take, Make, Write sheet
- fold sheet
- Parent Letter

SYSTEM **Orange**

NEW BOOK ***Fun at School***

GENRE **Nonfiction**

NEW BOOK
Fun at School, Level B

REREADING
So Big!, Level B

The Parade, Level A

Goals

- Use a wide range of simple phonogram patterns with a VC structure to solve words.
- Sort words by using the patterns and the sounds.
- Gain control of the entire alphabet, letter names, and sounds.
- Locate known words in continuous print.
- Notice a sequence of events.
- Read with control of voice-print match and close attention to print.
- Read with consistent self-monitoring and self-correction behavior.
- Write easy high-frequency words quickly.
- Understand that the book switches to a different connotation of *make* at the end (the concrete "making" of things to the abstract "making" of friends).

Analysis of New Book Characteristics

Fun at School, Level B

GENRE/FORM
- Narrative nonfiction

TEXT STRUCTURE
- Series of typical school activities
- Twist of meaning at the end

CONTENT
- Familiar school activities

THEMES AND IDEAS
- Friends
- Learning

LANGUAGE AND LITERARY FEATURES
- NA

SENTENCE COMPLEXITY
- Five-word sentence on every page
- Repeating pattern with no changes except for verbs and objects
- Present tense
- Prepositional phrases

VOCABULARY
- Verbs and objects: *read books, write stories, paint pictures, sing songs, eat lunch, play games, make puppets, make friends*
- Prepositions: *at*
- Pronoun: *we*
- Content word: *school*

WORDS
- High-frequency words: *we, at*
- One-syllable words with some two-syllable words
- See the Word Analysis Charts in the *Program Guide* for specific words in each category.

ILLUSTRATIONS
- Photographs of children and activities on each right page
- Close match between pictures and text

BOOK AND PRINT FEATURES
- Large font
- Ample space between words
- Two lines on each page of print
- Print on the left on a blank page; illustrations on the right page, except for last page
- Periods

▸ Rereading Books

- *The Parade*, Level A
- *So Big!*, Level B

PROMPTING GUIDE 1
Refer to *Prompting Guide 1* as needed.

- Invite children to reread *So Big!* and *The Parade.*
- Prompt children for word solving using the first letter, if needed; e.g., "Say the first part" or "Get your mouth ready to start the word."

▸ Phonics/Word Work

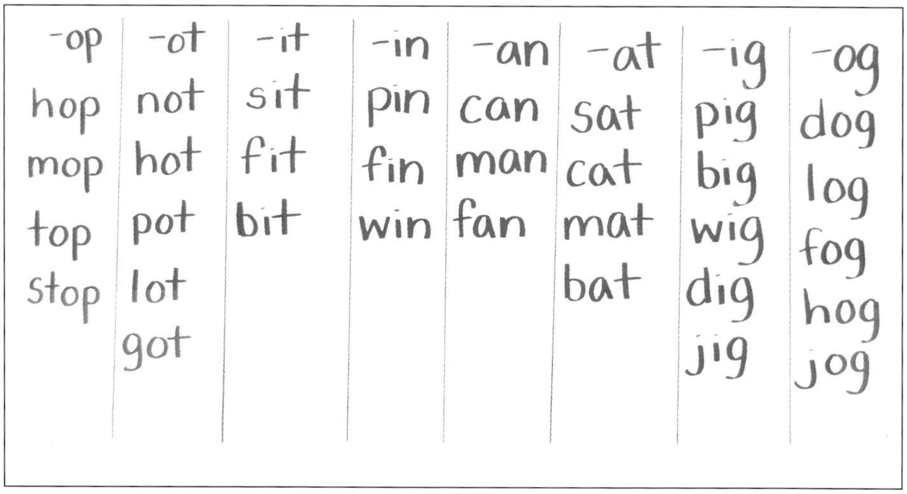

- **PRINCIPLE** Recognizing and using simple phonograms with a VC pattern (easiest): *-ad, -ag, -an, -am, -at, -ed, -en, -et, -ig, -in, -it, -og, -op, -ot, -ut*

"You can look at the pattern [part] you know to help you read a word."
"You can write words by using the patterns and the sounds."

- Post the phonogram chart from Lesson 46 for children to use as a reference. If you have not created all of the columns in the form of one chart, you can post several smaller charts.
- Point to and have the children read a word from each column.
- Suggested language: "You know many word parts or patterns. These parts can help you read and write words. Today you are going to make words with magnetic letters and then write them."
- Give each child a fold sheet. Then place in the middle of the table the CVC word cards of words with the phonograms *-op*, and *-og*. Also, give the children the magnetic letters: *b, f, h, i, m, s, t.*
- Demonstrate choosing a CVC word card and placing it in the first column of the fold sheet. Then make the same word with magnetic letters in the second column, and finally, write the word in the third column.
- Have the children choose, make, and write as many of these words as they can. (The words can be copied into *My Writing Book.*)

▸ Optional Letter/Word Work

- Have the children take their CVC word cards out of their word bags and lay the cards face down on a flat surface. Have children turn over one card at a time, read it, and then put the card back into their word bags.

Magnetic Letters

- Have children make a word with magnetic letters, so they can learn how to look at parts, e.g., *d-og, p-in, h-at, p-ig, h-en, m-at, m-an.*

My ABC Book

- Have the children practice breaking apart CVC words into the initial letter and the phonogram, e.g., *h-en.* Have the children write several words in *My ABC Book.*
- The goal of having children make, break, and remake words is to help them attend to word parts. As they read, they need to notice the parts to solve new words.

Classroom Connection

- Give children the fold sheet with sentence strip, *We play games at school.* Have each child cut up the words, place them on the fold sheet, and illustrate the sentence.
- Give the children the Take-Home Book *Fun at School* to reread.

Home/School Connection

- Give each child an envelope containing her cut-up sentence. Have children take home the fold sheet to read to family members.
- Give children the Take-Home Book *Fun at School* to read to family members.

Assessing Reading and Writing Behaviors

Observe to find evidence that children can:

- use a wide range of VC phonogram patterns to make and write words.
- demonstrate knowledge of the entire alphabet, letter names, and sounds.
- read with voice-print match.
- consistently self-monitor and self-correct.
- read the verb phrase and prepositional phrase by putting the words together.
- write with good spacing.
- write high-frequency words quickly.
- say words slowly to listen for, identify, and write easy-to-hear initial and final sounds.
- understand and discuss the concept of doing things at school.

Supporting English Language Learners

To support English language learners, you can:

- **help** children problem solve by teaching for understanding of "Try that again." "What else could it be?" and "What can you try?"
- **check** to be sure children understand and can say the words being used in Letter/Word Work.
- **use** the language of the text in a conversational way. Have children repeat the language several times to help them remember the syntax.
- **introduce** the vocabulary related to school, if necessary.
- **demonstrate** what this book makes you think of, and ask children to discuss their connections.
- **encourage** children to discuss what things the boy does that are the same as (or different from) what they do at school.
- **help** children to construct a syntactically correct sentence for Independent Writing.
- **ask** children to repeat words after you to work on articulation of the sounds in the word. Be sure the children say the words slowly themselves even if they hear a sound from your articulation.

Professional Development Links

When Readers Struggle: Teaching that Works
Chapter 13: Extending Reading Power: Writing to Read. Use this chapter to understand how writing can help children learn about print.

Interactive Writing: How Language and Literacy Come Together
Chapter 8 (p.109–120). Use this chapter to review how children can learn how words work through writing.

SYSTEM **Orange**

NEW BOOK ***My Big Brother***

GENRE **Nonfiction**

YOU WILL NEED

- Take-Home Book, *At School*
- *My Writing Book*
- phonogram chart from Lesson 47
- magnetic letters
- word bags

From the CD:

- *My ABC Book* ✓
- Take, Make, Write sheet
- word cards: CVC words with phonograms *-an, -ig*
- fold sheet
- Parent Letter

NEW BOOK

My Big Brother, Level B

REREADING

Fun At School, Level B

At School, Level A

Goals

- Use a wide range of simple phonogram patterns with a VC structure to read and write words.
- Sort words by using the patterns and the sounds.
- Make progress in gaining control of the entire alphabet, letter names, and sounds.
- Locate known words in continuous print.
- Notice word endings.
- Read with consistent self-monitoring and self-correction behaviors.
- Write many high-frequency words quickly.
- Read and understand a compound subject (*My brother and I*).
- Understand a category of activities related to what brothers can do together.

Analysis of New Book Characteristics

***My Big Brother*, Level B**

GENRE/FORM
- Narrative nonfiction

TEXT STRUCTURE
- Series of activities in which two brothers engage
- Concluding statement at the end, with expansion of the text

CONTENT
- Familiar play activities

THEMES AND IDEAS
- Family
- Brothers
- Caring

LANGUAGE AND LITERARY FEATURES
- NA

SENTENCE COMPLEXITY
- Nine-word sentences on most pages
- Repeating pattern with variation on several pages (verb form, different beginning)
- Present tense
- Prepositional phrases
- Conjunctions

VOCABULARY
- Verbs and objects: *paint pictures, ride bikes, read books*
- Prepositions: *with*
- Pronouns: *me, my*
- Name of family member: *brother*

WORDS
- High-frequency words: *my, big, likes, to, with, me, he, and, I, like*
- One-syllable words with some two-syllable words
- See the Word Analysis Charts in the *Program Guide* for specific words in each category.

ILLUSTRATIONS
- Photographs of children and activities on each right page
- Close match between pictures and text

BOOK AND PRINT FEATURES
- Large font
- Ample space between words
- Two, three, or four lines on each page of print
- Print on the left on a blank page; illustrations on the right page, except for last page
- Periods and exclamation point

▸ Rereading Books

- *Fun At School*, Level B
- *At School*, Level A

PROMPTING GUIDE 1
Refer to *Prompting Guide 1* as needed.

- Invite the children to reread *Fun at School* and *At School.*
- Prompt for solving words as needed; e.g., "Read that again and start the word." "Look at the beginning, or listen to how I start the word."

▸ Phonics/Word Work

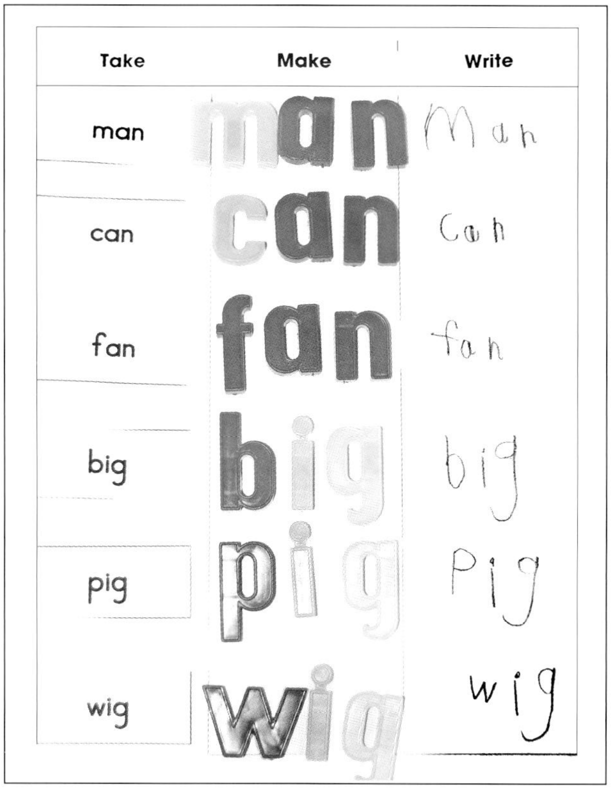

- **PRINCIPLE** Recognizing and using simple phonograms with a VC pattern (easiest): *-ad, -ag, -an, -am, -at, -ed, -en, -et, -ig, -in, -it, -og, -op, -ot, -ut*

"You can look at the pattern [part] you know to help you read a word."
"You can write words by using the patterns and the sounds."

- Post the phonogram chart from Lesson 47 for children to use as a reference.
- Suggested language: "You know many word parts or patterns. These parts can help you read and write words. Today you are going to make words with magnetic letters and then write them."
- Give each child a Take, Make, Write sheet. Then place in the middle of the table CVC word cards with the phonograms *-an* and *-ig.* Also, give the children the magnetic letters: *b, c, d, f, g, h, i, j, l, m, n, o, p, s, t, w, a.*
- Demonstrate choosing a CVC word card and placing it in the first column of the Take, Make, Write sheet. Then have them make the same word with magnetic letters in the second column, and finally, write the word in the third column.
- Have the children choose, make, and write as many words as they can. (The word sheet can be glued into *My Writing Book.*)

▸ New Book

***My Big Brother*,**
Level B

Introducing the Text

- Introduce the book by asking children to look at the big brother and the little brother on the cover. Suggested language: "In this book the little brother tells about all the things that his big brother likes to do with him." Read the title and look at pages 2 and 3 to see what the big brother likes to do with his little brother.
- "Turn to pages 4 and 5. What does the little brother say that his big brother likes to do with him? Yes, his big brother likes to ride bikes with him. So the boy says, 'My big brother likes to ride bikes with me.' Say *likes*. What letter comes first in *likes?* Find likes and put your finger under it. Get a good look and say it."
- "Turn to pages 8, 9, and 14." Have children predict what the little brother will say.
- And on page 14, have children say the word *with*. "What letter would you expect to see first in *with?* Find it and put your finger under it. Get a good look and say *with*."
- "Now turn back to the beginning of the book so the little boy can tell about all the things his big brother likes to do with him."

PROMPTING GUIDE 1
Refer to *Prompting Guide 1* as needed.

Reading the Text

- As the children read, notice careful pointing and independence in word solving.
- Prompt for the language structure, if needed, e.g., "What would sound right?" and have children check the word with the first letter.

Discussing and Revisiting the Text

Invite the children to talk about the brothers and what they like to do together. Some key understandings children may express are:

- The little boy tells about his big brother and the things they like to do together. [Extend by asking children to find pictures in the book that show what the brothers like to do together.]
- The brothers like each other. [Extend by asking children to tell how they know that.]
- This book reminds me of my brother, sister, friend, etc. [Encourage children to talk about their family or friend relationships.]

PROMPTING GUIDE 1
Refer to *Prompting Guide 1* as needed.

Teaching Points

- Based on your observations, use *Prompting Guide 1* to select a teaching point that will be most helpful to readers.
- Notice and reinforce control of voice-print match.

▸ Letter/Word Work

- Have the children take their CVC word cards out of their word bags and lay the cards face down on a flat surface. Have children turn over one card at a time, read it, and then put the card back into their word bags.

Magnetic Letters

- Have children make several CVC words with magnetic letters, so they can learn how to look at parts, e.g., *r-an, b-ut, s-it, g-ot.*
- The goal of having children make, break, and remake words is to help them attend to word parts.

My ABC Book

- Then have the children write some of the words in *My ABC Book.*

Classroom Connection

- Encourage the children to think of what they like to do at school that is like the boy in the story, *At School.*
- Give children the fold sheet to take back to the classroom. Have them write about and draw what they like to do at school. They may use what the boy does or think of ideas of their own.
- Give children the Take-Home Book *At School* to reread.

Home/School Connection

- Give children their fold sheets to take home to read to their family members.
- Give each child the Take-Home Book *At School* to share with the family.

Assessing Reading and Writing Behaviors

Observe to find evidence that children can:

- sort words by using the patterns and the sounds.
- demonstrate progress in gaining control of the entire alphabet, letter names, and connected sounds.
- read a compound subject (*my brother and I*).
- use more than one source of information in solving words.
- notice and read word endings.
- demonstrate consistent self-monitoring and self-correction behaviors.
- understand a category of activities related to what brothers can do together.
- understand why the narrator likes his big brother.

Supporting English Language Learners

To support English language learners, you can:

- **check** that children understand and can say the words being used in Letter/Word Work.
- **use** the language of the text in a conversational way. Have children repeat the language several times to help them remember the syntax. The sentence structures in *My Big Brother* are different from the sentence structures in other books that children have read up to this point, so check for understanding of "My brother and I" and "…with me."
- **name** the actions the boys do together.
- **use** the pictures to support children in talking about what the boys like to do and how the boys feel. Think aloud about how you know they are feeling happy; e.g., "I know the boys are happy on the slide because they are smiling. What did you notice?"
- **help** children discuss someone they like to play with and how they feel when playing with this person.
- **expand** children's language in a conversational way. For example, if children say, "Me and my cousin…," you can respond with, "So you might say/write, My cousin and I…"

Professional Development Links

When Readers Struggle: Teaching that Works
Chapter 11: Learning to Solve Words: Effective and Efficient Phonics. Use this chapter to help in understanding how readers use larger parts in words.

Teaching for Comprehending and Fluency: Thinking, Talking, and Writing About Reading, K–8
Chapter 4 (p. 47—Figure 4-3). Use this chapter to review building systems of strategic actions for monitoring and correcting reading.

SYSTEM **Orange**

NEW BOOK ***Getting Ready***

GENRE **Nonfiction**

YOU WILL NEED

- Take-Home Book, *My Big Brother*
- *My Writing Book*
- phonogram chart from Lesson 47
- magnetic letters
- sentence strips
- envelopes
- word bags

From the CD:

- *My ABC Book*✓
- Take, Make, Write sheet
- word cards: CVC words with phonograms *-at, -og*
- Recording Form for *My Big Brother*
- fold sheet
- Parent Letter

NEW BOOK

Getting Ready, Level A

REREADING

At School, Level A

My Big Brother, Level B

Goals

- Use a wide range of VC phonogram patterns to read and write words.
- Understand the entire alphabet, letter names, and sounds.
- Locate known words in continuous print.
- Use language structure, meaning, and visual information while reading.
- Demonstrate consistent self-monitoring and self-correction behaviors.
- Reread writing to check it.
- Start a sentence with an uppercase letter and use good spacing.
- Say words slowly to identify and write letters to represent easy-to-hear sounds.
- Understand that the person in the photograph is getting ready for a sporting event.
- Predict that the sport is baseball.
- Understand that the girl and her dad are going to play baseball and are dressed just alike.

Analysis of New Book Characteristics

Getting Ready, Level A

GENRE/FORM

- Narrative nonfiction

TEXT STRUCTURE

- Different items related to getting dressed
- Sequence of getting dressed building to surprise at the end

CONTENT

- Most objects and items of apparel familiar to children, although the relationship to baseball may need explanation
- Concept of baseball

THEMES AND IDEAS

- Sports
- Father-daughter relationship

LANGUAGE AND LITERARY FEATURES

- NA

SENTENCE COMPLEXITY

- One four-word simple sentence on every page
- Present tense
- Repeating pattern on each page with no variation
- Prepositional phrases

VOCABULARY

- Names of everything related to getting dressed: *pants, socks, shoes, shirt, cap, ball, bat, dad*

WORDS

- High-frequency words: *look, at, my*
- One-syllable words
- See the Word Analysis Charts in the *Program Guide* for specific words in each category.

ILLUSTRATIONS

- Photographs
- Close match between pictures and text
- Specialty clothing revealed through illustrations
- Key to girl's activity revealed on page 13
- Surprise at end revealed through illustration on last page

BOOK AND PRINT FEATURES

- Large font
- Ample space between words
- One line on each page of print
- Print on the left on a blank page; illustrations on the right page, except for last page
- Periods and exclamation point

▸ Rereading Books and Assessment

- *At School*, Level A
- *My Big Brother*, Level B

PROMPTING GUIDE 1
Refer to *Prompting Guide 1* as needed.

- Listen to one child read *My Big Brother* as you code the reading behavior on the Recording Form, have a brief comprehension conversation, and make a teaching point that you think will be most helpful to the reader. Score and analyze the Reading Record following the lesson.

- Have the other children reread *At School* and then *My Big Brother.*
- Prompt for word solving using patterns, if needed; e.g., "Look at the parts" or "Do you see a part that can help?"

▸ Phonics/Word Work

- **PRINCIPLE** Recognizing and using simple phonograms with a VC pattern (easiest): *-ad, -ag, -an, -am, -at, -ed, -en, -et, -ig, -in, -it, -og, -op, -ot, -ut*

"You can look at the pattern [part] you know to help you read a word."
"You can write words by using the patterns and the sounds."

- Post the phonogram chart from Lesson 47 for children to use as reference.
- Suggested language: "You know many word parts or patterns. These parts can help you read and write words. Today you are going to make words with magnetic letters and then write them."
- Give each child a Take, Make, Write sheet. Then place on the table word cards of words with the phonograms *-at, -og.* Also, give the children magnetic letters: *b, c, d, f, j, l, m, s, a, o.*
- Demonstrate choosing a CVC word card and placing it in the first column of the Take, Make, Write sheet. Then make the same word with magnetic letters in the second column, and finally, write the word in the third column.
- Have children choose, make, and write as many words as they can. (The word sheet can be glued into *My Writing Book.*)

▸ Writing About Reading

Dictated Writing

- **MY WRITING BOOK**
- **PROMPTING GUIDE 1**

Refer to *Prompting Guide 1* as needed.

- If time allows, you may want to begin by having each child read recent pages from *My Writing Book*. Occasionally ask the child to locate a word in a sentence read.
- Dictate the following sentence:

  My big brother likes to play ball with me.
- Prompt for quick writing of the easy high-frequency words. Encourage children to say words slowly and think about their sounds.
- Quickly write the words *brother* and *with* on the whiteboard to show children.
- Use sound boxes on the whiteboard for *big* and *likes* if needed.
- Ask the children to reread their sentence and illustrate it.
- If time allows, write the dictated sentence on a sentence strip, have children cut the strip into its individual words, mix them up, and put the sentence back together. You may want to cut apart the *s* from *likes* for a little challenge. (Alternatively, this activity can be done in the Home Connection section of the lesson.)

▸ New Book

Getting Ready,
Level A

Introducing the Text

- Introduce the children to the book by talking about what they wear to play their favorite sports. Suggested language: "The girl in this book is getting ready to play baseball."
- "Turn to the first page. On the first page she says, 'Look at my pants.' Say the word *at*. What letter would come first? Find at."
- "Now turn to page 8. What does she say to look at? Yes, she says, 'Look at my shirt.'"
- "On every page she will tell you something to look at until she is ready to play ball."
- "Turn back to the beginning and read *Getting Ready*. As you read, remember to point under each word."

PROMPTING GUIDE 1
Refer to *Prompting Guide 1* as needed.

Reading the Text

- The children should be able to read this quite independently.
- If children make errors that they do not notice, prompt for self-correction; e.g., "Try that again" or "Something wasn't right on that page."

Discussing and Revisiting the Text

Invite children to talk about the book. Some key understandings children may express are:

- The child in the story is getting ready to play baseball. [Extend by asking children to look at the cover and talk about why they think so.]
- The child in the story has lots of clothes and things to help get ready for a game of baseball. [Extend by asking children to support this statement by showing pictures from the book.]
- The child getting ready to play baseball is a girl. [Extend by asking why that might have been a surprise. Some children may have noticed clues. Ask those children to share the clues with the rest of the group.]
- The girl and her dad are dressed alike.

PROMPTING GUIDE 1
Refer to *Prompting Guide 1* as needed.

Teaching Points

- Based on your observations, use *Prompting Guide 1* to select a teaching point that will be most helpful to the readers.
- Reinforce crisp pointing and any self-correcting behavior you observed, especially if it is a new or emerging behavior; e.g., "You figured that out."

SYSTEM **Orange**

NEW BOOK ***Play and Ride***

GENRE **Fiction**

YOU WILL NEED

- Take-Home Book, *Getting Ready*
- *My Writing Book*
- magnetic letters
- word bags

From the CD:

- *My ABC Book*✓
- *My Poetry Book*✓
- Letters Made in Similar Ways document
- fold sheet
- Parent Letter

NEW BOOK
Play and Ride, Level C

REREADING
Getting Ready, Level A

My Big Brother, Level B

Goals

- Use word parts to solve words while reading.
- Use knowledge of word parts to write words.
- Self-monitor consistently.
- Check one source of information with another to correct errors.
- Self-correct some errors.
- Use known words as a tool in learning new words.
- Begin to read with phrasing and fluency.
- Use several sources of information (meaning, visual information, language structure) while reading for meaning.
- Understand opposites (*little* and *big*).
- Understand the use of contrast in the way the text is organized.
- Understand content (toys and real things; size as relative).
- Infer intentions or feelings of a character.

Analysis of New Book Characteristics

Play and Ride, Level C

GENRE/FORM
- Narrative Nonfiction

TEXT STRUCTURE
- Series of vehicles, shown first in toy form and then in life-size form
- Series of pairs showing compare/contrast

CONTENT
- Familiar toys and real vehicles

THEMES AND IDEAS
- Big and little
- Real and toy items
- Function of vehicles

LANGUAGE AND LITERARY FEATURES
- NA

SENTENCE COMPLEXITY
- Two sentences on each page of print
- Sentences five to six words long
- Repeating pattern over two-page spreads
- Present tense
- Prepositional phrases
- Adjectives

VOCABULARY
- Names of vehicles: *truck, boat, train, car*
- Names of action: *play, ride*
- Prepositions: *at, in, with*
- Pronouns: *I, we*
- Article: *this*
- Adjectives: *big, little*

WORDS
- High-frequency words: *look, at, this, little, I, can, with, big, in, we*
- One-syllable words with one two-syllable word
- See the Word Analysis Charts in the *Program Guide* for specific words in each category.

ILLUSTRATIONS
- Drawings of a single child and the child with parents on alternate pages
- Close match between pictures and text
- Illustrations showing contrast of *big* and *little*

BOOK AND PRINT FEATURES
- Large font
- Ample space between words
- Three lines on each page of print
- Print on the left on a blank page; illustrations on the right page, except for last page
- Periods

▸ Rereading Books

- *Getting Ready*, Level A
- *My Big Brother*, Level B

PROMPTING GUIDE 1
Refer to *Prompting Guide 1* as needed.

- Have the children reread *Getting Ready* and *My Big Brother.*
- Prompt readers to notice the parts of words, if needed, e.g., "Do you see a part you know?"

▸ Phonics/Word Work

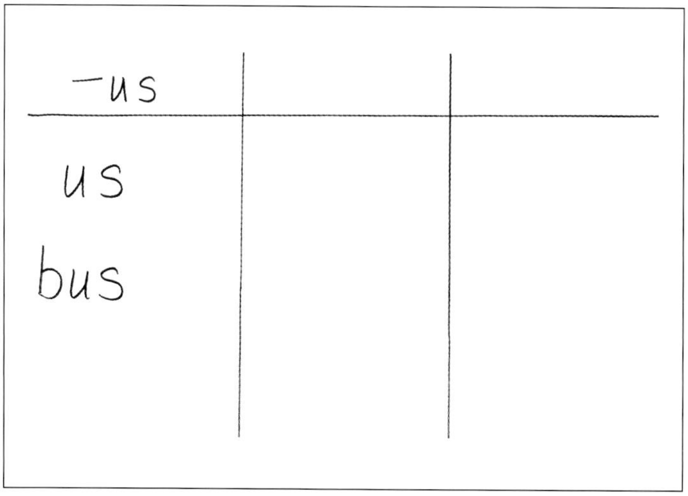

- **PRINCIPLE** Recognizing and using simple phonograms with a VC pattern (easiest): *-ad, -ag, -an, -am, -at, -ed, -en, -et, -ig, -in, -it, -og, -op, -ot, -us, -ut*

"You can look at the pattern [part] you know to help you read a word."
"You can write words by using the patterns and the sounds."

- Suggested language: "You can see another pattern or part in some words. It is the part *-us.* What letter would you write first to make the word *bus?*" Children respond. Then write the word *bus.*
- Start to build a three-column chart that you will use over the next two lessons. The first column will have *-us* words.
- Help children understand that *us* is a word but it is also a part of other words.
- Have children write *bus* and *us* in *My Writing Book.*

My ABC Book

- Have children read *My ABC Book,* starting in the middle and going back to the beginning to read the first part. Have them add the words *bus* and *us* to the alphabet book. Have them write the words or glue them in.
- If time allows, have them make *us* and *bus* with magnetic letters one at a time. Have them break apart *b-us* one or two times.

▸ New Book

Play and Ride,
Level C

Introducing the Text

- Introduce children to the book by showing the cover. Suggested language: "In this book, a little boy tells about things he plays with and big things he rides in."
- "Turn to pages 2 and 3. The boy says, 'Look at this little truck.' What can he do with the little truck? Yes, he can play with it. It is a toy."
- "On pages 4 and 5, what do you see? And what can the boy do with this truck? Yes, he can ride in this truck. This truck is real. Say the word *this*. It starts like *the*. Can you find *this* on page 4? Run your finger under it, and say it."
- "Turn to page 10. What does the boy want you to look at? Yes, that's a train. What can he do with the train? Yes, he can play with it because it is a toy."
- "Say the word *with*. What letter would you see first in *with?* Yes, it's a *w*. Find with, and put your finger under it. Get a good look, and say it."
- "Turn back to the beginning, and read *Play and Ride*. You will read about all the toy things the boy can play with and the real things he can ride in."

PROMPTING GUIDE 1
Refer to *Prompting Guide 1* as needed.

Reading the Text

- As the children read, prompt for them to check one source of information with another, e.g., "That makes sense, but does it look right?"

Discussing and Revisiting the Text

Invite children to talk about what the boy liked to do with his toys. Some key understandings children may express are:

- The boy plays with little toys, and then rides in big things that look like his toys. [Extend by asking for examples. Have children find the pages that support their ideas.]
- There are other things that people ride that can also be toys. [Elicit other toys and big things that could be in this story.]
- This story reminds me of ____________. [Accept any reasonable response that connects with the meaning of the story. Encourage children to provide details.]

PROMPTING GUIDE 1
Refer to *Prompting Guide 1* as needed.

Teaching Points

- Based on your observations, use *Prompting Guide 1* to select a teaching point that will be most helpful to the readers.
- You may want to prompt them to read without using a finger to point, e.g., "Read it with your eyes."

Letter/Word Work

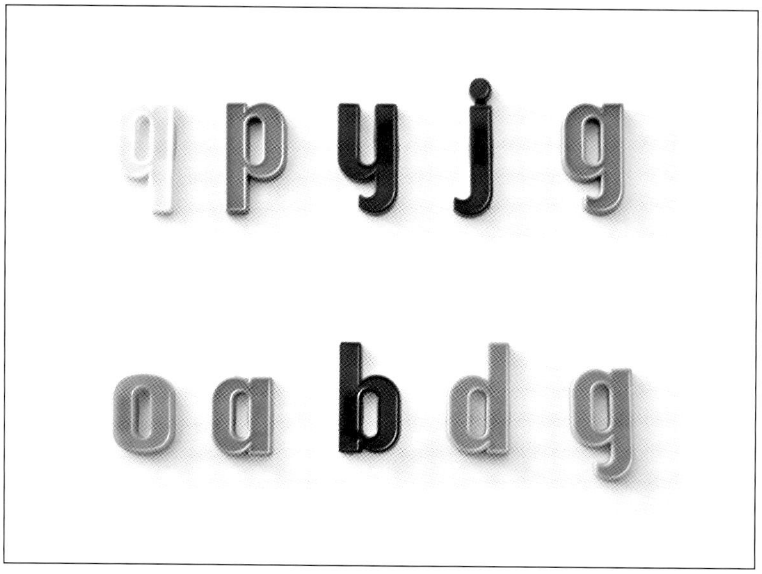

- Sort two groups of letters on the whiteboard. Have the children look at each and tell what is the same, e.g., letters with tails and letters with circles. Repeat with other categories (see Instructional Routines, Ways to Sort and Match Letters, in the *Program Guide*). Then have the children make two groups of letters and tell what is the same about the letters in their groups.

Word Bags

- Have the children lay out their word cards face down. Have children turn them over, one card at a time, read them, and put them back in the word bags.

My Poetry Book

- Have the children read from *My Poetry Book*.

Classroom Connection

Orange #51 Name: John

-us	-at	-it
us	hat	bit
bus	cat	sit
	sat	

- Give children the fold sheet with word cards at the bottom. At the top of each column is a pattern: *-us, -at, -it.*
- Have the children choose words that fit the pattern for each column from the following: *us, hat, sit, hit, bit, bus, cat, sat,* and glue them on the fold sheet.
- Have children read the words that they wrote under each column.
- Have children reread the Take-Home Book *Getting Ready.*

Home/School Connection

- Have the children take home their fold sheets with words.
- Suggest that children read the words they wrote to family members and add new words at home.
- Give them the Take-Home Book *Getting Ready.*

Assessing Reading and Writing Behaviors

Observe to find evidence that children can:

- identify and use word parts to solve words.
- begin to read with phrasing.
- use known words as a tool in learning new words (word connections).
- check one source of information with another.
- notice errors and self-correct them.
- understand the basic contrasts around which the book is organized (little things being toys and big things being real).

Supporting English Language Learners

To support English language learners, you can:

- **model** what you mean by "Do you see a part that you know?" by framing a known part of the word.
- **show** children what you mean by "Read it with your eyes" instead of "Point under each word."
- **use** the language of the text in a conversational way. Have children repeat the language several times to help them remember the syntax.
- **check** for understanding of *this* and the concepts of *with* and *in*.
- **name** the vehicles and have children repeat.
- **use** the pictures to support children in talking about what the boy means by "play with" and "ride in." Think aloud, and use evidence from the book to discuss how the boy feels and what the story makes you think of. Ask children to share their thoughts.
- **check** for understanding that the toys are little and the rides are big. Use the text as a support to discuss how the book is organized.
- **model** what you mean by "Make it sound like you're talking." Ask children to repeat after you.

Professional Development Links

When Readers Struggle: Teaching that Works
Chapter 11: Learning to Solve Words: Effective and Efficient Phonics
Use this chapter to understand how readers use larger parts in words.

Word Matters: Teaching Phonics and Spelling in the Reading/Writing Classroom
Chapter 3 (pp. 22–26). Use this chapter to investigate what it means to become a word solver.

Teaching for Comprehending and Fluency: Thinking, Talking, and Writing About Reading, K–8
Chapter 30 (p. 517—Figure 30-1). Use this chapter to explore teaching for fluent phrased reading in small group and individual contexts.

SYSTEM **Orange**

NEW BOOK ***My Bear***

GENRE **Fiction**

YOU WILL NEED

- Take-Home Book, *Play and Ride*
- *My Writing Book*
- phonogram chart from Lesson 51
- magnetic letters

From the CD:

- *My Poetry Book* ✓
- word cards: CVC words
- Recording Form for *Play and Ride*
- fold sheet
- Parent Letter

NEW BOOK
My Bear, Level A

REREADING
Play and Ride, Level C
Getting Ready, Level A

Goals

- Recognize a large number of high-frequency words quickly and easily.
- Check one source of information with another.
- Self-monitor consistently.
- Self-correct most errors.
- Use word parts to solve words while reading.
- Reread and use the first letter to begin to read a word.
- Use word parts to write words.
- Read with phrasing.
- Read without pointing.
- Say words slowly to identify easy-to-hear sounds and write the letters that represent them.
- Write easy high-frequency words quickly.
- Write with good spacing and end punctuation.
- Understand a sequence of activities, all of which are connected to a toy bear.
- Infer intentions or feelings of a character.

Analysis of New Book Characteristics

***My Bear*, Level A**

GENRE/FORM
- Fiction

TEXT STRUCTURE
- Series of actions that a girl does with her toy bear
- Implied sequence ending with sleeping with her bear

CONTENT
- Familiar activities

THEMES AND IDEAS
- Child's affection for stuffed bear

LANGUAGE AND LITERARY FEATURES
- NA

SENTENCE COMPLEXITY
- One six-word simple sentence on each page of print
- Present tense
- Repeating pattern on each page with no variation
- Prepositional phrases

VOCABULARY
- Names of actions: *ride, eat, dance, read, skate, paint, swing, sleep*
- Preposition: *with*
- Pronouns: *I, my*

WORDS
- High-frequency words: *I, can, with, my*
- One-syllable words
- See the Word Analysis Charts in the *Program Guide* for specific words in each category.

ILLUSTRATIONS
- Drawings on every right page
- Close match between pictures and text

BOOK AND PRINT FEATURES
- Large font
- Ample space between words
- One line on each page of print
- Print on the left on a blank page; illustrations on the right page, except for last page
- Periods

▸ Rereading Books and Assessment

- *Play and Ride*, Level C
- *Getting Ready*, Level A

PROMPTING GUIDE 1
Refer to *Prompting Guide 1* as needed.

- Listen to one child read *Play and Ride* as you code the reading behavior on the Recording Form, have a brief comprehension conversation, and select a teaching point that will be most helpful to the reader. Score and analyze the Reading Record following the lesson.
- Have the other children reread *Getting Ready* and then *Play and Ride.*
- Prompt for or reinforce self-correction behavior, if needed, e.g., "You made a mistake. Go back and see if you can fix it" or "You fixed that."

Take a Reading Record

▸ Phonics/Word Work

- **PRINCIPLE** Recognizing and using simple phonograms with a VC pattern (easiest): *-ad, -ag, -an, -am, -at, -ed, -en, -et, -ig, -in, -it, -og, -op, -ot, -us, -up, -ut*

"You can look at the pattern [part] you know to help you read a word."
"You can write words by using the patterns and the sounds."

- Suggested language: "Another part that you see in some words is *-up.* What letter would you write first to write the word *cup?*" Children respond. Then write the word *cup.*
- Continue to fill in the phonogram chart started in Lesson 51. The second column will have *-up* words.
- Help children understand that *up* is a word, but it is also a part of other words. Write *pup.* If children are finding this easy, you can write *puppy* and highlight the *-up* in the middle of the word.
- Have the children make *up, cup,* and *pup* one at a time with magnetic letters. Have them break the word *c-up* and *p-up* two or three times.
- Have children write *up, cup,* and *pup* in *My Writing Book.*

My Poetry Book

- Have the children reread the poem "Windshield Washer" (poem 4) from *My Poetry Book.* Show children the word *the* on the whiteboard. Then write the word *this* under it, and read it. Ask children to locate the word *this* in the poem.

▸ Writing About Reading

Interactive Writing

- **MY WRITING BOOK**
- **PROMPTING GUIDE 1**

Refer to *Prompting Guide 1* as needed.

- Talk about all the things the boy can play with and the things the boy can ride in.
- Use interactive writing to tell one thing the boy can play with and one thing he can ride in, e.g.,

  I can play with this train.
  He can ride in this truck.
- Emphasize saying words slowly and writing easy-to-hear consonant and vowel sounds. Use sound boxes on the whiteboard, if needed, for words such as *ride, play,* or *truck.*
- Prompt for quick writing of high-frequency words, such as *I, can, my, in.*
- Have the children reread the sentences.
- If time allows, write the sentences on sentence strips and cut them up. Ask the children to arrange and glue them in *My Writing Book* and illustrate them.

▸ New Book

My Bear,
Level A

Introducing the Text

- Introduce children to the book by showing them the cover. Suggested language: "This little girl can do lots of things with her bear. What are some of the things you think she can do with her bear?" Children respond.
- "Turn to pages 2 and 3. What can the girl do with her bear? Yes, so she says, 'I can ride with my Bear.' Say *with.* What letter would you see first in *with?* Find with, and run your finger under it, and say it."
- "Turn to page 10. What does the girl say she can do with her Bear? Say *can.* What letter comes first in *can?* Find can, run your finger under it, and say it."
- "Turn back to the beginning, and read all the things the girl says she can do with her Bear." At this point, children should have strong control of voice-print match and should not need to point. If voice-print match is not firm, you may allow a child to point a bit longer but work hard to get it controlled.

PROMPTING GUIDE 1
Refer to *Prompting Guide 1* as needed.

Reading the Text

- As children read, observe ease in problem solving. Reinforce self-correction behavior, e.g., "You fixed that."

Discussing and Revisiting the Text

Invite children to talk about the story. Some key understandings children may express are:

- The girl can do lots of things with her bear. [Extend by asking for examples. Encourage children to show the pages with these examples.]
- The girl must like her bear a lot. [Extend by asking why children think that.]

PROMPTING GUIDE 1
Refer to *Prompting Guide 1* as needed.

Teaching Points

- Based on your observations, use *Prompting Guide 1* to select a teaching point that will be most helpful to the readers.
- You may want to have the children locate *with* or *can* on two or three different pages.

▸ Optional Letter/ Word Work

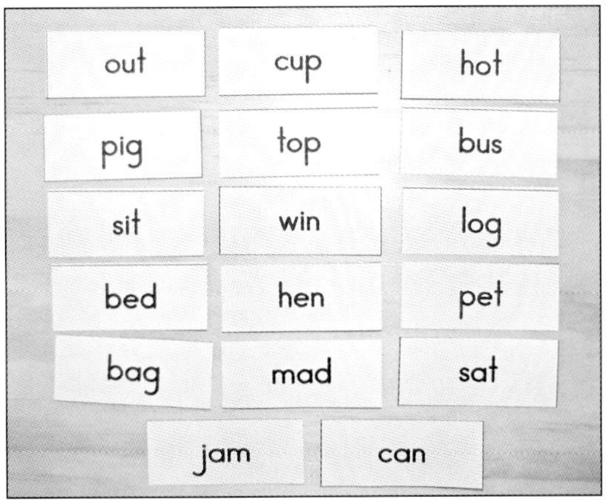

- Work with the children to develop flexibility with word parts using the CVC word cards. Have them read each word and then say the parts, e.g., *s-it, c-up.* Suggested words to select from: *bag, can, jam, mad, sat, bed, hen, pet, pig, win, sit log, top, hot, bus, cup,* and *out.*

Classroom Connection

- Give the children the Take-Home Book *Play and Ride.*
- Give children the fold sheet with the sentence from the story, *We can ride in this car.* Cut up the sentence for each child, and give the child the pieces to take back to class.
- In the classroom, children can put together the cut-up sentence and illustrate it on the fold sheet.
- Children may glue the sentence down or glue at home.

Home/School Connection

- Give children the Take-Home Book *Play and Ride* to read to family members.
- Have children take their cut up-sentence and fold sheet home to read to family members. They can also glue the cut-up sentence.

Assessing Reading and Writing Behaviors

Observe to find evidence that children can:

- self-monitor consistently.
- recognize high-frequency words quickly and easily.
- have full control of voice-print match.
- solve words using first letters and larger word parts.
- check one source of information with another.
- use word parts to write words.
- say words slowly to identify easy-to-hear sounds and write the letters that represent them.
- write easy high-frequency words quickly.
- infer intentions or feelings of a character.

Supporting English Language Learners

To support English language learners, you can:

- **teach** for understanding of "You made a mistake. Go back and see if you can fix it" or "You fixed that."
- **check** that children remember what a windshield wiper is.
- **use** the language of the text in a conversational way. Have children repeat the language several times to help them remember the syntax.
- **monitor** for understanding of all the actions.
- **support** children in using the pictures to recall what the girl and the bear like to do together and think about how the girl feels about her bear.
- **extend** children's language in a conversational way rather than correcting. If children say "She like reading" or "She readed," respond back, "Yes, she likes reading" or "Yes, she read with her bear."
- **check** to be sure children are saying the words to hear sounds.

Professional Development Links

When Readers Struggle: Teaching that Works
Chapter 12: Using Words: How to Build a Repertoire
Use this chapter to understand how readers use known words to solve new ones.

Word Matters: Teaching Phonics and Spelling in the Reading/Writing Classroom
Chapter 17 (pp. 220–226). Use this chapter to explore how systematic observation can support teaching for word solving.

Teaching for Comprehending and Fluency: Thinking, Talking, and Writing About Reading, K–8
Chapter 5 (pp. 55-56, Figure 5-5). Use this chapter to review strategic actions.

SYSTEM **Orange**

NEW BOOK ***What Is Very Long?***

GENRE **Nonfiction**

YOU WILL NEED

- Take-Home Book, *My Bear*
- *My Writing Book*
- magnetic letters: *t, h, e, i, s, b, u, t, c, n*
- phonogram chart from Lesson 52
- word bags

From the CD:

- *My Poetry Book*✓
- *My ABC Book*✓
- word card: *this*
- fold sheet
- Parent Letter

NEW BOOK

What Is Very Long?, Level C

REREADING

My Bear, Level A

Play and Ride, Level C

Goals

- Self-monitor consistently.
- Self-correct most errors.
- Recognize a core of high-frequency words.
- Recognize and use simple phonograms with a VC pattern.
- Use word parts to solve words while reading.
- Use word parts to write words.
- Connect words with beginning consonant digraphs.
- Use known words as a tool in learning new words.
- Begin to read with phrasing.
- Check one source of information with another.
- Understand that animals with something in common can form a category.
- Understand the difference between something physically long and a long name.

Analysis of New Book Characteristics

What Is Very Long?, Level C

GENRE/FORM

- Nonfiction

TEXT STRUCTURE

- Series of animals, each with an attribute that is long, presented on each page spread
- Emphasis on comparison (how animals are similar)
- Play on meaning on last page (long name instead of long body part)

CONTENT

- Some unfamiliar animal names
- Parts of animals' bodies

THEMES AND IDEAS

- Animal attributes
- How animals are similar

LANGUAGE AND LITERARY FEATURES

- NA

SENTENCE COMPLEXITY

- Two sentences on each page of print
- Sentences four, six, or seven words long
- Repeating pattern with variation for singular and plural
- Adjectives

VOCABULARY

- Names of animals and their body parts: *giraffe, neck, frog, legs, bird, beak, elephant, trunk, monkey, tail, rabbit, ears, walrus, teeth, hippopotamus*
- Articles: *a, this, the*
- Adjectives: *long, very*

WORDS

- High-frequency words: *this, is, a, the, has, here, an*
- One-syllable words with some multisyllable words
- See the Word Analysis Charts in the *Program Guide* for specific words in each category.

ILLUSTRATIONS

- Photographs of an animal on each right page
- Close match between pictures and text
- Illustrations showing the part of the animal that is long

BOOK AND PRINT FEATURES

- Large font
- Ample space between words
- Three lines on each page of print, with four on the last page
- Print on the left on a blank page; illustrations on the right page, except for last page
- Periods and exclamation point; question mark in title

▸ Rereading Books

- *My Bear*, Level A
- *Play and Ride*, Level C

PROMPTING GUIDE 1
Refer to *Prompting Guide 1* as needed.

- Invite the children to reread *Play and Ride* and *My Bear.*
- Prompt for phrasing, e.g., "Put these words together." Demonstrate how to read a group of words together, if needed.

▸ Phonics/Word Work

-us	-up	-ut
us	up	but
bus	cup	cut
	pup	nut

- **PRINCIPLE** Recognizing and using simple phonograms with a VC pattern (easiest): *-ad, -ag, -an, -am, -at, -ed, -en, -et, -ig, -in, -it, -og, -op,-ot, -us, -up, -ut*

"You can look at the pattern [part] you know to help you read a word."
"You can write words by using the patterns and the sounds."

- Suggested language: "You can see a pattern or part in some words. It is *-ut*. What letter would you write first to add *but* to the chart?"
- Continue to fill in the phonogram chart started in Lesson 51 and continued in Lesson 52. The third column will have *-ut* words.
- Write *cut* and *nut*, asking children to supply the first letter each time.
- Have the children make *but, cut,* and *nut* two or three times with magnetic letters and then break the words (*b-ut, c-ut, n-ut*).
- Then have them write the words *but, cut,* and *nut* in *My ABC Book.*

▸ New Book

What Is Very Long?, Level C

Introducing the Text

- Introduce children to the book by showing the cover. Suggested language: "The title of this book is *What Is Very Long?* In this book, you will learn about parts of animals that are very long. Do you know some parts of animals that are long?"
- "Turn to pages 2 and 3. What kind of animal is this? Yes, it is a giraffe, and what is long? Yes, the giraffe has a very long neck. Say the word *this*. It starts with *th*, just like *the*. Put your finger under *this*, and get a good look. Say *this*." Children respond.
- "Now turn to pages 4 and 5. What kind of animal is here? And what is long? Say the word *here*. What letter would come first? The word *here* starts this sentence so it has an uppercase *H*. Find here, and put your finger under it." Repeat for pages 14 and 16.
- "Look at the walrus on page 14. Say *walrus*. What is very long?"
- "Look at the hippopotamus on page 16. Say *hippopotamus*, and clap it with me. What is very long about that? Yes, the name!"
- "Now turn back to the beginning of the book, and read to find out all the parts of the animals that are very long."

PROMPTING GUIDE 1
Refer to *Prompting Guide 1* as needed.

Reading the Text

- As the children read, support the use of language structure, e.g., "Think what would sound right."
- Support the use of the first letter to solve new words, e.g., "Read that again, and get started on that word."
- Be sure to prompt for phrasing, if needed, e.g., "Put these words together."

Discussing and Revisiting the Text

Talk with the children about the different animals and what they noticed about them. You may want them to choose a page to read aloud. Some key understandings children may express are:

- This story is about animals that all have something long about them. [Extend by asking for examples of what is long on each animal.]
- Other animals with something long could be in this story. [Extend by asking for other animals with long body parts, e.g., a dog with a long tail.]
- Most animals in the story have a long body part. The hippopotamus doesn't have a long body part but has a long name. [Extend by asking what is different about the hippopotamus and why this animal is in the story.]

PROMPTING GUIDE 1
Refer to *Prompting Guide 1* as needed.

Teaching Points

- Based on your observations, use *Prompting Guide 1* to select a teaching point that will be most helpful to the readers.
- Select a page to revisit to confirm effective processing, e.g., checking the picture with the first letter of the word.

▸ Letter/Word Work

- Make *the* with magnetic letters, and ask children to read it. Suggested language: "Today you are going to learn a new word that starts like *the*." Make *this* on the whiteboard. Read it as you run your finger under it left to right, and ask children to talk about what they notice. They should say that the first two letters are the same.
- Have the children make the word *this* with magnetic letters and break it two or three times (*th-is*).

Word Bags

- Give children the word card *this* to read and add to their word bags.
- Have children lay out their word cards face down. Have them turn the words over one a time, read them, and put them away. Notice how quickly they recognize the word *this*.

My Poetry/Writing Book

- If time allows, have children read from *My Poetry Book* or *My Writing Book*.

Classroom Connection

Orange #53 Name: KIM

-us	-up	-ut
bus	cup	hut
us	pup	but
		nut

- Give children the fold sheet with the three-way sort printed on it and the words for patterns *-us, -up, -ut* (see *Lesson Resources CD*).
- In the classroom, have them cut the words apart and sort under the three patterns: *-us, -up, -ut.*
- Remind children to read the words after they have sorted them.
- Have children reread the Take-Home Book *My Bear.*

Home/School Connection

- Have the children take home their fold sheets.
- Have children sort the word cards into the three categories. They may glue them down.
- Give them the Take-Home Book *My Bear* to read to family members.

Assessing Reading and Writing Behaviors

Observe to find evidence that children can:

- use word parts to solve words while reading and to write words.
- check one source of information with another.
- use known words to learn new words.
- read with phrasing.
- understand that animals with something in common can form a category.
- understand the humor in the switch from something physically long to a long name.

Supporting English Language Learners

To support English language learners, you can:

- **be sure** children understand and can name the words and pictures being used in Letter/Word Work.
- **show** children what you mean by, "Put these words together."
- **use** the language of the text in a conversational way. Have children repeat the language several times to help them remember the syntax.
- **support** children with the names of the animals as well as the body parts. There is a lot of challenging vocabulary in this book. Do not allow children to become frustrated. If they forget the name of an animal or body part, tell them.
- **support** children in understanding the last page—the hippopotamus has a long name.
- **use** the pictures to support children in talking about what animals have a long part. Tell children some other things that are long and see if they can name some too.
- **model** what you mean by "Make it sound like you're talking." Ask them to repeat some of the phrases after you.

Professional Development Links

When Readers Struggle: Teaching that Works
Chapter 11: Learning to Solve Words: Effective and Efficient Phonics
Use this chapter to help in understanding how readers use larger parts in words.

Guided Reading: Good First Teaching for All Children
Chapter 12: Teaching for Strategies. Use this chapter to understand supporting early reading strategies for maintaining fluency, detecting and correcting error, and problem-solving new words. There are a number of examples of children's reading.

LESSON **54** LEVEL **C**

SYSTEM **Orange**

NEW BOOK ***The Play***

GENRE **Nonfiction**

YOU WILL NEED

- Take-Home Book, *What Is Very Long?*
- *My Writing Book*
- magnetic letters
- phonogram chart from Lesson 53
- "Jack and Jill," enlarged poem
- word bags

From the CD:

- *My Poetry Book* ✓
- *My ABC Book* ✓
- Recording Form for *What Is Very Long?*
- Take, Make, Write sheet
- word cards: CVC words
- fold sheet
- Parent Letter

NEW BOOK
The Play, Level A

REREADING
What Is Very Long?, Level C

My Bear, Level A

Goals

- Recognize many high-frequency words quickly and easily.
- Check one source of information with another while reading.
- Self-monitor consistently while reading.
- Self-correct most errors.
- Recognize and use simple phonograms with a VC pattern.
- Use word parts to solve words while reading.
- Use word parts to write words.
- Connect words by beginning consonant digraphs.
- Use known words as a tool in learning new words.
- Read with phrasing and fluency.
- Use more than one source of information (meaning, visual information, language structure) while reading.
- Write easy high-frequency words quickly.
- Write with good spacing.
- Start a sentence with an uppercase letter and write end punctuation.
- Understand the concept of a play with masks.

Analysis of New Book Characteristics

The Play, Level A

GENRE/FORM
- Narrative Nonfiction

TEXT STRUCTURE
- Series of scenes showing actors in a play
- Characters holding masks
- No sequence

CONTENT
- Familiar animals
- Concept of a play

THEMES AND IDEAS
- Children acting parts
- Using props for a play

LANGUAGE AND LITERARY FEATURES
- NA

SENTENCE COMPLEXITY
- One four-word simple sentence on each page of print
- Present tense
- Repeating pattern on each page with no variation

VOCABULARY
- Names of players: *mouse, hen, cat, duck, dog, cow, horse*
- Content word: *play*

WORDS
- High-frequency words: *here, is, the*
- One-syllable words
- See the Word Analysis Charts in the *Program Guide* for specific words in each category.

ILLUSTRATIONS
- Photographs on every right page
- Close match between pictures and text

BOOK AND PRINT FEATURES
- Large font
- Ample space between words
- One line on each page of print
- Print on the left on a blank page; illustrations on the right page, except for last page
- Periods and exclamation point

▸ Rereading Books and Assessment

PROMPTING GUIDE 1
Refer to *Prompting Guide 1* as needed.

- *What Is Very Long?*, Level C
- *My Bear*, Level A

- Listen to one child read *What Is Very Long?* as you code the reading behavior on the Recording Form, have a brief comprehension conversation, and select a teaching point that will be most helpful to the reader. Score and analyze the Reading Record following the lesson.
- Have the other children reread *My Bear* and then *What Is Very Long?*
- Prompt readers to use phrasing, e.g., "Put your words together so that it sounds like talking."

▸ Phonics/Word Work

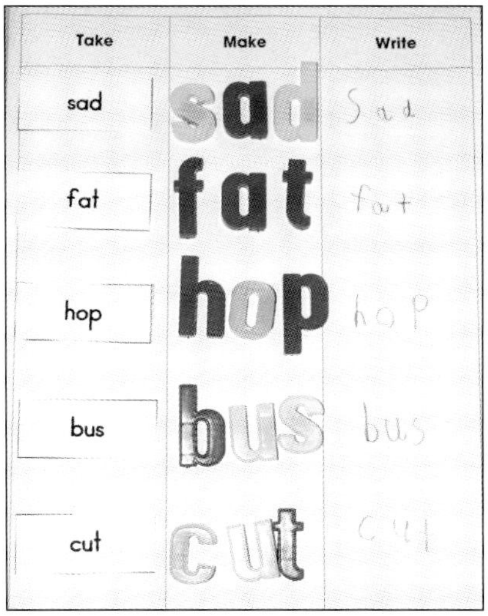

- **PRINCIPLE** Recognizing and using simple phonograms with a VC pattern (easiest): *-ad, -ag, -an, -am, -at, -ed, -en, -et, -ig, -in,-it, -og, -op, -ot, -us, -up, -ut*

"You can look at the pattern [part] you know to help you read a word."
"You can write words by using the patterns and the sounds."

- Suggested language: "You have learned many parts that are in words. These parts can help you read and write words. Today you are going to make words with magnetic letters and then write them."
- Give each child a Take, Make, Write sheet and place word cards for all of the patterns in the middle of the table.
- Demonstrate choosing a CVC word card, making it with magnetic letters, and then writing it.
- Have the children choose, make, and write as many words as they can. (The sheet can be glued into *My Writing Book.*)

My Poetry Book

- Introduce the new poem "Jack and Jill" (poem 9). Talk about the meaning of the poem. Children may have heard this rhyme, but read it to them and then invite them to read it with you several times. Have them locate the word *up* as they read the poem in *My Poetry Book.*

▸ Writing About Reading

Dictated Writing

- **MY WRITING BOOK**
- **PROMPTING GUIDE 1**

Refer to *Prompting Guide 1* as needed.

- If time allows, you may want to begin by having each child read recent pages from *My Writing Book*. Occasionally ask the child to locate a word in a sentence read.
- Dictate the following sentences:

  Here is a frog.
  The frog has very long legs.
- Help the children think about how to write the high-frequency words *here, is, a, the, has.* You can expect them to start *very* and *long,* but you will need to write the rest on the whiteboard for them. You may want to use sound boxes to help them listen for and identify the four sounds and letters in *frog* and *legs.*
- If time allows, have children locate two or three words in the writing and illustrate the sentences.

▸ New Book

The Play,
Level A

Introducing the Text

- Introduce children to the book by talking about children's experience with plays, perhaps with the school play, for example. Suggested language: "In this book, the children are putting on a play with different animal characters. The children are holding masks in front of their faces so they can play the animals. Each child tells the animal that will be in the play."
- "Turn to pages 2 and 3. What animal is here? Yes, the child says, 'Here is the mouse.' Find <u>here</u>. Put your finger under it and say it."
- "Turn to pages 4 and 5. What animal is here?" Yes, the child says, 'Here is the hen.' "
- "Turn back to the beginning, and read *The Play*."

PROMPTING GUIDE 1
Refer to *Prompting Guide 1* as needed.

Reading the Text

- As the children read, reinforce self-monitoring, if needed, e.g., "You noticed something wasn't right."
- The children should be able to read the text accurately and independently.

Discussing and Revisiting the Text

Invite children to talk about the book. Some key understandings children may express are:

- The children are in a play.
- The play has characters in it. [Extend by asking for examples. Have children turn to the pages that support these examples.]
- The children like being in the play. [Extend by asking why children think that.]

PROMPTING GUIDE 1
Refer to *Prompting Guide 1* as needed.

Teaching Points

- Based on your observations, use *Prompting Guide 1* to select a teaching point that will be most helpful to the readers.
- You may want to have the children revisit a page where they did some effective problem solving. You can ask them to reread or to "find the tricky part" and then demonstrate problem solving.

▸ Optional Letter/ Word Work

- Have the children lay out their CVC word cards face down. Have them turn the words over one at a time, read them, and put them back in the word bags.

My ABC Book

- Have the children read *My ABC Book* page by page, reading the letters, saying the names of the pictures, and reading the words they have written. Then, children can add words by thinking of a word they want to write and writing it on the appropriate page.

Classroom Connection

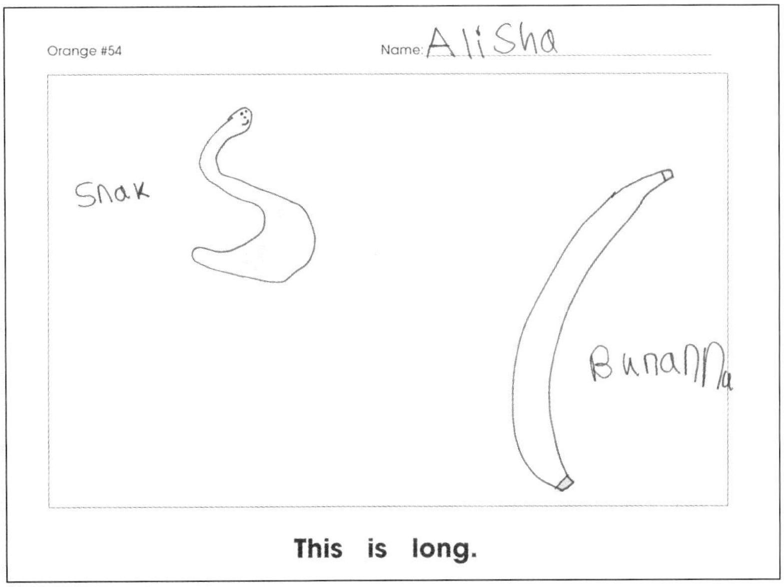

- Give the children the fold sheet with the sentence: *This is long.* Have them draw pictures of things that are long and label them.
- Give children the Take-Home Book *What Is Very Long?*
- Give children any retired words (words that are well known and can be read quickly) from their word cards to read in the classroom.

Home/School Connection

- Have children take home their fold sheets to read and add more items to.
- Have children take the Take-Home Book *What Is Very Long?* to read to family members.
- Have children take home retired words for games.

Assessing Reading and Writing Behaviors

Observe to find evidence that children can:

- recognize high-frequency words quickly.
- self-monitor and self-correct errors.
- use word parts to solve words while reading, and write words.
- use known words to learn new words.
- read with phrasing.
- check one source of information with another while reading.
- write easy high-frequency words quickly.
- write with good spacing.
- start a sentence with an uppercase letter and write end punctuation.
- understand the concept of a play with masks.

Supporting English Language Learners

To support English language learners, you can:

- **read** "Jack and Jill" several times so children begin to feel comfortable joining in. Discuss its meaning. Jack falls down and hurts his head, and so does Jill.
- **be sure** children understand all the pictures and words used in Phonics/Letter Word Work.
- **use** the language of the text in a conversational way. Name each animal.
- **check** for understanding of the concepts of a play and masks.
- **help** children in using the pictures to recall what animals the children pretend to be in the play.
- **ask** children to repeat the sentence with you several times when dictating the sentence.
- **remind** children to say the words slowly and listen for the sounds they hear.
- **demonstrate** saying words slowly as a model for articulation.
- **be sure** children say the word slowly themselves even if they hear a sound from your articulation.
- **tell** children that some words they know well so they can be written quickly.

Professional Development Links

When Readers Struggle: Teaching that Works
Chapter 12: Using Words: How to Build a Repertoire
Use this chapter to understand how readers use known words to solve new ones.

Word Matters: Teaching Phonics and Spelling in the Reading/Writing Classroom
Chapter 2 (pp. 16–19). Use this chapter to investigate teaching for word-solving strategies.

YOU WILL NEED

- Take-Home Book, *The Play*
- *My Writing Book*
- "The Itsy, Bitsy Spider," enlarged poem
- magnetic letters
- phonogram chart from Lesson 53
- sticks or pencils for puppets

From the CD:

- Ways to Sort and Match Letters
- Take, Make, Write sheet
- word cards: CVC words, *up*
- Letters Made in Similar Ways document
- fold sheet
- Parent Letter

SYSTEM **Orange**

NEW BOOK ***Our Pets***

GENRE **Nonfiction**

NEW BOOK
Our Pets, Level C

REREADING
The Play, Level A
What Is Very Long?, Level C

Goals

- Self-monitor consistently.
- Self-correct most errors.
- Check one source of information with another (e.g., pictures with the first letter).
- Understand how patterns in words can help in spelling words.
- Use patterns to solve words in reading and word writing.
- Locate words with specific patterns in continuous text.
- Locate a word using the first letter.
- Read with phrasing and fluency.
- Use more than one source of information (meaning, visual information, language structure) while reading.
- Understand the concept of pets.
- Bring background knowledge to the idea of pets.
- Infer why people like their pets.

Analysis of New Book Characteristics

***Our Pets*, Level C**

GENRE/FORM
- Narrative Nonfiction

TEXT STRUCTURE
- Series of children and pets, each described

CONTENT
- Familiar animal names, with some not usually thought of as pets
- Attributes of animals

THEMES AND IDEAS
- Concept of pets
- Taking care of animals

LANGUAGE AND LITERARY FEATURES
- NA

SENTENCE COMPLEXITY
- Three sentences on each page, except last page
- Sentences four to seven words long
- Repeating pattern of meaning with variation in order of sentences on last page
- Adjectives

VOCABULARY
- Names of pets: *mouse, snake, bird, horse, cat, goldfish, pig, cow*
- Pronouns: *it, I, this*
- Adjectives: *little, long, yellow, big, soft, wet, fat, black, white*
- Conjunction: *and*

WORDS
- High-frequency words: *this, is, a, little, it, I, like, big, and*
- One-syllable words with some multisyllable words
- See the Word Analysis Charts in the *Program Guide* for specific words in each category.

ILLUSTRATIONS
- Photographs of a child and animal on every right page, except the last page
- Close match between pictures and text

BOOK AND PRINT FEATURES
- Large font
- Ample space between words
- Three lines on each page of print
- Print on the left on a blank page; illustrations on the right page, except for last page
- Periods and exclamation point

▸ Rereading Books

- *The Play*, Level A
- *What Is Very Long?*, Level C

PROMPTING GUIDE 1
Refer to *Prompting Guide 1* as needed.

- Invite the children to reread *The Play* and *What Is Very Long?*
- If needed, prompt readers to use phrasing, e.g., "Read it all at once."

▸ Phonics/Word Work

The Itsy, Bitsy Spider

The itsy, bitsy spider
Climbed up the waterspout.
Down came the rain
And washed the spider out.

Out came the sun
And dried up all the rain.
And the itsy, bitsy spider
Climbed up the spout again.

- **PRINCIPLE** Recognizing and using simple phonograms with a VC pattern (easiest): *-ad, -ag, -an, -am, -at, -ed, -en, -et, -ig, -in, -it, -og, -op, -ot, -us, -up, -ut*

"You can look at the pattern [part] you know to help you read a word."
"You can write words by using the patterns and the sounds."

- Introduce the poem "The Itsy, Bitsy Spider" (poem 10), and talk with children about what is happening. Children may be familiar with this rhyme, but read it to them and then ask them to join in a few times using shared reading. Check children's knowledge of rhymes by having them identify words that rhyme. Have them look for any words or parts of words they know. Have them locate and highlight the word *up* and locate the word on the phonogram chart.

Magnetic Letters

- Tell children, "You have learned many patterns or parts that are in words. The patterns can help you read and write words. Today you are going to make words with magnetic letters and then write them."
- Give each child a Take, Make, Write sheet and place CVC word cards for all of the patterns on the table.
- Demonstrate choosing a CVC word, reading it, making it with magnetic letters, and then writing it.
- Have the children choose, make, and write as many words as they can. (The sheet can be glued into *My Writing Book*.)

▸ New Book

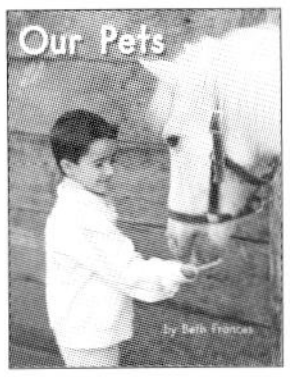

Our Pets,
Level C

Introducing the Text

- Introduce children to the book by talking about animals that people have as pets. Suggested language: "Pets can be lots of fun. What pets do you like?" Children respond. Show the cover of *Our Pets.* "In this book, you will learn about different kinds of pets children have. Each child tells about a pet and what it looks like. The book is called *Our Pets.*"
- "Turn to pages 2 and 3. This is a little pet. What kind of pet is this? Yes, this is a mouse, and it is little. Say the word *this.* It starts like *the.* It starts with a *th-*. Find this with an uppercase *T.* Run your finger under it, and say *this.*"
- "Turn to the next page. What kind of pet is this? Yes, this is a snake. And how does it look? Say the word *it.* What letter would come first in *it?* Look for it with an uppercase *I.* Put your finger under the word, and say *it.*"
- Have them look at pages 10 and 12 and name the pets.
- "You will be surprised to see the pet at the end."
- Now have children turn to the beginning and read to learn about *Our Pets.* Insist on no pointing so the children will read in word groups.

PROMPTING GUIDE 1
Refer to *Prompting Guide 1* as needed.

Reading the Text

- As the children read, you may want to reinforce effective problem solving. If appropriate, help children notice how to check the name of the animal with the first letter of the word.
- If needed, reinforce phrased reading, e.g., "Make it sound like talking."

Discussing and Revisiting the Text

Invite the children to talk about all the pets and what they noticed about them. You may want them to select a page to read. Some key understandings children may express are:

- This story is about all different types of pets. [Extend by asking for examples of the different pets in the book. Have children find the pages that show their examples.]
- The children in the story like their pets. [Extend by asking how they know that.]
- This story reminds me of ___________. [Accept any reasonable connection such as my pet rabbit.]
- Each pet has something that makes it different from the other animals. [Extend by asking for examples such as one is big; another is long; another is soft, etc.]

PROMPTING GUIDE 1
Refer to *Prompting Guide 1* as needed.

Teaching Points

- Based on your observations, use *Prompting Guide 1* to select a teaching point that will be most helpful to the readers.
- You may want to go to the word *this* and clarify that it means the pet that is being shown on the page.

▸ Letter/Word Work

- Add the word card *up* to children's word bags.
- Have the children lay out their CVC word cards face down. Have them turn the cards over one at a time, read the word, and put them back in the word bags.

Letter Sort

- Have the children say and sort magnetic letters two or three different ways (see Instructional Routines, Ways to Sort and Match Letters, in the *Program Guide*).

Classroom Connection

- Give children the fold sheet with the sentences, "Here is the mouse" and "Here is the cat" written under the pictures.
- Have them read the sentences and illustrate them. Then have them cut out the animals and tape them to the ends of pencils or Popsicle sticks to make puppets. Children may "act out" the part of the story *The Play* with the mouse and cat.
- Give children the Take-Home Book *The Play* to reread.

Home/School Connection

- Have the children take home their stick puppets to share with their families.
- Give children the Take-Home Book *The Play* to read to family members.

Assessing Reading and Writing Behaviors

Observe to find evidence that children can:

- check one source of information with another.
- use sound/letter relationships and patterns in words to spell words in writing.
- make comparisons among items in the larger category of pets.
- use phrasing while reading.
- use more than one source of information (meaning, visual information, language structure) while reading.
- understand the idea that people like their pets for some of the same reasons but also for different reasons.

Supporting English Language Learners

To support English language learners, you can:

- **read** "The Itsy Bitsy Spider" several times. Ask children if they hear the rhyming words. "Do you hear words that sound the same at the end?"
- **be clear** when using the language from the book while still being conversational. It is the first time they will hear/read three different sentences on each page.
- **have** children repeat some of the language of the book several times.
- **help** children with the names of a wide variety of pets.
- **talk** to children about the adjectives that describe each pet. Check for understanding of these words.
- **prevent** children from becoming frustrated with the vocabulary. If children get stuck, ask them to tell you the first sound of the word. Then, tell them the word, if necessary. This will support them in using the visual information.
- **use** the pictures to support children in talking about all the different kinds of pets. Ask children if any of the pets surprised them.
- **model** what you mean by "Make it sound like you're talking."

Professional Development Links

When Readers Struggle: Teaching that Works
Chapter 12: Using Words: How to Build a Repertoire
Use this chapter to understand the benefit of overlearning some words.

Teaching for Comprehending and Fluency: Thinking, Talking, and Writing About Reading, K–8
Chapter 4. Use this chapter to explore helping students develop systems of strategic actions to sustain processing. There are individual charts that explain solving words, monitoring and correcting, searching for and using information, summarizing, maintaining fluency, and adjusting the reading.

SYSTEM **Orange**

NEW BOOK ***Making a Pizza***

GENRE **Nonfiction**

YOU WILL NEED

- Take-Home Book, *Our Pets*
- *My Writing Book*
- "There Once Was a Queen," enlarged poem
- phonogram chart from Lesson 53
- magnetic letters: *h, e, r, e*
- word bags

From the CD:

- *My Poetry Book*✓
- word card: *her*
- Recording Form for *Our Pets*
- fold sheet
- Parent Letter

NEW BOOK
Making a Pizza, Level A

REREADING
Our Pets, Level C
The Play, Level A

Goals

- Recognize and write many high-frequency words.
- Locate words with patterns within continuous print.
- Use known words to solve new words.
- Read with effective word solving while attending to meaning.
- Read without finger pointing.
- Use meaning, language structure, and visual information to monitor and self-correct reading.
- Say words slowly to listen for and identify easy-to-hear sounds in sequence and write the letters that represent them.
- Understand a step-by-step process, in sequence.
- Infer what happened between pages 15 and 16.
- Understand why the book ends the way it does.
- Understand that the organization of the book is circular (ends the way it began).

Analysis of New Book Characteristics

Making a Pizza, Level A

GENRE/FORM
- Narrative Nonfiction

TEXT STRUCTURE
- Sequential steps in making a pizza
- Each page spread showing one step, building through cooking and eating
- Circular narration--from empty pan to empty pan

CONTENT
- Familiar food for most children
- Concept of cooking step by step

THEMES AND IDEAS
- Food preparation

LANGUAGE AND LITERARY FEATURES
- NA

SENTENCE COMPLEXITY
- One four-word simple sentence on each page of print
- Present tense
- Repeating pattern on each page with no variation

VOCABULARY
- Names of items: *pan, dough, sauce, cheese, pepperoni, oven, pizza*
- Content words related to the pizza

WORDS
- High-frequency words: *here, is, the*
- One-syllable words with one two-syllable and one four-syllable word
- See the Word Analysis Charts in the *Program Guide* for specific words in each category.

ILLUSTRATIONS
- Photographs on every right page
- Close match between pictures and text

BOOK AND PRINT FEATURES
- Large font
- Ample space between words
- One line on each page of print
- Print on the left on a blank page; illustrations on the right page, except for last page
- Periods

▸ Rereading Books and Assessment

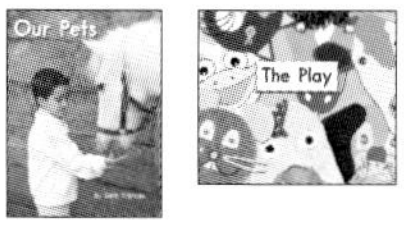

- *Our Pets*, Level C
- *The Play*, Level A

PROMPTING GUIDE 1
Refer to *Prompting Guide 1* as needed.

- Listen to one child read *Our Pets* as you code the reading behavior on the Recording Form, have a brief comprehension conversation, and select a teaching point that will be most helpful to the reader. Score and analyze the Reading Record following the lesson.
- Have the other children reread *The Play* and then *Our Pets.*
- Prompt readers to monitor using meaning, visual information, or language structure, e.g., "Try that again, and make it look right (or make sense)."

▸ Phonics/Word Work

There Once Was a Queen

There once was a queen
Whose face was green.
She ate her milk
And drank her bread,
And got up in the morning
To go to bed.

- **PRINCIPLE** Recognizing and using simple phonograms with a VC pattern (easiest): *-ad, -ag, -an, -am, -at, -ed, -en, -et, -ig, -in, -it, -og, -op, -ot, -us, -up, -ut*

"You can look at the pattern [part] you know to help you read a word."
"You can write words by using the patterns and the sounds."

- Introduce the new poem "There Once Was a Queen" (poem 11). Read it to the children, and talk about the humor in the poem. Then ask children to join in a few times using shared reading.
- Have children locate and highlight the word *up.* Have them locate the word on the phonogram chart from Lesson 53.
- Have children reread both "The Itsy, Bitsy Spider"(poem 10) and "There Once Was a Queen" in *My Poetry Book.* Have them highlight the word *up* and then turn a page and write two words with patterns that they know. Have them write the word and then highlight the pattern. They can use the charts to help them or check their words.

▸ Writing About Reading

Dictated Writing

- **MY WRITING BOOK**
- **PROMPTING GUIDE 1**

Refer to *Prompting Guide 1* as needed.

- If time allows, you may want to begin by having each child read recent pages from *My Writing Book.* Occasionally ask the child to locate a word in a sentence read.
- Dictate the following sentences:

  This is a big pet.
  This is a snake.

- The children should be able to write the high-frequency words *this, is, a* quickly and easily. Ask them to say words like *big, pet,* and *snake* slowly, and help them listen for the sounds and write the letters in sequence using sound boxes. You will want to show the other letters, e.g., *e* in *snake.*
- Have them reread the sentences and illustrate them.

▸ New Book

Making a Pizza,
Level A

Introducing the Text

- Introduce children to the book by talking about what children think of pizza. Suggested language: "Have you ever made a pizza? What are some of the things you need?" Children respond.
- Show the cover of *Making a Pizza*. "Do you see the pepperoni pizza on the cover? In this book, you will read about all the things that are here to make a pizza."
- "Turn to page 2. What do you see? Yes, here is the pan."
- "Now turn to page 4, and what do you see? Yes, here is the dough. Put your finger under *here*."
- "Turn to page 10, and what do you see? Yes, the pepperoni."
- "Now the pizza is ready, so what do we need? Turn to page 12 to find out. Yes, the oven to cook the pizza in."
- "Turn to the beginning, and read about all the things you need for making a pizza."

PROMPTING GUIDE 1
Refer to *Prompting Guide 1* as needed.

Reading the Text

- During reading, you may want to reinforce effective problem solving, e.g., "You figured that out" or "You checked the picture with the word."
- Go back to a tricky part to revisit effective problem solving.

Discussing and Revisiting the Text

Invite children to talk about the sequence of making a pizza. Some key understandings children may express are:

- The book tells how to make a pizza. [Extend by asking children to describe some of the steps. You may want to make a simple circular diagram.]
- They ate the pizza after they made it. [Extend by asking children why they think that.]
- The book ends with just the pan, like on the first page. [Extend by completing the circular drawing.]

PROMPTING GUIDE 1
Refer to *Prompting Guide 1* as needed.

Teaching Points

- Based on your observations, use *Prompting Guide 1* to select a teaching point that will be most helpful to the readers.
- You may want to revisit a page where the children engaged in self-correction.

▸ Optional Letter/ Word Work

he
her
here

- Write the word *he* on the whiteboard. Ask children to read it.
- Then write the word *her* under it. Suggested language: "If you know a word like *he*, it can help you to read a word like *her*. *Her* starts like *he*, but it has an *r* at the end and that makes the *e* sound different. Let's read both words. What do you notice?"
- Children can talk about the parts that are the same and different.
- Then write the known word *here* under *he* and *her*. "*Here* starts with *he*. All three of these words look alike and sound alike at the beginning, but they sound different in the middle and end."

Magnetic Letters

- Have them make *he, her,* and *here* with magnetic letters two or three times.

Word Bags

- Give children the new word card *her* to add to their word bags.
- Have children lay out their word cards face down. Have them turn the words over one at a time, read them, and put them back in the word bags.

Classroom Connection

Poem #11

There Once Was a Queen

There once was a queen
Whose face was green.
She ate her milk
And drank her bread,
And got up in the morning
To go to bed.

- Have the children take the fold sheet with "There Once Was a Queen" back to their classrooms to read.
- Have children draw a picture of the green queen.
- Encourage children to write about the queen on the back of the sheet.
- Give the children the Take-Home Book *Our Pets*. They can read it in the classroom and color the pictures.

Home/School Connection

- Have the children take home the Take-Home Book *Our Pets*.
- Have them take home the fold sheet to read to family members.

Assessing Reading and Writing Behaviors

Observe to find evidence that children can:

- use self-monitoring and self-correction behavior.
- use known words to solve new words.
- use effective word solving while attending to meaning.
- read without finger pointing.
- read with phrasing.
- use meaning, language structure, and visual information to monitor and self-correct reading.
- write easy high-frequency words quickly.
- say words slowly to listen for and identify easy-to-hear sounds in sequence and write the letters that represent them.
- understand a step-by-step process.
- infer what happened between pages 15 and 16.

Supporting English Language Learners

To support English language learners, you can:

- **read** "The Green Queen" several times so children begin to feel comfortable joining in. Discuss its meaning. The queen does the opposite of what she is supposed to.
- **use** *he* and *her* each in a sentence to support the meaning of each word.
- **use** the language of the text in a conversational way. Have children repeat the ingredients used in making a pizza. Discuss why the ingredients need to be placed in order.
- **help** children in using the pictures to recall what someone does to make a pizza.
- **make** a wondering statement to see what the children are thinking about the last page. "This book ends like it started. I am wondering why they showed the pizza pan again."
- **check** for understanding of the surprise ending.
- **use** words such as *first, next,* and *after that* when discussing the book, but don't expect children to use those terms.
- **ask** children to repeat the sentence with you several times when dictating the sentence.
- **remind** children to say the words slowly and listen for the sounds they hear.

Professional Development Links

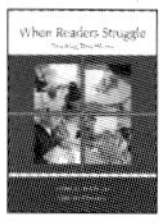

When Readers Struggle: Teaching that Works
Chapter 12: Using Words: How to Build a Repertoire. Use this chapter to understand how readers use known words to solve new ones.

Word Matters: Teaching Phonics and Spelling in the Reading/Writing Classroom
Chapter 16: The Writing Workshop: Support for Word Learning. Use this chapter to understand how writing helps readers learn about words.

SYSTEM **Orange**

NEW BOOK ***A Visit from Aunt Bee***

GENRE **Fiction**

YOU WILL NEED

- Take-Home Book, *Making a Pizza*
- magnetic letters
- word bags

From the CD:

- *My ABC Book* ✓
- Take, Make, Write sheet
- word card set
- fold sheet
- Parent Letter

NEW BOOK

A Visit from Aunt Bee, Level C

REREADING

Making a Pizza, Level A

Our Pets, Level C

Goals

- Recognize many high-frequency words easily.
- Recognize and use simple phonograms with a VCe pattern.
- Use patterns and word parts you know to read and write words.
- Make and/or read new words by substituting a new first consonant letter.
- Locate known and unknown high-frequency words in a text.
- Self-monitor consistently.
- Read in phrases with the eyes and without finger pointing.
- Use meaning, visual information, and language structure to solve words.
- Search actively for information in the pictures.
- Process dialogue as part of a story.
- Begin to realize that quotation marks and the word *said* indicate that someone is talking.
- Understand events typical of home and family, such as a visit by a relative.
- Recognize what makes the story humorous at the end.

Analysis of New Book Characteristics

A Visit From Aunt Bee, Level C

GENRE/FORM

- Fiction

TEXT STRUCTURE

- Narrative
- Seven brief episodes leading up to Aunt Bee's arrival

CONTENT

- Familiar home activities

THEMES AND IDEAS

- Having relatives visit
- Anticipation

LANGUAGE AND LITERARY FEATURES

- Character with a name

SENTENCE COMPLEXITY

- One or two sentences on each page of print
- Sentences four to six words long
- Repeating pattern of meaning on several pages with change in activity
- Present tense
- Dialogue on one page, with speaker assignment after the quote

VOCABULARY

- Names of activities--verb and object: clean the house, pick some flowers, blow up balloons, make a cake, set the table, make a card
- Pronoun: *we*

WORDS

- High-frequency words: *is, said, we, the, up, make, a, here*
- One-syllable words with some multi-syllable words
- See the Word Analysis Charts in the *Program Guide* for specific words in each category.

ILLUSTRATIONS

- Amusing drawings on every right page
- Close match between pictures and text

BOOK AND PRINT FEATURES

- Large font
- Ample space between words
- Two lines on each page of print, except last page
- Print on the left on a blank page; illustrations on the right page, except for last page
- Periods, exclamation points, quotation marks

▸ Rereading Books

- *Making a Pizza*, Level A
- *Our Pets*, Level C

PROMPTING GUIDE 1
Refer to *Prompting Guide 1* as needed.

- Invite children to reread *Our Pets* and *Making a Pizza.*
- If needed, prompt readers to solve words using known words and word parts, e.g., "Do you know a word like that?" or "Do you see a part that you know?"

▸ Phonics/Word Work

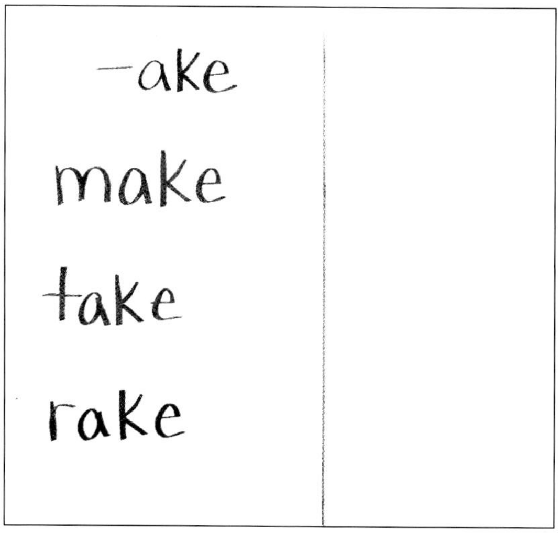

- **PRINCIPLE** Recognizing and using phonograms with a vowel-consonant-silent *e* (VCe) pattern: *-ade, -ace, -age, -ake, -ale, -ame, -ane, -ape, -ate, -ice, -ide, -ike, -ile, -ime, -ine, -ite, -ive, -obe, -oke, -ope*

"You can look at the pattern [part] you know to help you read a word."
"You can write words by using the patterns and the sounds."

- Suggested language: "You have learned many patterns or parts that are in words. The patterns can help you read and write words. Another pattern that you see in words is *-ake.* Look at the word *make.*"
- Write *make* on the chart under *ake*, and ask children what they notice. They may respond that there is an *e* at the end. "There is an *e* at the end of this pattern. It is a silent *e.* You cannot hear it. But it makes the *a* in *make* sound like the name of the letter. Say it slowly, and listen for the *a.*"
- You may want to have children say it slowly several times. Then repeat for *take* and *rake.*
- "Today you are going to make words with magnetic letters and then write them."
- Give each child a Take, Make, Write sheet and place word cards for CVCe words with the *-ake* pattern on the table.
- Demonstrate choosing a CVCe word card, reading it, making it with magnetic letters, and then writing it.
- Children choose, make, and write as many words as they can. (The sheet can be glued into *My Writing Book.*)

▸ New Book

A Visit from Aunt Bee, Level C

Introducing the Text

- Introduce children to the book by talking about what they might do at home to prepare for a relative's visit. Show the cover of *A Visit from Aunt Bee.* Suggested language: "Do you have a special aunt in your family? Aunt Bee is a very special aunt, and she is coming to visit her family. The family wants to get ready for Aunt Bee's visit. They do lots of things to make everything special for her."
- "Turn to pages 2 and 3. Who do you see? Yes, and Mom said to the children 'Aunt Bee is coming.' Can you say the word *said?* What letter would you see first in *said?* Yes, it starts with *s.* Find said, and run your finger under it. Get a good look, and say it."
- "Now turn to pages 6 and 7. Say the name *Aunt Bee. Aunt* starts with an uppercase *A.* Find the word aunt, and say it."
- "What are the children and Mom doing to get ready? Yes, they pick flowers, so they say, 'We pick some flowers.' "
- "Say *we.* What letter comes first in *we?* Yes, it's a *w,* and it starts the sentence so *we* starts with an uppercase *W.* Find we, and put your finger under it. Get a good look, and say *we.*"
- "Now turn to page 9. Every time you turn a page, you will see what the family does to get ready for Aunt Bee." Repeat for pages 14 and 15. Turn back to the beginning to find out what happens."

PROMPTING GUIDE 1
Refer to *Prompting Guide 1* as needed.

Reading the Text

- As the children read, prompt for their search and use of meaning and language structure, e.g., "Try that again, and think what would make sense" or "Try that again, and think what would sound right."

Discussing and Revisiting the Text

Engage the children in talking about all the things the family did for Aunt Bee's visit. Some key understandings children may express are:

- Aunt Bee is coming to visit, so the mom and children are getting ready for her arrival. [Extend by asking for examples of what they do to prepare for Aunt Bee's arrival. Have children find the pages that support their ideas.]
- This story reminds me of __________.
- The children could have done other things to get ready for Aunt Bee. [Extend by asking for examples, such as make a nice dinner, dress up, etc.]
- Next in the story, the children and their aunt will __________. [Invite children to predict what might happen next in the story.]

PROMPTING GUIDE 1
Refer to *Prompting Guide 1* as needed.

Teaching Points

- Based on your observations, use *Prompting Guide 1* to select a teaching point that will be most helpful to the readers.
- Revisit the text if needed to reinforce how to check the picture with the first letter of the word. Use the prompts for fluency, if needed.

▸ Letter/Word Work

- Make the word *he* on the board. Ask the children to read it.
- Then make the word *me* under it. Suggested language: "If you know a word like *he*, it can help you to read a word like *me*. Listen: *he, me.* What do you notice?"
- Make *he* with magnetic letters. "I can make *he*. Then, if I want to make *me*, I take away the *h* and put an *m* at the beginning. This says *me*."
- Change the first letter to *w* and ask the children what it says.
- Give the children magnetic letters (*h, e, m, w*), and have them make each word by changing the letter.

Word Bags

- Children lay out their word cards face down. They turn the words over one at a time, read them, and put them back in the word bags.

Classroom Connection

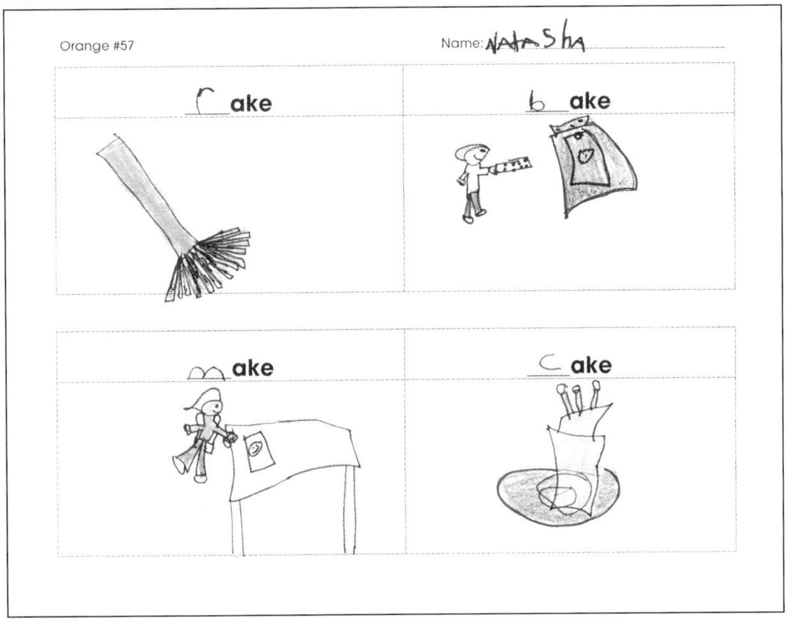

- Give children the fold sheet with the *-ake* phonogram written on it four times: *-ake, -ake, -ake, -ake* (see *Lesson Resources CD*).
- Children write a different letter in front of each phonogram to make real words.
- Have them draw a picture for each word.
- Then have them choose one of the words to use to write and illustrate a sentence.
- Give children the Take-Home Book *Making a Pizza* to reread.

Home/School Connection

- Children take home their fold sheets to read to family members.
- Give them the Take-Home Book *Making a Pizza* to reread.
- Give them *My ABC Book* to read.

Assessing Reading and Writing Behaviors

Observe to find evidence that children can:

- use self-monitoring behaviors consistently.
- recognize and use phonogram patterns (VCe) in reading and writing.
- make/read new words by substituting a new first consonant letter.
- use meaning, visual information, and language structure to solve words.
- be aware of dialogue (noticing the word *said* and quotation marks) and read it with phrasing.
- understand a typical home and family event, such as a visit by a relative.

Supporting English Language Learners

To support English language learners, you can:

- **teach** for understanding of "Do you know a word like that? or "Do you see a part that you know?" by showing/telling the word part that children know.
- **use** *he, me,* and *we* each in a sentence to clarify the meaning of each word. Use examples from the group in your sentences; e.g., *We are reading together today. He* (pointing towards one of the children) *came to see me.*
- **monitor** for understanding of an *aunt.*
- **explain** that *Aunt Bee is coming* means she will be visiting. She is on her way.
- **check** each picture and name the action of the family.
- **give** explicit attention to the picture on the last page either in the introduction or the discussion so that children understand what is funny (duplicated efforts).
- **use** the pictures to support children in talking about what the family does to get ready for Aunt Bee, what might happen next, and how the family feels about Aunt Bee.
- **demonstrate** the difference in how the reading sounds between *Aunt Bee is coming* and *Aunt Bee is coming!*

Professional Development Links

When Readers Struggle: Teaching that Works
Chapter 12: Using Words: How to Build a Repertoire. Use this chapter to understand the importance of rapid word solving.

Teaching for Comprehending and Fluency: Thinking, Talking, and Writing About Reading, K–8
Chapter 4 (Figure 4-3 p. 47). Use this chapter to review strategic actions for monitoring and correcting reading and Chapter 30 (pp. 515–518) to review teaching for fluent, phrased reading.

SYSTEM **Orange**

NEW BOOK ***Birds***

GENRE **Nonfiction**

YOU WILL NEED

- Take-Home Book, *A Visit from Aunt Bee*
- *My Writing Book*
- phonogram chart from Lesson 57
- magnetic letters
- word bags

From the CD:

- Lotto cards
- word cards for Lotto
- Take, Make, Write sheet
- word card sets
- word card: *by*
- Recording Form for *A Visit from Aunt Bee*
- fold sheet
- Parent Letter

NEW BOOK
Birds, Level A

REREADING
Making a Pizza, Level A

A Visit from Aunt Bee, Level C

Goals

- Self-monitor and self-correct consistently.
- Check one source of information with another.
- Recognize and use phonogram patterns with silent *e*.
- Use phonogram patterns to write words.
- Sort words by phonogram patterns.
- Notice and use the *-ing* ending on words.
- Write easy high-frequency words quickly.
- Say words slowly to listen for and identify easy-to-hear sounds and letters.
- Write letters to represent many sounds
- Reread sentences to know what to write next.
- Understand actions in a simple category (what birds can do).
- Remember some information about birds after reading the book.

Analysis of New Book Characteristics

Birds, Level A

GENRE/FORM
- Nonfiction

TEXT STRUCTURE
- Different bird taking a different action on each page spread
- Surprise at the end
- No sequence

CONTENT
- Familiar concept "bird," even if names are not known
- Familiar actions

THEMES AND IDEAS
- Nature
- Wildlife–birds and what they do

LANGUAGE AND LITERARY FEATURES
- NA

SENTENCE COMPLEXITY
- One four-word simple sentence on every page
- Present tense
- Repeating pattern on each page with no variation
- Speech bubble on last page

VOCABULARY
- Action words: *flying, swimming, drinking, eating, walking, running, sleeping, talking*
- Content word: *bird*

WORDS
- High-frequency words: *this, is*
- One- and two-syllable words
- See the Word Analysis Charts in the *Program Guide* for specific words in each category.

ILLUSTRATIONS
- Photographs on every right page
- Close match between pictures and text

BOOK AND PRINT FEATURES
- Large font
- Ample space between words
- One line on each page of print
- Print on the left on a blank page; illustrations on the right page, except for last page
- Periods and exclamation point

▸ Rereading Books and Assessment

- *Making a Pizza*, Level A
- *A Visit from Aunt Bee*, Level C

PROMPTING GUIDE 1
Refer to *Prompting Guide 1* as needed.

- Listen to one child read *A Visit from Aunt Bee* as you code the reading behavior on the Recording Form, have a brief comprehension conversation, and make a teaching point that you think will be most helpful to the reader. Score and analyze the Reading Record following the lesson.
- Have the other children reread *A Visit from Aunt Bee* and then *Making a Pizza*.

Take a Reading Record

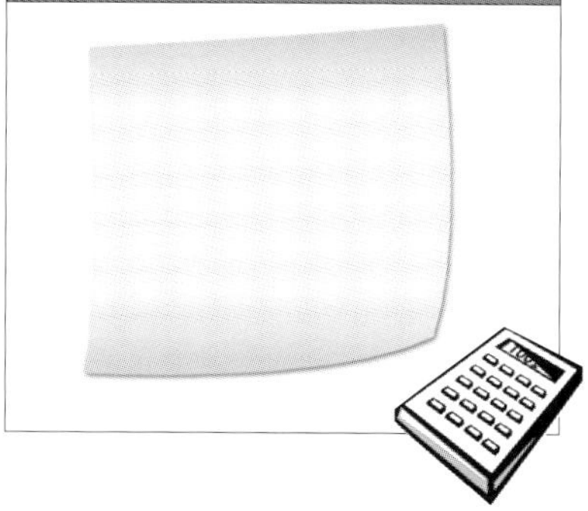

▸ Phonics/Word Work

-ake	-ike
make	like
take	bike
rake	hike

- **PRINCIPLE** Recognizing and using phonograms with a vowel-consonant-silent *e* (VCe) pattern: *-ade, -ace, -age, -ake, -ale, -ame, -ane, -ape, -ate, -ice, -ide, -ike, -ile, -ime, -ine, -ite, -ive, -obe, -oke, -ope*

"You can look at the pattern [part] you know to help you read a word."
"You can write words by using the patterns and the sounds."

- Have children read the phonogram chart from Lesson 57 with words that have the *-ake* pattern. Remind children that the silent *e* usually means that the vowel sound is like its name. You can leave room on the chart for more columns or add columns by stapling or taping them later.
- Suggested language: "You have learned many patterns or parts that are in words. The patterns help you read and write words. Another pattern that you see in words is *-ike*. Look at *like*." Write *like* on the chart under *-ike*, and ask children what they notice. "There is an *e* at the end of this pattern. It is a silent *e*. You cannot hear it. But it makes the *i* in *like* sound like the name of the letter." Repeat for *bike* and *hike*.

Take, Make, Write Sheet

- "Today you are going to make words with magnetic letters and then write them."
- Give each child a Take, Make, Write sheet. Also give children word cards with CVCe words with the *-ake* and *-ike* patterns and the magnetic letters.
- Demonstrate and then have the children choose, make, and write as many words as they can.

▸ Writing About Reading

Interactive Writing

- **MY WRITING BOOK**
- **PROMPTING GUIDE 1**

Refer to *Prompting Guide 1* as needed.

- Start by writing *Aunt Bee is coming!* on the chart. Then ask the children to tell some things that the family says they do to get ready for Aunt Bee's visit. Engage children in composing sentences such as:

    We clean the house.
    We make a cake.
    Aunt Bee is here!

- You will want to use the high-frequency words *we* and *a*, because all the children should know how to write these words.
- Encourage children to slowly say words such as *make, cake,* or *clean* to listen for and identify the easy-to-hear beginning sounds and letters. You will want to write the rest.
- With words such as *house* or *card*, get children to say the word and listen for the first sound and letter. Then finish writing the word. After you share the pen to let children write two or three sentences on the whiteboard, write *Aunt Bee is here!*
- Have the children reread the sentences with you.
- You may want to type the sentences, copy them onto strips for each child, and cut them up. Children can put them together and glue the sentence strips into *My Writing Book* to reread and illustrate.

▸ New Book

Birds,
Level A

Introducing the Text

- Introduce children to the book by showing the cover. Suggested language: "This book is about different kinds of birds and all the things they are doing. What can birds do?"
- "Turn to pages 2 and 3. What is this bird doing? Yes, this bird is flying."
- "Now turn to page 6 to see what a different bird is doing. What is this bird doing? Say *this*. What two letters come first in *this?* Yes, *th*. Find this and put your finger under it. Say *this*.
- "Now turn to page 10. What is this bird doing? Yes, this bird is walking."
- "Turn back to the beginning and read about what all the different birds are doing."

PROMPTING GUIDE 1
Refer to *Prompting Guide 1* as needed.

Reading the Text

- As the children read, you may need to reinforce self-correction behavior, e.g., "You noticed that wasn't right, and you fixed it."
- Also prompt for reading without pointing, e.g., "Read it with your eyes."

Discussing and Revisiting the Text

Invite children to talk about the different kinds of birds in the book. Some key understandings children may express are:

- There are a lot of different kinds of birds. [Extend by asking for examples of the birds. Invite children to talk about how the birds look alike and how they look different. Encourage children to use the photographs in the book as evidence.]
- The book is about all the things that birds can do. [Extend by asking children to use the photographs to find examples and show them.]

PROMPTING GUIDE 1
Refer to *Prompting Guide 1* as needed.

Teaching Points

- Based on your observations of reading behavior, use *Prompting Guide 1* to select a teaching point that will be most helpful to the readers.
- You may want to call children's attention to the words that end in *-ing*. Have children cover the *-ing* ending and say the first part of the word; then have them say the *-ing* ending; and finally the whole word.

Optional Letter/ Word Work

- Write the word *my* on the whiteboard. Ask children to read it.
- Then write the word *by* below *my*. Suggested language: "If you know a word like *my*, it can help you to read a word like *by*. Listen: *my, by.* What do you notice?"
- Give children the word card for *by* to add to their word bags. Ask them to find the word card for *my* and read both of the words.

Lotto

- Have children play a game of Lotto using known phonogram patterns (see *Lesson Resources CD*).
- Hold up word cards with familiar phonogram patterns. As you hold up a card, say the word on the card.
- Have the children listen for the pattern and also look at the word. If the word is on their cards, children read it and place a marker on that word.

Classroom Connection

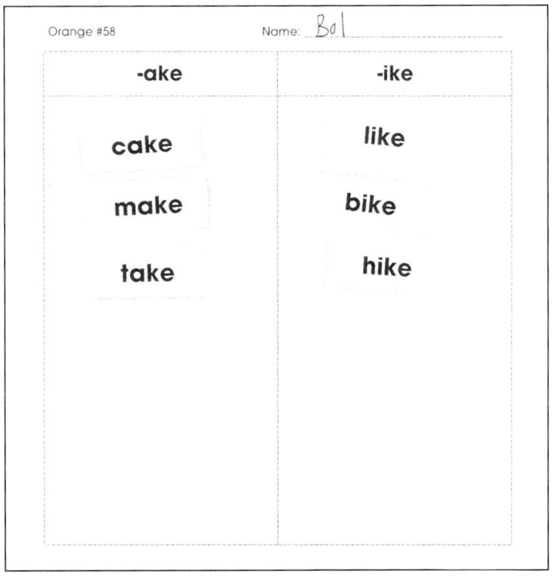

- Give the children the Take-Home Book *A Visit from Aunt Bee* to reread in the classroom.
- Give children the two-column fold sheet with the phonograms *-ake* and *-ike* at the top of each column and the word cards: *make, take, cake, bike, like, hike.*
- Have children cut the word card sheet apart and glue each word in the column under the appropriate pattern. Finally, have children read the words.

Home/School Connection

- Have the children take home their fold sheet of sorted words to read with their families.
- Give children the Take-Home Book *A Visit from Aunt Bee* to read to their families.

Assessing Reading and Writing Behaviors

Observe to find evidence that children can:

- consistently self-monitor and self-correct as they read.
- show evidence of phased, fluent reading.
- work flexibly with phonogram patterns.
- use word parts to solve new words.
- say words slowly to listen for and identify easy-to-hear sounds and letters.
- write letters to represent many sounds.
- reread sentences to know what to write next.
- remember and talk about some of the information about birds

Supporting English Language Learners

To support English language learners, you can:

- **demonstrate** what you mean by "Read it with your eyes."
- **use** clear language and clear demonstration when teaching children to use the word *my* to write *by*.
- **check** to be sure children know and understand all the words and pictures used in both Phonics and Letter/Word Work.
- **use** the language of the text in a conversational way. Have children repeat the language to be sure they understand the structure.
- **monitor** for understanding of all the actions of the birds.
- **ask** children to use the pictures to talk about what the birds can do.
- **discuss** the new information that children learned about birds.
- **support** children in constructing syntactically correct sentences about getting ready for Aunt Bee. Support their use of language in a conversational way.
- **ask** children to repeat with you several times the sentences about getting ready for Aunt Bee written on the whiteboard.
- **demonstrate** saying words slowly. Remind children that they must say the words slowly and listen for the sounds they hear.

Professional Development Links

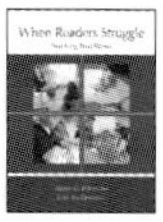

When Readers Struggle: Teaching that Works
Chapter 13: Extending Reading Power: Writing to Read. Use this chapter to understand how writing helps children learn about print.

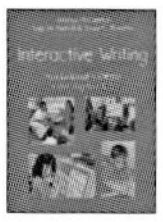

Interactive Writing: How Language and Literacy Come Together, K–2
Chapter 13 (pp. 188–194). Use this chapter to explore making decisions for effective teaching in interactive writing. Figure 13-1 provides examples of making teaching decisions in interactive writing.

SYSTEM **Orange**

NEW BOOK ***Flap, Flap, Fly***

GENRE **Nonfiction**

YOU WILL NEED

- Take-Home Book, *Birds*
- magnetic letter set

From the CD:

- *My ABC Book* ✓
- picture cards: *cake, ice cream*
- word card: *they*
- Letters Made in Similar Ways document
- fold sheet
- Parent Letter

NEW BOOK

Flap, Flap, Fly, Level C

REREADING

A Visit from Aunt Bee, Level C

Birds, Level A

Goals

- Recognize many high-frequency words.
- Use simple phonograms with silent *e* to read and write words.
- Understand that two different sounds can be associated with *a*.
- Connect words to solve them.
- Read and understand a text with three sentences on a page and three lines of print.
- Read with phrasing and fluency.
- Read with the eyes and without pointing.
- Solve words while reading by using more than one source of information.
- Use meaning, structure, and visual information to self-monitor and self-correct while reading.
- Follow a series of episodes and understand the conclusion of a text.

Analysis of New Book Characteristics

Flap, Flap, Fly, Level A

GENRE/FORM
- Narrative nonfiction

TEXT STRUCTURE
- Series of paired episodes in which little ducks repeat the mother duck's actions
- Builds to the end, when the little ducks learn to fly

CONTENT
- Familiar animals
- Concept of a mother duck teaching babies

THEMES AND IDEAS
- Adult and baby animals
- Caring for and teaching baby animals
- Baby animals learning and growing

LANGUAGE AND LITERARY FEATURES
- Rhythmic language
- Illustrations that communicate caring between the mother duck and babies and playfulness on the part of the young
- Suspense at the end

SENTENCE COMPLEXITY
- One or two sentences on each page
- Sentences two- to three-words long
- Repeating pattern of meaning, alternating between the mother and babies' activities
- Present tense
- Prepositional phrases

VOCABULARY
- Names of activities: *walk, eat, swim, fly*
- Pronouns: *she, they*
- Adjective: *little*
- Prepositions: *in, by*

WORDS
- High-frequency words: *can, she, and, by, the, little, they, in*
- One-syllable words with one two-syllable word
- See the Word Analysis Charts in the *Program Guide* for specific words in each category.

ILLUSTRATIONS
- Soft pastel paintings across both page spreads
- Close match between pictures and text

BOOK AND PRINT FEATURES
- Large font
- Ample space between words
- Three lines on each page of print except the last two
- Print on the left on a blank page highlighted in white
- Periods, exclamation point, ellipses

▸ Rereading Books

- *A Visit from Aunt Bee*, Level C
- *Birds*, Level A

PROMPTING GUIDE 1
Refer to *Prompting Guide 1* as needed.

- Invite children to reread *A Visit from Aunt Bee* and *Birds.*
- If needed, prompt children to read without finger pointing; e.g.,"Read it with your eyes."

▸ Phonics/Word Work

- **PRINCIPLE** Recognizing and using phonograms with a vowel-consonant-silent *e* (VCe) pattern: *-ade, -ace, -age, -ake, -ale, -ame, -ane, -ape, -ate, -ice, -ide, -ike, -ile, -ime, -ine, -ite, -ive, -obe, -oke, -ope*

"You can look at the pattern [part] you know to help you read a word."
"You can write words by using the patterns and the sounds."
"A vowel can have a sound like its name."

- Have children read the phonogram chart from Lesson 58 with words that have the *-ake* and *-ike* patterns. Remind children that the silent *e* means that the vowel sounds like its name.
- Have children turn to and read the *Aa* page of *My ABC Book.*
- Suggested language: "You have learned two sounds for *a.* It can sound like *a* as in *cat.* It can also sound like *a* as in *cake.*" Give children the picture card for *cake.* Have them glue it on the "*ape* page" of *My ABC Book,* write *cake* under it, and highlight the *a* in *ape* and *cake.*
- Repeat the process for *i,* using the picture card for *ice cream* and the *Ii* pages of *My ABC Book.*

▸ New Book

Flap, Flap, Fly,
Level C

Introducing the Text

- Introduce the book by asking children to look at the cover. Suggested language: "This book is called *Flap, Flap, Fly*. This is Mother Duck and these are her little ducks, and they live by a pond. Can you see the pond? In the story you will find out all the things Mother Duck can do and that her little ducks can do the same things."
- "Turn to pages 2 and 3. What can Mother Duck do? Yes, she can walk. She walks by the pond. Say the word *she*. She starts with *sh-*. The word *she* starts the sentence so it starts with an uppercase *S*. Find she. Put your finger under *she* and say it. Oh, you found *she* again. It is on the page two times."
- "Turn to pages 4 and 5. Mother Duck can walk by the pond, so what can her little ducks do? Yes, they can walk by the pond, too. Say the word *by*. What letter would come first in *by?* Yes, now put your finger under *by* and say it." Repeat for pages 14 and 15.
- "Well, turn the page and see what can the little ducks do. Yes, they can flap, flap, flap, fly! Can you say that?"
- "Turn back to the beginning and read about Mother Duck and her little ducks and all the things they can do by the pond."

PROMPTING GUIDE 1
Refer to *Prompting Guide 1* as needed.

Reading the Text

- As the children read, prompt for self-monitoring as needed, e.g., "Were you right?" or "Did that sound right?"
- Also, demonstrate or support fluent, phrased reading.

Discussing and Revisiting the Text

Invite children to talk about how the little ducks learned to fly. Some key understandings children may express are:

- Whenever Mother Duck does something, the little ducks do the same thing. [Extend by asking children to show examples.]
- The baby ducks learn to do things by copying the mother duck.
- This reminds me of how I learned to__________.
- It seems like flying might be new for the little ducks. [Extend by asking why they think this, e.g., they flap, flap, flap before they fly.]
- At first, the little ducks were probably scared to fly, and then, they were proud that they learned.

PROMPTING GUIDE 1
Refer to *Prompting Guide 1* as needed.

Teaching Points

- Based on your observations, use *Prompting Guide 1* to select a teaching point that will be most helpful to readers.
- You may want to help children notice when they are not right and initiate working it out.

▸ Letter/Word Work

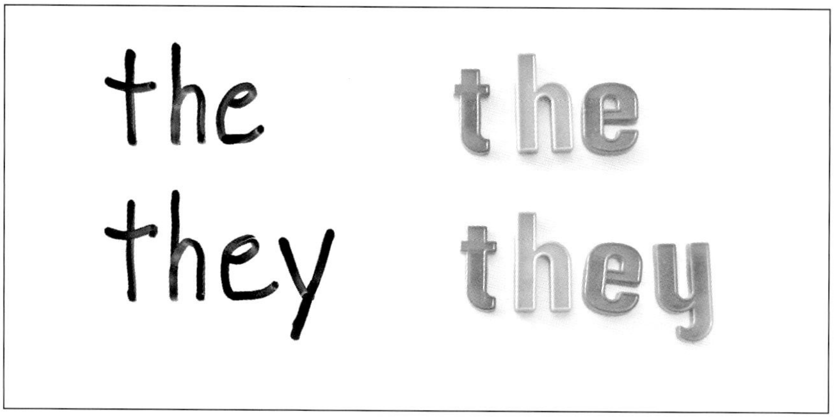

- Write the word *the* on the whiteboard. Ask children to read it.
- Suggested language: "If you know a word like *the*, it can help you to read a word like *they*." Say *the* and *they*. "What do you notice?"
- Children may respond that the two words sound alike at the beginning. Write *they* on the whiteboard below *the*. Show children that the two words are almost the same except that *they* has a *y* on the end. Also tell children that *they* and *the* sound different at the end.
- Give children magnetic letters *t, h, e, y* and have them make *the* and *they* several times.
- Also give children the word card for *they* to add to their word bags.

Letter Sort

- If time allows, have the children say and sort magnetic letters two or three different ways (see Instructional Routines, Ways to Sort and Match Letters, in the *Program Guide*).

Classroom Connection

- Give the children the two-column fold sheet with a picture of an apple at the top of one half and an ape at the top of the other half (see *Lesson Resources CD*) and the word cards: *cake, cat, sat, make, that, rake, came, hat.*
- Have children cut apart the word cards and place each card under the picture that represents the appropriate vowel sound.
- Children may glue the word cards under the appropriate vowel sound or may take the cards home to glue them.
- Have children reread the Take-Home Book *Birds*.

Home/School Connection

- Give children their fold sheet with sorted word cards to take home and read to their families. If they have not glued their word cards to the fold sheet in the classroom, children can do this at home.
- Have children take home the Take-Home Book *Birds* to share with family members.
- Have children do a letter sort with magnetic letters.

Assessing Reading and Writing Behaviors

Observe to find evidence that children can:

- use their knowledge of phonograms to solve words.
- understand that one vowel may be connected to two different sounds.
- sustain reading over three sentences on a page.
- notice and use periods.
- read without finger pointing and read with phrasing.
- use meaning, structure, and visual information to self-monitor and self-correct while reading.
- follow a series of episodes and (with the help of pictures) remember and discuss them.
- infer what has happened to the ducklings.

Supporting English Language Learners

To support English language learners, you can:

- **monitor** for understanding of "Read it with your eyes" and "Were you right?"
- **check** to be sure children know what you mean by "A vowel can have a sound like its name."
- **use** *they* in a sentence to support the meaning.
- **explain** the concept of baby ducks learning new things, if necessary.
- **discuss** the meaning of *flap*, *she*, and *walks by the pond*.
- **make** the organization of the text explicit (first the mother duck is doing something and then the little ducks are doing it).
- **use** the language of the text in a conversational way, having children repeat some of the language of the book several times.
- **make** links between the ducks' actions and the pictures.
- **use** the pictures to support children in discussing all the things the baby ducks learned.
- **clarify** the meaning of the ending and ask children how the ducks must feel now that they can fly.
- **think aloud** about a time you learned something new and ask children to share a similar learning experience of their own.

Professional Development Links

When Readers Struggle: Teaching that Works
Chapter 13: Extending Reading Power: Writing to Read. Use this chapter to understand how writing helps children learn about print.

Teaching for Comprehending and Fluency: Thinking, Talking, and Writing About Reading, K–8
Chapter 30 (pp. 520–521). Use this chapter to explore teaching students to read without pointing to words with a finger.

SYSTEM **Orange**

NEW BOOK ***At the Pond***

GENRE **Nonfiction**

YOU WILL NEED

- Take-Home Book, *Flap, Flap, Fly*
- *My Writing Book*
- magnetic letter set
- phonogram chart from Lesson 58
- word bags

From the CD:

- Lotto Game Board
- word card: *walk*
- Recording Form for *Flap, Flap, Fly*
- fold sheet
- Parent Letter

NEW BOOK
At the Pond, Level A

REREADING
Birds, Level A

Flap, Flap, Fly, Level C

Goals

- Use all sources of information while reading.
- Self-monitor and self-correct consistently.
- Use phonogram patterns to read words.
- Say words slowly to hear sounds and write letters in words.
- Make connections between words.
- Say words slowly, listen for the sounds, and identify the letters that represent them.
- Write several high-frequency words.
- Start a sentence with an uppercase letter and write end punctuation.
- Understand the category of the kinds of things that can be seen at a pond.
- Remember and discuss the collection of things that can be seen at a pond.

Analysis of New Book Characteristics

At the Pond, Level A

GENRE/FORM
- Narrative nonfiction

TEXT STRUCTURE
- Father and daughter seeing different things at a pond
- Different animal on each page
- No sequence

CONTENT
- Familiar animals for most children
- Concept of a pond

THEMES AND IDEAS
- Nature
- Wildlife in and around a pond
- Family activities

LANGUAGE AND LITERARY FEATURES
- NA

SENTENCE COMPLEXITY
- One five-word simple sentence on every page
- Present tense
- Repeating pattern on each page with no variation except switch from *a* to *the*

VOCABULARY
- Names of animals: *frog, turtle, fish, fox, butterfly, snake, turtle*
- Content word: *pond*
- Pronoun: *we*

WORDS
- High-frequency words: *we, can, see, a, the*
- One- and two-syllable words and one three-syllable word
- See the Word Analysis Charts in the *Program Guide* for specific words in each category.

ILLUSTRATIONS
- Photographs on every right page
- Close match between pictures and text

BOOK AND PRINT FEATURES
- Large font
- Ample space between words
- One line on each page of print
- Print on the left on a blank page; illustrations on the right page, except for last page
- Periods and exclamation point

▸ Rereading Books and Assessment

- *Birds*, Level A
- *Flap, Flap, Fly*, Level C

PROMPTING GUIDE 1
Refer to *Prompting Guide 1* as needed.

- Listen to one child read *Flap, Flap, Fly* as you code the reading behavior on the Recording Form, have a brief comprehension conversation, and make a teaching point that you think will be most helpful to the reader. Score and analyze the Reading Record following the lesson.
- Have the other children reread *Birds* and then *Flap, Flap, Fly.*
- Prompt readers to notice and use punctuation; e.g., "Let your voice go down when you see a period. "Make your voice go up when you see a question mark. Make your voice excited when you see an exclamation point."

▸ Phonics/Word Work

-ake	-ike	-ice	-ate	
make	like	nice	late	
take	bike	mice	gate	
rake	hike	rice		

- **PRINCIPLE** Recognizing and using phonograms with a vowel-consonant-silent *e* (VCe) pattern: *-ade, -ace, -age, -ake, -ale, -ame, -ane, -ape, -ate, -ice, -ide, -ike, -ile, -ime, -ine, -ite, -ive, -obe, -oke, -ope, -ore*

"You can look at the pattern [part] you know to help you read a word."
"You can write words by using the patterns and the sounds."
"A vowel can have a sound like its name."

- Read the phonogram chart from Lesson 58 with words that have the *-ake* and *-ike* patterns. Remind the children of the silent *e* that means the vowel sounds like its name.
- Write *-ice* at the top of the third column (or a new chart).Write *nice, mice,* and *rice* and read the words to the children. Ask them what they notice. Point out the long *i* sound and the silent *e.* Ask them to think of other words, e.g., *rice.* Repeat the process with *-ate.* Repeat to add a fourth column with the phonogram *-ate.*

Lotto

- Play Lotto with word cards with the *-ake, -ike,* -*i*ce, and *-ate* phonogram patterns for children to read.

▸ Writing About Reading

Independent Writing

- **MY WRITING BOOK**
- **PROMPTING GUIDE 1**

Refer to *Prompting Guide 1* as needed.

- If time allows, you may want to begin by having each child read recent pages from *My Writing Book*. Occasionally ask the child to locate a word in a sentence read.
- Invite the children to write one or two sentences about what the little ducks can do by the pond, e.g.,

  The ducks can eat by the pond.
  They can walk.
  They can fly.

- For a word like *duck*, use sound boxes on the opposite page and have the children say it slowly, listen to the three sounds, and identify the letters that represent the three sounds. Then add the *c* so they can notice how it looks.
- You will expect both accurate writing of high-frequency words like *can, by, the*, and *they*. You can also expect that children can write the letters for easy-to-hear sounds.
- If time allows, invite children to illustrate their sentences.

▸ New Book

***At the Pond*,**
Level A

Introducing the Text

- Introduce children to the book by showing the cover. Suggested language: "A little girl and her dad are at this pond. What are some of the things they might see at the pond?"
- "On each page of this book, the little girl and her dad will tell one thing that they can see at the pond."
- "Turn to pages 2 and 3. What do the girl and her dad say they can see? Yes, so what will they say? Yes, they say, 'We can see a frog.' Find can and put your finger under it."
- "Now turn to page 8 to see what else the girl and her dad can see."
- "Turn more pages to see what other things they can see."
- "Now turn back to the beginning and read *At the Pond.*

PROMPTING GUIDE 1
Refer to *Prompting Guide 1* as needed.

Reading the Text

- As the children read, you may need to reinforce checking behaviors, e.g., "You knew something wasn't right."

Discussing and Revisiting the Text

Invite children to talk about the things the girl and her dad saw at the pond. Some key understandings children may express are:

- The girl and her father saw lots of things at the pond. [Extend by asking children to use the pictures on the pages to show examples.]
- My favorite part was ______. [Encourage children to talk about what they liked in the story.]
- The little girl and her dad like to go to the pond. [Extend by asking children why they think that.]

PROMPTING GUIDE 1
Refer to *Prompting Guide 1* as needed.

Teaching Points

- Based on your observations, use *Prompting Guide 1* to select a teaching point that will be most helpful to the readers.
- You may want children to locate one or two high-frequency words, e.g., *can, see,* and *we.*

▸ Optional Letter/ Word Work

- Help the children think about words they know and how those words help them to learn other words. Use magnetic letters to make the word *my* and change it to *by*. Do the same with *he* and *here*, *we* and *me*, *no* and *go*, *got* and *lot*, *hot* and *not*. Ask them how the words are the same and different.

Word Bags

- Show children the word card *walk* and read it. Then write the word letter-by-letter on the whiteboard, saying it slowly. Suggested language: "This is the word *walk* that you read yesterday. What sound can you hear at the beginning?" Children respond with *w*.The last part says */ok/* and it is spelled like this.
- Write *talk* under *walk*, and invite children to look at and read both words. Give them the word card *walk* to add to their word bags.

Classroom Connection

- Give the children the Take-Home Book *Flap, Flap, Fly* to read in the classroom.
- Give children the fold sheet that says, "The little ducks can ____." (see *Lesson Resources CD*)
- Have children read the sentence, fill in the ending, and illustrate the sentence.
- Send home two Lotto cards and the word cards for word patterns they know, *-ake, -ike, -ate, -ice* so they can play Lotto at home.

Home/School Connection

- Have children take home the Take-Home Book *Flap, Flap, Fly* and their fold sheet.
- Give children two Lotto cards and the word cards for word patterns that they know to play the game at home.

Assessing Reading and Writing Behaviors

Observe to find evidence that children can:

- demonstrate self-monitoring and self-correcting behavior.
- use language structure, visual information, and meaning to self-monitor and self-correct reading.
- make and talk about the connections in words.
- use phonogram patterns to read words.
- say words slowly, listen for the sounds, and identify the letters that represent them.
- write several high-frequency words.
- start a sentence with an uppercase letter and write end punctuation.
- remember and discuss the things that can be seen at a pond.

Supporting English Language Learners

To support English language learners, you can:

- **use** *walk* and *talk* in sentences to support meaning.
- **demonstrate** what you mean by finding two words that go together in some way.
- **introduce** the concept of a pond, if necessary.
- **use** the language of the text in a conversational way. Have children repeat the language to be sure they understand the structure.
- **have** children say and point to the pictures to learn the labels for everything they see at the pond.
- **ask** children to use the pictures, if necessary, to talk about what they see at the pond.
- **support** children in constructing syntactically correct sentences about what the ducks can do at the pond. Support their use of language in a conversational way.
- **ask** children to repeat the sentence with you several times.
- **demonstrate** saying words slowly. Remind children that they themselves must say the words slowly and listen for the sounds they hear.
- **tell** children that there are some words that one just needs to know from how they look. For example, *walk* and *talk*.

Professional Development Links

When Readers Struggle: Teaching that Works
Chapter 13: Extending Reading Power: Writing to Read. Use this chapter to understand how writing helps children learn about print.

Interactive Writing: How Language and Literacy Come Together
Chapter 6: Learning About the Writing Process: Composing a Text. Use this chapter to understand how to help children compose sentences to express their ideas.

YOU WILL NEED

- Take Home Book, *At the Pond*
- magnetic letter set
- *My Writing Book*
- phonogram chart from Lesson 60
- word bags

From the CD:

- word cards: *on, and*
- fold sheet
- Parent Letter

SYSTEM **Orange**

NEW BOOK ***Going on a Train Ride***

GENRE **Fiction**

NEW BOOK
Going on a Train Ride, Level C

REREADING
At the Pond, Level A

Flap, Flap, Fly, Level C

Goals

- Recognize and use phonogram patterns with silent *e*.
- Make and talk about connections between words.
- Reflect the meaning of the punctuation through raising and lowering the voice.
- Use known words, first letters, and some word parts to self-monitor and self-correct while reading.
- Use meaning, language structure, and visual information to solve problems while reading.
- Understand the concept of pretending.
- Understand and talk about the idea that a whole family would pretend in order to amuse a young child.

Analysis of New Book Characteristics

Going on a Train Ride, Level A

GENRE/FORM
- Fiction

TEXT STRUCTURE
- Narrative
- Series of scenes as a boy tells about each family member who will go on a train ride
- Scenes build to the end, with the surprise being an imaginary train ride

CONTENT
- Familiar home activities
- Concept of a train ride as well as playing train

THEMES AND IDEAS
- Family playing together
- Humoring an imaginative child

LANGUAGE AND LITERARY FEATURES
- Building of plot to surprise conclusion
- Child narrator

SENTENCE COMPLEXITY
- Two- to three-sentences on each page
- Sentences four- to eight-words long
- Repeating pattern of meaning on several pages with change in the order of sentences
- Present tense
- Prepositional phrases
- Use of *too*, set off by commas, meaning *also*

VOCABULARY
- Names of family members: *dad, sister, brother, Gram, Gramps, Bear*
- Pronouns: *I, he, she, us*
- Onomatopoetic word: *choo! choo!*

WORDS
- High-frequency words: *I, like, am, going, on, a, my, likes, he, can, go, the, too, little, come, big, she, with, us, and*
- One- and two-syllable words
- See the Word Analysis Charts in the *Program Guide* for specific words in each category.

ILLUSTRATIONS
- Drawings on every right page
- Close match between pictures and text, although family members accumulate (with finally all present), so attention to print is required

BOOK AND PRINT FEATURES
- Large font
- Ample space between words
- Three lines on each page of print
- Print on the left on a blank page; illustrations on the right page, except for last page
- Periods and exclamation point

▸ Rereading Books

- *At the Pond*, Level A
- *Flap, Flap, Fly*, Level C

PROMPTING GUIDE 1
Refer to *Prompting Guide 1* as needed.

- Invite children to reread *At the Pond* and *Flap, Flap, Fly.*
- Prompt for phrasing if needed, e.g., "Put your words together to sound like talking."

▸ Phonics/Word Work

-ake	-ike	-ice	-ate	-ide
make	like	nice	late	hide
take	bike	mice	gate	side
rake	hike	rice		tide
				wide

- **PRINCIPLE** Recognizing and using phonograms with a vowel-consonant-silent *e* (VCe) pattern: *-ade, -ace, -age, -ake, -ale, -ame, -ane, -ape, -ate, -ice, ide, -ike, ile, -ime, -ine, -ite, -ive, -obe, -oke, -ope, -ore*

"You can look at the pattern [part] you know to help you read a word."
"You can write words by using the patterns and the sounds."
"A vowel can have a sound like its name."

- Read the chart from Lesson 60 containing words that have the *-ake, -ike, -ice,* and *-ate* patterns. Remind children of the silent *e* that means the vowel sounds like its name.
- Suggested language: "There is another pattern that has *i* and a silent *e* like the pattern in *like*. This pattern is *-ide*. Watch while I write the word *ride*." Write *-ide* at the top of the fifth column. This column will have *-ide* words.
- Slowly write *ride* on the whiteboard, and then read the word while running a finger under it left to right. Ask children what they notice about the word. Then repeat the process for the words *hide, side, tide,* and *wide* on the chart. (Choose words that children understand.)

My Writing Book

- Have children write a couple of *-ide* words in *My Writing Book* and then highlight the *i*.

▸ New Book

***Going on a Train Ride*,**
Level C

Introducing the Text

- Introduce the book by talking to children about trains and showing them the cover of the book. Suggested language: "Have you ever been on a train ride? Well, this little boy is pretending he is going on a train ride."
- Point to the boy on the cover. Tell children that the conductor is the person who drives the train and he wears a hat like the boy.
- "Turn to pages 2 and 3. What do you notice? Yes, the boy is thinking about trains because he likes them. And he says, 'I am going on a train ride.'"
- "Turn the page. The boy is saying to himself, 'My dad can go on the train ride, too.' Say the word *can*. What letter would you see first in *can*? Run your finger under the word.
- "Now turn to pages 6 and 7. What other person does the boy think can come on the train ride? Yes, his sister can come, too. The little boy sees lots of people in his house who can go on the train ride."
- "Now turn to pages 14 and 15. Who else likes trains? Yes, and Bear likes trains, too. Say *and*. What letter would come first in *and*? It would be an uppercase *A* because it starts the sentence. Find and with an uppercase *A* and run your finger under it."
- "Turn back to the beginning and read about all the people in the boy's family who are going on a train ride."

PROMPTING GUIDE 1
Refer to *Prompting Guide 1* as needed.

Reading the Text

- As the children read, demonstrate or prompt for problem solving, e.g., "Try that again and think what would sound right" or "That makes sense, but does it look right?"
- Prompt for phrasing or reading the punctuation, if needed.

Discussing and Revisiting the Text

Invite children to talk about the boy and his train. Some key understandings children may express are:

- The boy is pretending that he is going on a train ride with his whole family. [Extend by asking children to tell what clues in the story made them think this.]
- The family lines up chairs to make a pretend train. [Extend by asking children how they think this line is like a train.]
- The boy is happy at the end of the story because his dream of riding on a train came true. [Extend by asking why they think this.]

PROMPTING GUIDE 1
Refer to *Prompting Guide 1* as needed.

Teaching Points

- Based on your observations, use *Prompting Guide 1* to select a teaching point that will be most helpful to the readers.

▸ Letter/Word Work

- Give the children word cards with two new high-frequency words, *on* and *and*. Also give them the magnetic letters: *o, n, a, d*. Have children look closely at each new high-frequency word, make it two or three times with magnetic letters, and then write it in *My Writing Book*. Have them add the words to their word bags.
- Have the children read their word cards from their word bags.

Magnetic Letters

- Use magnetic letters to show how to use a known word to help with other words, e.g., *an–and, but–buy, his–has, get–got, come–came,* and *look–book*.

Classroom Connection

Orange #61 Name: Tyler

rake	hike	tide
make cake flake take	 bike like Mike	ride hide Slide

- Give children the three-column fold sheet with the words *rake, hike,* and *tide* at the top of each column.
- Have children take the sheet back to their classrooms and write two or three words with the same phonogram pattern in each column.
- Give children the Take-Home Book *At the Pond* to reread.

Home/School Connection

- Give children their three-column fold sheets to take home to read with their families.
- Challenge children to add more words to each column at home.
- Give children the Take-Home Book *At the Pond* to read to their families.

Assessing Reading and Writing Behaviors

Observe to find evidence that children can:

- look at phonogram patterns, letters, and other parts of words to connect them.
- use meaning, language structure, and visual information to solve problems while reading.
- demonstrate evidence of self-monitoring and self-correcting.
- understand the central idea of the story, which is that the family plays a pretend game to amuse a young child.

Supporting English Language Learners

To support English language learners, you can:

- **check** to be sure children understand all the words being used in Phonics and Letter/Word Work.
- **help** children in understanding the concept of a family pretending together.
- **use** the language of the text in a conversational way having children repeat some of the language of the book several times.
- **self-monitor** to be sure children understand the phrase "come with us."
- **use** the pictures to support children in recognizing and naming the family members.
- **ask** children to repeat unfamiliar names like *Gram* and *Gramps*.
- **give** a clear demonstration of using punctuation while reading. For example, "When you see this little mark," (point out the comma) "take a short breath."
- **ask** children to use the pictures, if necessary, to discuss what the family does together.
- **think** aloud about what this story makes you think of and ask children to do the same.
- **encourage** children's language in a conversational way, rather than correcting. For example, if the child says, "He brang his bear," respond with, "Yes, he brought his bear on the train."

Professional Development Links

When Readers Struggle: Teaching that Works
Chapter 13: Extending Reading Power: Writing to Read. Use this chapter to understand how writing can help children extend thinking and understanding.

Guided Reading: Good First Teaching for All Children
Chapter 12. Use this chapter to understand supporting early reading strategies.

Teaching for Comprehending and Fluency: Thinking, Talking, and Writing About Reading, K–8
Chapter 16 (pp. 245, 250). Use this chapter to explore how a teacher's facilitative talk can support children in discussing texts. Figure 16-9 has examples of comments, demonstrations, and questions that you might use with children.

SYSTEM **Orange**
NEW BOOK ***Spots***
GENRE **Nonfiction**

YOU WILL NEED

- Take-Home Book, *Going on a Train Ride*
- *My Writing Book*
- "Zoom, Zoom, Zoom," enlarged poem
- magnetic letters
- word bags

From the CD:

- *My Poetry Book* ✓
- word card: *going*
- Recording Form for *Going on a Train Ride*
- fold sheet
- Parent Letter

NEW BOOK
Spots, Level A

REREADING
At the Pond, Level A
Going on a Train Ride, Level C

Goals

- Self-monitor and self-correct consistently.
- Use a known word to solve an unknown word.
- Read high-frequency words quickly.
- Use known words, first letters, and word parts to self-monitor and self-correct while reading.
- Use meaning, language structure, and visual information to solve problems while reading.
- Write high-frequency words quickly.
- Say words slowly, identify the easy-to-hear sounds, and write the letters that represent them.
- Start a sentence with an uppercase letter and use end punctuation.
- Understand and discuss the concept that ties the book together (that many animals have spots, but a clown also has spots).
- Notice the surprise at the end of the book.

Analysis of New Book Characteristics

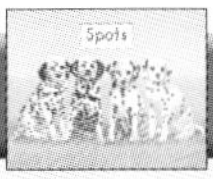

Spots, Level A

GENRE/FORM
- Nonfiction

TEXT STRUCTURE
- Different animal with spots on every page, with surprise switch on the last page
- No sequence other than ending

CONTENT
- Familiar animals for most children
- Concept of spots in nature

THEMES AND IDEAS
- Nature
- Animals
- Patterns

LANGUAGE AND LITERARY FEATURES
- NA

SENTENCE COMPLEXITY
- One four-word simple sentence on every page
- Present tense
- Repeating pattern on each page with no variation except switch from *a* to *the*

VOCABULARY
- Names of animals and person: *dog, cow, pig, ladybug, frog, fish, cat, clown*
- Content word: *spots*

WORDS
- High-frequency words: *the, has, a*
- One-syllable words and one two-syllable word
- See the Word Analysis Charts in the *Program Guide* for specific words in each category.

ILLUSTRATIONS
- Photographs on every right page
- Close match between pictures and text

BOOK AND PRINT FEATURES
- Large font
- Ample space between words
- One line on each page of print
- Print on the left on a blank page; illustrations on the right page, except for last page
- Periods and exclamation point

▸ Rereading Books and Assessment

- *At the Pond,* Level A
- *Going on a Train Ride,* Level C

PROMPTING GUIDE 1
Refer to *Prompting Guide 1* as needed.

- Listen to one child read *Going on a Train Ride* as you code the reading behavior on the Recording Form, have a brief comprehension conversation, and make a teaching point that you think will be most helpful to the reader. Score and analyze the Reading Record following the lesson.
- Have the other children reread *At the Pond* and then *Going on a Train Ride.*

▸ Phonics/Word Work

Zoom, Zoom, Zoom

Zoom, zoom, zoom
I'm going to the moon.
If you want to take a trip,
Climb aboard my rocket ship.
Zoom, zoom, zoom,
I'm going to the moon.

Leisha is playing.

Tara is going to school.

- **PRINCIPLE** Recognizing and using endings that add *-ing* to a verb to denote the present participle: *play/playing; send/sending*

"Some words have *-ing* at the end to show you are doing something now."

- Read the new poem, "Zoom, Zoom, Zoom," (poem 12) to the children, and then invite them to read it with you several times using shared reading. Talk about the meaning.
- Have children locate some known words in the poem, such as *the* and *to.*
- Write *I* on the whiteboard and then write *I'm,* telling children that *I'm* is a contraction—a short way to say "I am." Point out the apostrophe. Have children locate *I'm* and read the first line of the poem again. Then have children locate a few unknown words, first predicting the first letter: *want, moon, rocket, take.*

Word Bags

- Write *go* on the whiteboard, and tell children that some words have *-ing* at the end to show that something is being done right now. Write *going* and ask children what they notice about the two words. Have children say and read *going.*
- Give children the word card *going* and have them read the word. Cut off the *-ing,* so that children can put *go* and *-ing* together again.

▸ Writing About Reading

Interactive Writing

- **MY WRITING BOOK**
- **PROMPTING GUIDE 1**

Refer to *Prompting Guide 1* as needed.

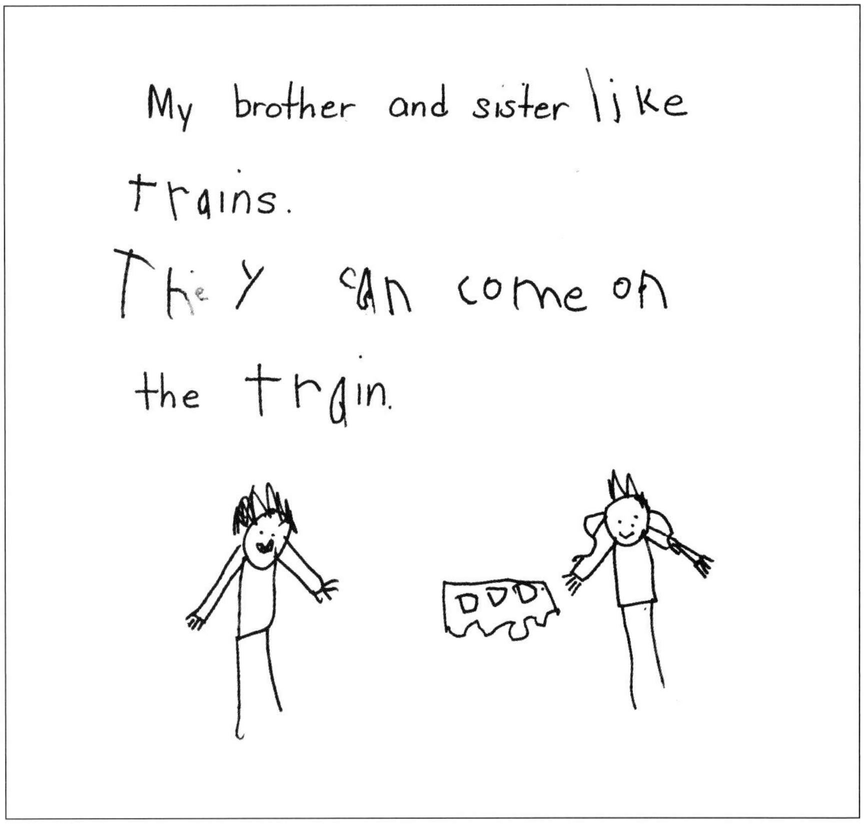

- Invite the children to talk about all the people who went on the train ride. Together, compose two or three sentences about the story, e.g.,

  My brother and sister like trains.
  They can come on the train.

- Use interactive writing to construct the sentences.
- Write those high-frequency words that children already know very well, such as *can, on, the, my.*
- Involve children in saying words slowly to contribute the first letter of harder words such as *brother, sister,* or *train.* As they slowly repeat these words, encourage children to listen closely to the sounds that they hear. Have them record the letters that stand for those easy-to-hear sounds.
- Use sound boxes for words with easy-to-hear sounds, as in *like.*
- If there is time, children can copy the sentences into *My Writing Book.*

▸ New Book

Spots,
Level A

Introducing the Text

- Introduce children to the book by showing the cover. Point out that the dogs on the cover have lots and lots of spots. Suggested language: "This book tells about lots of things that have spots. What are some things you know that have spots?"
- "Turn to pages 2 and 3. What has spots? Yes, the dog has spots. Say *has*. Find has on page 2. Run your finger under it and say *has*."
- "Turn the pages to see what other things have spots."
- Look at page 10. "What do you see that has spots? Yes, the frog has spots. Put your finger under *has* and say it."
- "Now turn back to the beginning of the story and read about all the things that have spots."

PROMPTING GUIDE 1
Refer to *Prompting Guide 1* as needed.

Reading the Text

- The children should be able to read the text with independence and accuracy. Reinforce self-correction behavior, if appropriate.

Discussing and Revisiting the Text

Invite children to talk about animals with spots. Some key understandings children may express are:

- Lots of animals have spots. [Extend by asking for children to name some of the animals with spots and show their pictures in the book.]
- A clown has spots. [Extend by asking why this page was surprising or funny. Ask how the clown is different from the other things in the book.]

PROMPTING GUIDE 1
Refer to *Prompting Guide 1* as needed.

Teaching Points

- Based on your observations, use *Prompting Guide 1* to select a teaching point that will be most helpful to the readers.
- If the children engaged in problem solving, reinforce what was effective.

▸ Optional Letter/Word Work

cat	cats
dog	dogs
cake	cakes
hat	hats
ball	balls

"Add *s* to some words to show you mean more than one."

- Suggested language: "Today we talked about words that have *-ing* added at the end. Sometimes you add *-s* to the end of a word to show that there is more than one."
- Write some known words such as *cat, dog, cake, hat, ball* on the whiteboard or chart paper. Beside each word, write its plural: *cats, dogs, cakes, hats, balls.* Have children read the singular and then the plural form.
- Ask children what they notice about each word pair. Children will respond that you are just adding an *s.*
- Have the children make two or three words with magnetic letters and add *s* to them.

Classroom Connection

- Give children the two-column fold sheet with the following words printed on the left side in four squares: *ball, cat, dog, hat.*
- Have children take the fold sheet back to the classroom and draw a picture of the word in each of the squares. In the second column, children should write the word again and add -s to make the word plural.
- Have them illustrate the new plural words.
- Give children the Take-Home Book *Going on a Train Ride* to read.

Home/School Connection

- Give children their fold sheets to take home to read to family members.
- Give children the Take-Home Book *Going on a Train Ride.*

Assessing Reading and Writing Behaviors

Observe to find evidence that children can:

- use meaning, language structure, and visual information to solve problems while reading.
- demonstrate evidence of self-monitoring and self-correcting.
- reflect the meaning of the punctuation through varying the voice.
- actively search for information.
- quickly write high-frequency words.
- say words slowly, identify the easy-to-hear sounds, and write the letters that represent them.
- start a sentence with an uppercase letter and use end punctuation.
- understand the central idea of the book (that animals have spots).
- understand why the book was a surprise at the end.

Supporting English Language Learners

To support English language learners, you can:

- **read** the poem, "Zoom, Zoom, Zoom" several times until children feel comfortable joining in.
- **monitor** children's understanding of "Zoom, Zoom, Zoom" by asking them what is happening in the poem.
- **monitor** for understanding of "Some words have *-ing* at the end to show you are doing something now."
- **use** clear language (and even drawings if necessary) to explain the concept of plurals. (Some languages do not have plurals. They just use the same noun with a number word before or after it to show more than one.)
- **help** children in pronouncing the plural nouns. Listen for articulation of */s/*. Explain that when */s/* is not said at the end of a word, the meaning of the word changes.
- **use** the language of the text in a conversational way. Have children repeat the language to be sure they understand the structure. Name the animals in the book.
- **help** children in constructing syntactically correct sentences about the train ride. Support their use of language in a conversational way.
- **ask** children to repeat the sentence with you several times.
- **remind** children to say words slowly and listen for the sounds.

Professional Development Links

When Readers Struggle: Teaching that Works
Chapter 15: Processing Texts: Teaching for Independence. Use this chapter to understand the importance of background knowledge in comprehending a text.

Interactive Writing: How Language and Literacy Come Together, K–2
Chapter 8 (pp. 113–114). Use this chapter to learn more about how to show children how words work.

Word Matters: Teaching Phonics and Spelling in the Reading/Writing Classroom
Chapter 9 (pp. 88–90). Use this chapter to review how to support children in writing high-frequency words.

YOU WILL NEED

- Take-Home Book, *Spots*
- *My Writing Book*
- highlighter pen
- stick-on notes

From the CD:

- picture cards and matching word cards: *cat, hat, bus, man, fan*
- fold sheet
- Parent Letter

SYSTEM **Orange**

NEW BOOK ***Playing with Blocks***

GENRE **Fiction**

NEW BOOK

Playing with Blocks, Level C

REREADING

Going on a Train Ride, Level C

Spots, Level A

Goals

- Search for and use meaning and language to solve words.
- Use the first letter of words to solve them.
- Reread a sentence to search for and use language structure.
- Consistently self-monitor reading, correcting when needed.
- Read several high-frequency words quickly and easily.
- Read with phrasing and smoothness.
- Recognize and use the *-ay* part to solve words.
- Notice and use the last letter and sound in words.
- Understand the sequence of events in the story.
- Infer the relationship between Pam and Tim.

Analysis of New Book Characteristics

Playing with Blocks, Level C

GENRE/FORM

- Fiction

TEXT STRUCTURE

- Narrative
- Series of scenes showing two children playing with blocks, culminating in a big building toppling

CONTENT

- Familiar home activities
- Concept of building with blocks
- Concept of balance in building

THEMES AND IDEAS

- Children playing together
- Competition and cooperation
- Friends

LANGUAGE AND LITERARY FEATURES

- Building of plot to surprise conclusion
- Characters with names
- Dialogue

SENTENCE COMPLEXITY

- Two sentences on each page, except on the last two pages
- Sentences four- to ten-words long
- No repetition of sentence patterns
- Past tense
- Prepositional phrases
- Dialogue between two speakers
- Speech bubble on last page

VOCABULARY

- Names of things the children built: *house, wall, road, bridge, tunnel, building*
- Content words: *made, blocks*
- Pronouns: *we, it*

WORDS

- High-frequency words: *look, at, the, I, it, with, said, big, this, a, we, can, make, no*
- One-syllable words with some two-syllable words
- See the Word Analysis Charts in the *Program Guide* for specific words in each category.

ILLUSTRATIONS

- Drawings on every right page
- Close match between pictures and text, although interpretation required to identify the objects built with blocks

BOOK AND PRINT FEATURES

- Large font
- Ample space between words
- Four lines on each page of print, except on last two pages
- Print on the left on a blank page; illustrations on the right page, except for last page
- Periods, commas, exclamation point, quotation marks

▸ Rereading Books

- *Going on a Train Ride*, Level C
- *Spots*, Level A

PROMPTING GUIDE 1
Refer to *Prompting Guide 1* as needed.

- Invite children to reread *Going on a Train Ride* and *Spots*.
- If needed, prompt children to read without finger pointing; e.g., "Read it with your eyes."

▸ Phonics/Word Work

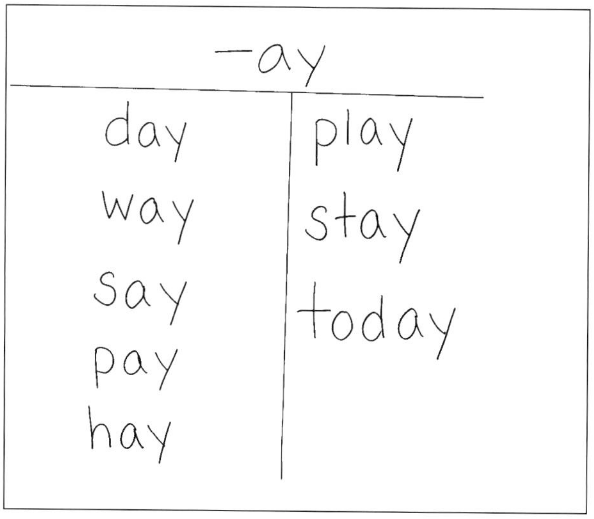

- **PRINCIPLE** Recognizing and using letter combinations that represent long vowel sounds: *ai, ay, ee, ea, oa, ow, ie, ei*

"You can look at the pattern [part] you know to help you read a word."
"You can write words by using the patterns and the sounds."
"A vowel can have a sound like its name."

- Suggested language: "You have been learning about patterns or parts that help you to read or write words. Here is another pattern." Write *-ay* at the top of the chart and then write *day* below it in the first column. "This word is *day*. Watch while I write another word."
- Write *way* slowly and then read it while running a finger under it left to right. Then do the same for *say*.
- Ask the children what they notice about the words. They should respond that all of the words have *-ay* at the end, and they may say that the *a* has a sound like its name. Generate and write several more words that children understand.
- Write *play* at the top of the second column. Run your finger under the two letters *pl*. "Now we have the two letters *p* and *l* at the beginning." Tell children that these two letters go together at the beginning of many words. Repeat the process with *stay*. If children seem to understand this, try writing *today* and discussing it. Highlight the *-ay* in *today* on the chart.
- Have children write a couple of *-ay* words in *My Writing Book*. Then have them use yellow highlighter to mark the *-ay*.

▸ New Book

Playing with Blocks, Level C

Introducing the Text

- Introduce the book by showing children the cover. Suggested language: "This little girl is called Pam. The little boy is Tim. What do you think that Pam and Tim are doing? Yes, Pam and Tim are playing with blocks and they are going to build a city with their blocks. So this book is called *Playing with Blocks*."
- "Turn to pages 2 and 3 to see what Pam made. Yes, Pam made a house, so she said to Tim, 'I made a house with blocks.'"
- "Now turn to pages 4 and 5 to see what Tim made. Yes, he made a wall with the blocks. Say the word *with*. What letter would you see first in *with?* Find with. Run your finger under it and say *with*."
- "Now turn to pages 8 and 9 to see what Pam made. Yes, she made a tunnel with the blocks."
- "And on pages 12 and 13, what did Tim make? Yes, he made a building for the city. What are you thinking about the building?"
- "Turn back to the beginning of the book and read to find what happened to the city that Pam and Tim built."

PROMPTING GUIDE 1
Refer to *Prompting Guide 1* as needed.

Reading the Text

- As the children read, prompt for self-correction, as needed, e.g., "Something wasn't quite right."
- Also prompt for solving new words, as needed, e.g., "Read that again and get your mouth ready for that word."
- Be sure to support fluent reading, if needed.

Discussing and Revisiting the Text

Talk about what happened with the blocks. Encourage children to share their building experiences. Some key understandings children may express are:

- A boy and girl are playing with blocks. [Extend by asking children to show pictures from the text as examples.]
- The big building of blocks falls down. [Extend by asking why they think the building fell down. Accept any plausible response such as the blocks got too high or Pam knocked them over.]
- Pam and Tim felt ________ when the building fell down. (Accept any reasonable response such as surprised, sad, etc.)
- Pam and Tim seem like friends. [Extend by asking why they think that, e.g., they like playing together.]

PROMPTING GUIDE 1
Refer to *Prompting Guide 1* as needed.

Teaching Points

- Based on your observations, use *Prompting Guide 1* to select a teaching point that will be most helpful to the readers.

▸ Letter/Word Work

- Suggested language: "The ending sound of a word can help you read or write the word. I'm going to show you some pictures. I want you to say the name of the picture and think about the ending sound. Then I will show you the first part of the word so you can predict the ending letter of the word." (Have assorted picture cards and matching word cards with a stick-on note over the last letter. The goal is for children to transfer what they have learned about the sounds of consonants to identifying ending sounds. Suggested pictures and words: *cat, hat, bus, man, fan.*)
- Say the word and then show children the word card with the last letter covered. Have children predict the last letter (see *Lesson Resources CD* for suggested cards).
- Have the children write two or three words in *My Writing Book.*

Classroom Connection

- Give children a three-column fold sheet with an ending sound *-t*, *-s*, *-n* printed at the top of each column. Also give children picture cards with the same ending sounds.
- Have children say the names of the picture cards. Then have them sort the cards according to the ending sounds they hear.
- Have children sort and glue the pictures according to the categories on the fold sheet or take them home to glue.
- Give children the Take-Home Book *Spots* to reread.

Home/School Connection

- Have children take home the Take-Home Book *Spots* to read to family members.
- Give children the fold sheet with picture cards to take home and share. Have them glue the pictures in the appropriate columns.

Assessing Reading and Writing Behaviors

Observe to find evidence that children can:

- search for and use meaning and language structure while reading.
- reread a sentence to search for and use the language structure to solve words.
- read several high-frequency words quickly.
- read with phrasing and smoothness.
- understand the sequence of the story.
- infer the relationship between the two characters in the text.

Supporting English Language Learners

To support English language learners, you can:

- **use** clear language (and even drawings if necessary) to explain the concept of plurals.
- **monitor** for understanding of "listening for the end sound."
- **use** the language of the text in a conversational way. Have children repeat the language to be sure they understand the structure. Support children in understanding the dialogue and the past tense.
- **be explicit** when telling children how the book is organized (Pam tells something she built. Tim tells what he built.)
- **have** children point to and name each item the children built.
- **use** the pictures to support children in discussing what Tim and Pam do together—they build a small city—and the surprise ending.
- **expand** children's language in a conversational way. For example, children might say *builded*. Respond with the correct verb, *Yes, they built....*

Professional Development Links

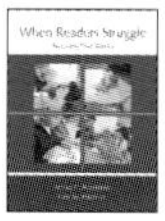

When Readers Struggle: Teaching that Works
Chapter 4: Reading Behavior: What Does It Tell Us? Use this chapter to learn about how to observe the precise reading behaviors of the child and think about what it tells you he controls.

Guided Reading: Good First Teaching for All Children
Chapter 14 (pp. 177–182). Use this chapter to explore how the processing system for reading changes over time. Figure 14-1 has detailed descriptions of how reading instruction changes over time.

SYSTEM **Orange**
NEW BOOK ***Drawing***
GENRE **Fiction**

YOU WILL NEED

- Take-Home Book, *Playing with Blocks*
- *My Writing Book*
- word bags

From the CD:

- letter cards: *p, g, l, d, t, m*
- picture cards: *rug, net, jeep, bird, bed, girl, cup, carrot, sheep, drum, dog, flag, goat, ball, jam*
- Recording Form for *Playing with Blocks*
- fold sheet
- Parent Letter

NEW BOOK
Drawing, Level A

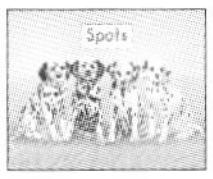

REREADING
Spot, Level A
Playing with Blocks, Level C

Goals

- Self-correct and self-monitor consistently.
- Use what is known about a word to solve an unknown word.
- Read high-frequency words quickly.
- Use known words, first letters, and word parts to self-monitor and self-correct while reading.
- Use meaning, language structure, and visual information to solve problems while reading.
- Say words slowly, identify the easy-to-hear sounds, and write the letters that represent them.
- Start sentences with an uppercase letter and use end punctuation.
- Understand and discuss the concept that ties the book together (the members of a family, drawn one at a time).

Analysis of New Book Characteristics

Drawing, Level A

GENRE/FORM
- Fiction

TEXT STRUCTURE
- Girl drawing family members one at a time
- Cumulative, with each page adding another family member
- Summary picture at end

CONTENT
- Familiar family names
- Concept of drawing and adding to the drawing

THEMES AND IDEAS
- Art
- Family members

LANGUAGE AND LITERARY FEATURES
- NA

SENTENCE COMPLEXITY
- One five-word simple sentence on every page
- Present tense
- Repeating pattern on each page with no variation except switch from *a* to *my*

VOCABULARY
- Names of people and pets: *mom, dad, girl, boy, baby, dog, cat*
- Content words: *draw, family*

WORDS
- High frequency words: *I, can, a, my*
- One-syllable words, one two- and one three-syllable word
- See the Word Analysis Charts in the *Program Guide* for specific words in each category.

ILLUSTRATIONS
- Photographs on every right page
- Close match between pictures and text
- Labels on each item in the picture

BOOK AND PRINT FEATURES
- Large font
- Ample space between words
- One line on each page of print
- Print on the left on a blank page; illustrations on the right page, except for last page
- Periods and exclamation point

▸ Rereading Books and Assessment

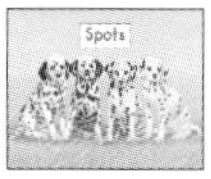

- *Spots*, Level A
- *Playing with Blocks*, Level C

PROMPTING GUIDE 1
Refer to *Prompting Guide 1* as needed.

- Listen to one child read *Playing with Blocks* as you code the reading behavior on the Recording Form, have a brief comprehension conversation, and make a teaching point that you think will be most helpful to the reader. Score and analyze the Reading Record following the lesson.
- Have the other children reread *Spots* and then *Playing with Blocks.*
- Prompt for use of language structure; e.g., "Think what would sound right?" or "Listen to this. Does that sound right?"

▸ Phonics/Word Work

- **PRINCIPLE** Recognizing and using ending consonant sounds and the letters that represent them: *b, m, t, d, g, n, p, f, l, r, s, z, x, ss, ll, tt, ck*

"Words can end with the same sound and letter."
"You can match letters and sounds at the end of a word."

- Suggested language: "You have been learning about the ending sound in words. Today you are going to match ending sound with a letter."
- Place letter cards *p, g, l, d, t, m* in the right column of the pocket chart. (If children are still having trouble with ending sounds, cut down on the number of letters.)
- Show picture cards *rug, net, jeep, bird, bed, girl, cup, carrot, sheep, drum, dog, flag, goat, ball, jam* one at a time. Have children say the word pictured, listen to the ending sound, match the ending sound to its letter, and place the picture card in the left column across from the letter card.
- Notice how quickly children are able to identify the ending consonant sounds.

My Writing Book

- Have children choose one picture with an ending sound that they know well. Have them glue the picture into *My Writing Book* and write the word, focusing on the last letter. Then have children highlight the last letter.

▸ Writing About Reading

Independent Writing

- **MY WRITING BOOK**
- **PROMPTING GUIDE 1**

Refer to *Prompting Guide 1* as needed.

- If time allows, you may want to begin by having each child read recent pages from *My Writing Book.* Occasionally ask the child to locate a word in a sentence read.
- Talk with the children about things the boy and girl built in their city. Ask children to write about two or three of them in *My Writing Book.* For example:

  Pam made a house with blocks.
  Tim made a wall with blocks.
- You should expect accurate writing of easy high-frequency words. When children want to write words such as *made, Pam, Tim,* use sound boxes to have them say the word slowly and write letters for the sounds that they hear. Fill in the rest.
- Use the whiteboard to show how to write words like *house* and *blocks.*
- Prompt for an uppercase letter to start the sentences and for end punctuation.
- If time allows, you may want to write a sentence on a strip for each child, cut the strip apart, and have children put the sentence together again.

▸ New Book

Drawing,
Level A

PROMPTING GUIDE 1
Refer to *Prompting Guide 1* as needed.

PROMPTING GUIDE 1
Refer to *Prompting Guide 1* as needed.

Introducing the Text

- Introduce children to the book by talking about the kinds of things that the children like to draw. Suggested language: "This little girl is drawing a picture. In the story, she will tell about all of the things that she can draw."
- "Turn to page 2. What does the girl say she can draw? Yes, she says she can draw a mom. Say the word *can*. Find can and put your finger under it."
- "Now turn to page 6. What does the girl say she can draw? Yes, she says she can draw a girl."
- "Turn back to the beginning and read *Drawing* to find out about all the things the girl can draw."

Reading the Text

- You should expect the children to read the text accurately. If they make errors, simply say, "Something wasn't quite right" to show that you expect that the child will be able to fix it.

Discussing and Revisiting the Text

Invite children to talk about the book. Some key understandings children may express are:

- The girl is drawing a lot of things. [Extend by asking for examples, showing the pages, e.g., mom, dad, girl, boy, baby, dog, cat.]
- The girl drew her whole family. [Extend by asking children who they would draw.]

Teaching Points

- Based on your observations, use *Prompting Guide 1* to select a teaching point that will be most helpful to the readers.
- You may want them to locate one or two words in the text.

▸ Optional Letter/ Word Work

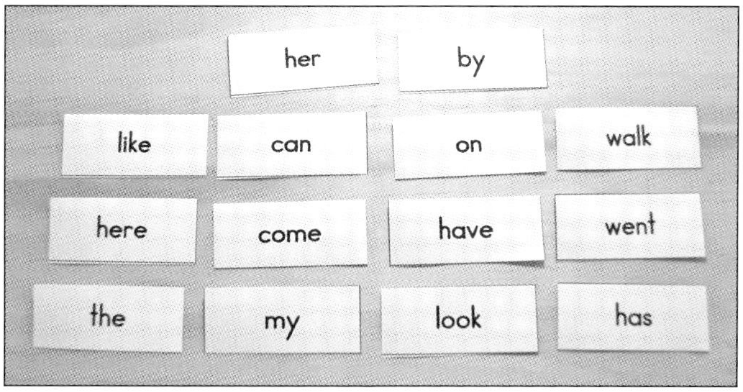

- Tell children to take out their high-frequency word cards from their word bags and read the cards.
- Have children lay out their high-frequency word cards for a game. As you name a feature of a word, have children find the word card, read it, and put it into their word bags. Suggested language: "Find a word that begins with *c*." "Find a word that ends in *s*." "Find a word that ends with a silent *e*." "Find a word that ends with *k*." Help children gain flexibility in following the directions for finding known words.

Classroom Connection

- Give the children the fold sheet with the cut-up sentence, *I made a building with the blocks.* Have children cut up the sentence and take it back to the classroom (see *Lesson Resources CD*).
- Have children put the sentence together and illustrate it on their fold sheet.
- Have the children reread the Take-Home Book *Playing With Blocks.*

Home/School Connection

- Give them the Take-Home Book *Playing with Blocks* to read to family members.
- Have children take home their fold sheets and cut--up sentence to remake and glue on the sheet.
- Have children play a word sorting game.

Assessing Reading and Writing Behaviors

Observe to find evidence that children can:

- use meaning, language structure, and visual information to solve problems while reading.
- demonstrate self-monitoring and self-correcting.
- reflect the meaning of the punctuation through varying the voice.
- actively search for information.
- say words slowly, identify the easy-to-hear sounds, and write the letters that represent the sounds.
- start sentences with an uppercase letter and use end punctuation.
- understand that the girl is drawing her family.
- make connections to their own lives.

Supporting English Language Learners

To support English language learners, you can:

- **recognize** that using the prompts, "Think what would sound right" or "Does that sound right?" might not be helpful for English language learners because these children are just learning the structure of English.
- **demonstrate** what you mean by "matching ending sounds with letters." Be sure children understand the concept of "ending."
- **name** the picture cards for children, if necessary.
- **think aloud** about your own family when discussing the book with children. Encourage children to talk about their family or friends.
- **extend** children's language in a conversational way, rather than correcting.
- **support** children using the past-tense verbs.
- **ask** children to repeat a sentence with you several times to reinforce the structure.
- **demonstrate** saying words slowly and be sure children say them.
- **tell** children that there are some words that they don't need to say slowly. These are words that they just know how to write quickly.

Professional Development Links

When Readers Struggle: Teaching that Works
Chapter 16: Processing Texts: Teaching for Fluency. Use this chapter to understand the importance of pausing and phrasing in early reading.

Guided Reading: Good First Teaching for All Children
Chapter 14 (pp. 177–182). Use this chapter to explore how the processing system for reading changes over time. Figure 14-1 has detailed descriptions of how reading instruction changes over time.

Voices on Word Matters: Learning About Phonics and Spelling in the Literacy Classroom
Chapter 9 (pp. 106–107). Use this chapter to review the importance of picture sorting.

SYSTEM **Orange**

NEW BOOK ***Helping***

GENRE **Fiction**

YOU WILL NEED

- Take-Home Book, *Drawing*
- "Zoom, Zoom, Zoom," enlarged poem
- highlighter tape

From the CD:

- *My Poetry Book*✓
- Lotto cards
- word cards for Lotto
- fold sheet
- Parent Letter

NEW BOOK

Helping, Level C

REREADING

Playing with Blocks, Level C

Drawing, Level A

Goals

- Self-monitor and self-correct reading
- Recognize and use ending consonant sounds.
- Connect words by ending consonant sounds.
- Notice and use punctuation--exclamation point and comma.
- Reflect the meaning of the punctuation through raising and lowering the voice.
- Use known words, first letters, and word parts to self-monitor and self-correct while reading.
- Use meaning, language structure, and visual information to solve problems while reading.
- Make connections between events in a text and children's own lives.
- Understand that the text is showing what children can do to help the family.

Analysis of New Book Characteristics

Helping, Level C

GENRE/FORM

- Fiction

TEXT STRUCTURE

- Narrative
- Series of eight scenes showing two children helping with chores
- Scenes build to the last page when they "help" eat ice cream.

CONTENT

- Familiar home activities
- Concept of doing chores to help the family

THEMES AND IDEAS

- Family--helping grandmother
- Cooperation
- Sharing chores

LANGUAGE AND LITERARY FEATURES

- Relationships shown in illustrations
- Nameless characters who have good attributes

SENTENCE COMPLEXITY

- Two sentences on each page, except last page
- Sentences three- to seven-words long, except on last page
- Repetition of sentence patterns with variation in the tasks and some variation in order of sentences
- Present tense
- Verbs and objects
- Use of *too*, set off by commas, to mean *also*

VOCABULARY

- Names of chores: *make the beds, pick up the books, pick up the toys, feed the cat, wash the dishes, rake the leaves, carry the bags, eat the ice cream*
- Pronouns: *us, we*

WORDS

- High-frequency words: *look, at, us, we, can, make, the, up, and, too*
- One-syllable words with one two-syllable word
- See the Word Analysis Charts in the Program Guide for specific words in each category.

ILLUSTRATIONS

- Drawings on every right page
- Close match between pictures and text

BOOK AND PRINT FEATURES

- Large font
- Ample space between words
- Three to four lines on each page of print
- Print on the left on a blank page; illustrations on the right page, except for last page
- Periods, commas, exclamation point

▸ Rereading Books

- *Playing with Blocks*, Level C
- *Drawing*, Level A

PROMPTING GUIDE 1
Refer to *Prompting Guide 1* as needed.

- Invite children to reread *Playing with Blocks* and *Drawing*.
- Prompt for solving words by using known words, e.g., "Do you know a word like that?"

▸ Phonics/Word Work

Zoom, Zoom, Zoom

Zoom, zoom, zoom
I'm going to the moon.
If you want to take a trip,
Climb aboard my rocket ship.
Zoom, zoom, zoom,
I'm going to the moon.

- **PRINCIPLE** Recognizing and using ending consonant sounds and the letters that represent them: *b, m, t, d, g, n, p, f, l, r, s, z, x, ss, ll, tt, ck*

"Words can end with the same sound and letter."
"You can match letters and sounds at the end of a word."

- Display the chart with the poem "Zoom, Zoom, Zoom" (poem 12). Reread it with the class, then have children read it in *My Poetry Book*.
- Suggested language: "You have been learning about ending sounds of words. Look at your poem and find a word that ends in *n*. Say the word, and then highlight the -*n* ending." Children should locate *moon*, say it, and highlight it with highlighter tape or a marker.
- Repeat the process with *m, d, t, p*. Children should notice more than one word for *m* and *p*.
- "Now find and say a word with the -*ing* ending. Highlight the -*ing* ending." Children should find *going* and highlight the -*ing*. "Noticing the ending of a word can help you read it."

▸ New Book

Helping,
Level C

Introducing the Text

- Introduce the story by talking with children about how they help around the house. Tell them that the boy on the cover is helping to rake the leaves. Then read the title, *Helping*. Suggested language: "What are some ways you can help your family around your house? The children in this story like to help in the house. They tell all the ways they can help."
- "Turn to page 2. The boys say, 'Look at us!' What letter comes first in *look?* Yes, and it's an uppercase *L* because it is the beginning of the sentence. Find look and put your finger under it. Get a good look at it and say *look*."
- "And what else can the boys do to help? Yes, so they say, 'We can help make the beds.' Say *we*. What letter comes first in *we?* Find the word we and put your finger under it. Get a good look and say *we*."
- "Turn to pages 4 and 5. What can the boys help to do now?" Repeat with pages 10 and 11, 12 and 13, and page 16.
- "Now turn to the beginning of the book and read about all the ways the boys say that they can help."

PROMPTING GUIDE 1
Refer to *Prompting Guide 1* as needed.

Reading the Text

- As the children read, prompt for self-monitoring, or checking on themselves, e.g., "Were you right?"
- You may also need to prompt for solving new words, e.g., "That would make sense but does it look right?"

Discussing and Revisiting the Text

Invite children to talk about what happened in the story. Some key understandings children may express are:

- The boys tell how they can help around the house [Extend by asking children to use the pictures in the story to talk about how they help.]
- The boys also helped to eat ice cream. [Extend by asking why this was different from the other ways the boys help in the story.]
- They probably got the ice cream as a reward for all of their hard work. [Extend by asking children to talk about this.]
- This story reminds me of _________. (Accept any reasonable response, e.g., ways that children help in their homes.)

PROMPTING GUIDE 1
Refer to *Prompting Guide 1* as needed.

Teaching Points

- Based on your observations, use *Prompting Guide1* to select a teaching point that will be most helpful to the readers.
- You may want to have the children revisit a page or two so you can demonstrate or reinforce how they can check on themselves.

▸ Letter/Word Work

- Have the children play Lotto with picture cards and ending sounds. (See *Lesson Resources CD* for cards and words.)
- First, have children say the words that the pictures on their cards represent. Have children think about the ending sound.
- Lay out a pile of word cards, draw a card one at a time, show it to children and together say the word. If the child has a picture card with the same ending sound, he can cover the word on the Lotto card. (The word and the picture do **not** need to be an exact match. They only need to have the same ending sound.) The first child to cover the entire Lotto card is the winner.

Classroom Connection

- Give the children a fold sheet with the sentence printed on it: *I can draw my family* (see *Lesson Resources CD*).
- Have them highlight the capital letter (word *I*) at the beginning and the period at the end.
- Have them draw pictures of their families and label them like the girl did in the story.
- Give children the Take-Home Book *Drawing* to reread.

Home/School Connection

- Have the children take home their fold sheets to read to their families.
- If time allows, have them add other family members like aunts and uncles and label them.
- Give them the Take-Home Book *Drawing*.

Assessing Reading and Writing Behaviors

Observe to find evidence that children can:

- hear and identify ending sounds and connect them with letters.
- connect words using ending sounds.
- use meaning, language structure, and visual information to solve problems while reading.
- self-monitor and self-correct while reading.
- reflect the meaning of the punctuation through vocal modulation.
- actively search for information.
- understand the concept of helping, remember some examples of how the boys helped around the house, and understand the ending.

Supporting English Language Learners

To support English language learners, you can:

- **review** the meaning of "Zoom, Zoom, Zoom."
- **review** the concept of ending sounds.
- **help** children in discussing what they do to help at their homes. "At home my children help wash the dishes. What do you do?"
- **expand** children's language in a conversational way, rather than correcting.
- **use** the language of the text in a conversational way. Have children repeat the language to be sure they understand the structure.
- **demonstrate** how the reading of a sentence sounds different when there is an exclamation point.
- **have** children point to and name each way the boys in the story help.
- **use** the pictures to support children in discussing how the boys in the story help out at home. Support children in making connections to what they do at home.
- **ask** children if they were surprised by the ending. If not, ask how they knew what would happen. If they were surprised, show how the bags gave a little hint as to the ending of the book.

Professional Development Links

When Readers Struggle: Teaching that Works
Chapter 16: Processing Texts: Teaching for Fluency. Use this chapter to understand the importance of pausing and phrasing in early reading.

Teaching for Comprehending and Fluency: Thinking, Talking, and Writing about Reading, K–8
Chapter 4 (pp. 47–48). Use this chapter to revisit supporting children in monitoring and correcting reading and searching for and using information.

Chapter 5 (pp. 54–55). Use this chapter to support children in making connections to their personal knowledge, knowledge of the world, and knowledge of text.

SYSTEM **Orange**

NEW BOOK ***Baking***

GENRE **Fiction**

YOU WILL NEED

- Take-Home Book, *Helping*
- *My Writing Book*
- magnet letter set
- word bags

From the CD:

- word cards: *get, want, us*
- Recording Form for *Helping*
- fold sheet
- Parent Letter

NEW BOOK
Baking, Level A

REREADING
Drawing, Level A

Helping, Level C

Goals

- Use what is known about a word to solve an unknown word.
- Read high-frequency words quickly.
- Use known words, first letters, and word parts to self-monitor and self-correct while reading.
- Use meaning, language structure, and visual information to solve problems while reading.
- Say words slowly, identify many sounds, and write the letters that represent those sounds.
- Write high-frequency words quickly.
- Start a sentence with an uppercase letter and write end punctuation.
- Understand and discuss the idea that the monkeys are baking.
- Understand the conclusion (that they have a shop).
- Read the labels on the food in the shop.

Analysis of New Book Characteristics

Baking, Level A

GENRE/FORM
- Fiction

TEXT STRUCTURE
- Two monkeys baking something different on every page
- Summary picture of everything baked at the end

CONTENT
- Familiar foods for most children, although some may need explanation
- Concept of cooking
- Concept of a store

THEMES AND IDEAS
- Food preparation
- Bakery or other food shop

LANGUAGE AND LITERARY FEATURES
- NA

SENTENCE COMPLEXITY
- One four-word simple sentence on every page
- Past tense
- Repeating pattern on each page with no variation.

VOCABULARY
- Names of food: *pizza, bread, pies, brownies, cupcakes, cookies, cake, pie*
- Content words: *baked*

WORDS
- High-frequency words: *we, the*
- One-syllable words and four two-syllable words
- See the Word Analysis Charts in the *Program Guide* for specific words in each category.

ILLUSTRATIONS
- Photographs on every right page
- Close match between pictures and text
- Label on each item in the picture on the last page

BOOK AND PRINT FEATURES
- Large font
- Ample space between words
- One line on each page of print
- Print on the left on a blank page; illustrations on the right page, except for last page
- No print on last page except labels on food items
- Periods

▸ Rereading Books and Assessment

- *Drawing*, Level A
- *Helping*, Level C

PROMPTING GUIDE 1
Refer to *Prompting Guide 1* as needed.

- Listen to one child read *Helping* as you code the reading behavior on the Recording Form, have a brief comprehension conversation, and make a teaching point that you think will be most helpful to the reader. Score and analyze the Reading Record following the lesson.
- Have the other children reread *Drawing* and then *Helping*.
- Prompt readers to each look for and use visual information; e.g., "Does ___ look right?" or, "Think about how the word looks."

▸ Phonics/Word Work

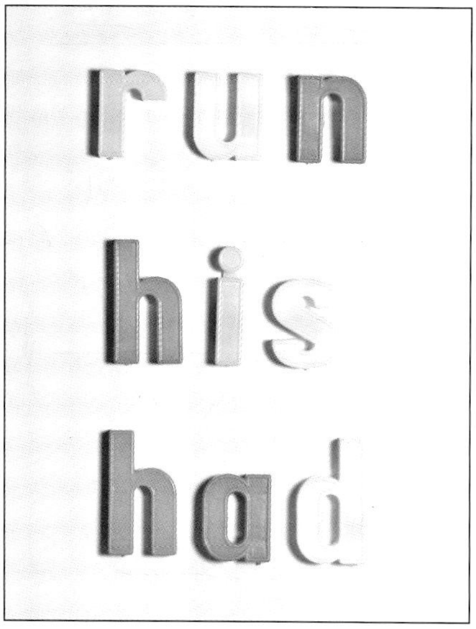

- **PRINCIPLE** Using what you know about a word to solve an unknown word *(her, mother)*

"You can use what you know about a word to read a new word."

- Suggested language: "When you come to a word that is new to you, you can use what you know to read it or write it."
- Show the word *make* with magnetic letters on the whiteboard and have children read it. Then change the *m* to *b* and have them read the new word. Repeat with the letter *r*. Continue showing a word, having the children read it and then making a new word for them to read. Suggested words: *big, bag, bags; run, ran, can; his, him, ham; had, has, hat; rice, nice; an, and, ant; the, then, they;* and *the, this, that.*
- "So you can think about a word you know to help you with new words."

▸ Writing About Reading

Dictated Writing

- **MY WRITING BOOK**
- **PROMPTING GUIDE 1**

Refer to *Prompting Guide 1* as needed.

- If time allows, you may want to begin by having each child read recent pages from *My Writing Book.* Occasionally ask the child to locate a word in a sentence read.
- Dictate the following sentences:

  We can help make the beds.
  We can help feed the cat.
- Encourage the children to write most of the high-frequency words quickly, e.g., *we, can, the.* Show the word *help* quickly on the whiteboard. Use sound boxes to help the children say the other words slowly, listen for the sounds, and hear and write the letters that represent them (e.g., *make, beds, feed, cat*).
- If time allows, write one sentence on a strip for each child, cut the sentence apart, and have the children put the sentence back together again to glue into *My Writing Book* and illustrate.

▸ New Book

Baking,
Level A

Introducing the Text

- Introduce children to the book by showing the cover. Suggested language: "The monkeys on the cover have special hats on. Bakers wear these kinds of hats. And the name of this book is *Baking*. Have you ever baked something with your family? What are some of the things you baked? Well, the monkeys in this story have a bakery. They tell about all the things they baked to sell in their store."
- "Turn to page 2. What did the monkeys bake? Yes, they baked the pizza." Point out the *d* in *baked*.
- "Turn to page 8. What else did they bake?" Children respond.
- "And on the last page you can see all of the things that the monkeys baked."
- "Turn back to the beginning and read *Baking*.

PROMPTING GUIDE 1
Refer to *Prompting Guide 1* as needed.

Reading the Text

- As the children read, you can expect independent problem solving. Reinforce effective problem-solving behaviors.

Discussing and Revisiting the Text

Invite children to talk about the monkeys and what they baked. Some key understandings children may express are:

- Two monkeys are baking lots of things. [Extend by asking children to show pages with pictures of what the monkeys are baking and to describe the pictures.]
- My favorite food in the book is the ________. (Elicit which foods are the children's favorites of what the monkeys made.)
- The monkeys are baking for their shop. [Extend by asking children to explain how they know this.]

PROMPTING GUIDE 1
Refer to *Prompting Guide 1* as needed.

Teaching Points

- Based on your observations, use *Prompting Guide 1* to select a teaching point that will be most helpful to the readers..
- You may also want to revisit a page or two to reinforce self-monitoring or self-correcting behavior.

Optional Letter/ Word Work

- Do more work with the whiteboard, going from known words, or parts, to unknown words.
- Suggested word connections: *mad, made; my, by, try; her, here; got, get, met; went, want; us, bus; mop, stop; the, then.*

Word Bags

- Give children word cards for the new words *get, want,* and *us* and have them read them and add these cards to their word bags.
- Have the children read through their word cards quickly.

Classroom Connection

- Give the children a fold sheet (see *Lesson Resources CD*). At the bottom, it says, *I can help* ________.
- Have the children finish the sentence.
- Have them highlight the capital letter at the beginning of the sentence.
- Have them take the fold sheet back to the classroom to draw a picture.
- Give them the Take-Home Book *Helping* to take back to the classroom and read.

Home/School Connection

- Give the children the Take-Home Book *Helping* to read to their families.
- Have them take home the fold sheet to share.
- If time allows, have children draw and write about ways they can help.

Assessing Reading and Writing Behaviors

Observe to find evidence that children can:

- use meaning, language structure, and visual information to solve problems while reading.
- demonstrate self-monitoring and self-correcting.
- actively search for information.
- say words slowly, identify many sounds, and write the letters that represent them.
- write high-frequency words quickly.
- start a sentence with an uppercase letter and write end punctuation.
- understand the concept of baking and having a shop.
- make connections to their own lives.

Supporting English Language Learners

To support English language learners, you can:

- **monitor** for understanding of "When you come to a word that is new to you, you can use what you know to read it or write it." Use clear and explicit language when demonstrating examples.
- **introduce** the concept of a bakery, if necessary.
- **use** the language of the text in a conversational way. Have children repeat the language structure to become familiar with the past tense word *baked*.
- **explain** to children that *baked* means that the monkeys already cooked it.
- **spend** some time on page 16 to help the children use the labels for the items of food.
- **use** the pictures as support for discussing the story and how the monkeys feel. Be sure children understand that the monkeys did all the baking for the bakery.
- **extend** children's language in a conversational way, rather than correcting. Children might say *bakeded*. Respond with, *Yes, they baked.*
- **ask** children to repeat the dictated sentence with you several times to reinforce the structure.

Professional Development Links

When Readers Struggle: Teaching that Works
Chapter 16: Processing Text: Teaching for Fluency. Use this chapter to understand the importance of pausing and phrasing in early reading.

Teaching for Comprehending and Fluency: Thinking, Talking, and Writing About Reading, K–8
Chapter 30 (pp. 521–522). Use this chapter to review teaching, reinforcing, and prompting for fluent, phrased reading.

YOU WILL NEED

- Take-Home Book, *Baking*
- magnetic letters
- word bags

From the CD:

- Verbal Path for the Formation of Letters✓
- Letters Made in Similar Ways
- word cards: *out, play, you, your*
- fold sheet
- Parent Letter

SYSTEM **Orange**

NEW BOOK ***Out to Play***

GENRE **Fiction**

NEW BOOK
Out to Play, Level C

REREADING
Baking, Level A
Helping, Level C

Goals

- Recognize and use phonogram patterns with *-ay*.
- Make and talk about connections between words.
- Reflect the meaning of the punctuation through raising and lowering the voice.
- Use known words, first letters, and some word parts to monitor and self-correct while reading.
- Use meaning, language structure, and visual information to solve problems while reading.
- Notice the problem and solution in the story.
- Make connections between texts.

Analysis of New Book Characteristics

Out to Play, Level C

GENRE/FORM

- Fiction
- Simple Animal Fantasy
- Series (No. 3 in the Bunny series)

TEXT STRUCTURE

- Narrative
- Series of events in which Bunny prepares to go out
- Story problem and resolution

CONTENT

- Familiar activities
- Concepts of umbrella and rain

THEMES AND IDEAS

- Family—relationship mother and daughter
- Problem solving

LANGUAGE AND LITERARY FEATURES

- Character of Bunny similar to young child
- Story carried by dialogue
- Illustrations showing personality of Bunny

SENTENCE COMPLEXITY

- One to two sentences on each page of print
- Sentences three to nine words long
- No repetition of sentence patterns
- Present and past tense
- Dialogue between two speakers
- Prepositional phrases

VOCABULARY

- Names of familiar objects and apparel: *shoes, hat, toys, umbrella*
- Pronouns: *I, you, your, her, my, she*
- Prepositions: *at, out*

WORDS

- High-frequency words: *I, want, to, go, out, said, you, can, get, your, got, her, look, not, my, and, she, went*
- One-syllable words with two multisyllable words
- See the Word Analysis Charts in the *Program Guide* for specific words in each category.

ILLUSTRATIONS

- Soft pastel paintings on every right page
- Close match between pictures and text

BOOK AND PRINT FEATURES

- Large font
- Ample space between words
- One to four lines on each page of print
- Print on the left on a blank page; illustrations on the right page, except for last page
- Periods, commas, exclamation point, quotation marks

▸ Rereading Books

- *Baking*, Level A
- *Helping*, Level C

PROMPTING GUIDE 1
Refer to *Prompting Guide 1* as needed.

- Invite children to reread *Baking* and *Helping.*
- Prompt for solving words, e.g., "Look at the beginning," or "Listen to how I start it."

▸ Phonics/Word Work

- **PRINCIPLE** Using efficient and consistent motions to form letters

"You can make the shape of a letter."
"You can say words that help you learn how to make a letter."

- Suggested language: "When you start letters the right way, you can write them easily. Watch me as I make the letter *l.* Pull down. Watch me as I make the letter *d.* Pull back, around, up and down."
- After you model forming a letter, have the children make it in the air and then in *My Writing Book* a few times. Select those letters that the children are not forming efficiently and work with several letters that start the same way. Be sure you have the children say the language as they form the letter. Eventually, they will not need to use the language. Practice several letters as time allows. (See Letters Made in Similar Ways in the *Lesson Resources CD* and the Verbal Path in *Prompting Guide 1.*)

▸ New Book

Out to Play**,**
Level C

Introducing the Text

- Introduce children to the book by showing the cover. Suggested language: "Look at Bunny Rabbit. Bunny wanted to go out to play, so she said to her mom, 'I want to go out to play.' "
- "Turn to page 2. Say the word *said.* What letter would come first in *said?* Find the word said, and put your finger under it. Get a good look, and say it."
- "Turn to pages 4 and 5. Bunny's mom told Bunny she can go out, but she told Bunny to get some things before she goes. What did she tell Bunny to get?" Children respond. "Say the word *get.* What letter would come first in *get?* Find get, and run your finger under it, and say *get.*"
- "Turn to pages 8 and 9. What did Bunny's mom tell her to get?"
- "Turn to pages 12 and 13. What is the problem?" Children respond. "So what do you think Bunny's mom will tell her about going out to play?"
- "Turn back to the beginning, and read to find out if Bunny went out to play."

PROMPTING GUIDE 1
Refer to *Prompting Guide 1* as needed.

Reading the Text

- As the children read, prompt for using multiple sources of information, e.g., "That makes sense, but does it look right?"
- Prompt for phrased reading and reading the punctuation, if needed.

Discussing and Revisiting the Text

Invite the children to talk about the bunny and how she got ready to go out. Some key understandings children may express are:

- Bunny gets ready to go outside to play. [Extend by asking for examples of what she does. Have children show the pages with their examples.]
- Bunny is excited to go outside. [Extend by asking why.]
- The problem is Bunny's mom says she can't go outside because it's raining. [Extend by asking Bunny's solution to this problem.]
- Bunny felt sad when she thought she couldn't go out to play and happy when she was able to. [Extend by asking why they think this.]
- This story reminds me of other Bunny stories. [Extend by showing the children *My Family* and *Hop, Hop, Hop* and inviting conversations.]

PROMPTING GUIDE 1
Refer to *Prompting Guide 1* as needed.

Teaching Points

- Based on your observations, use *Prompting Guide 1* to select a teaching point that will be most helpful to the readers.
- You may want to revisit any parts of the story in which the children needed support.
- Demonstrate or reinforce the use of more than one kind of information.

▸ Letter/Word Work

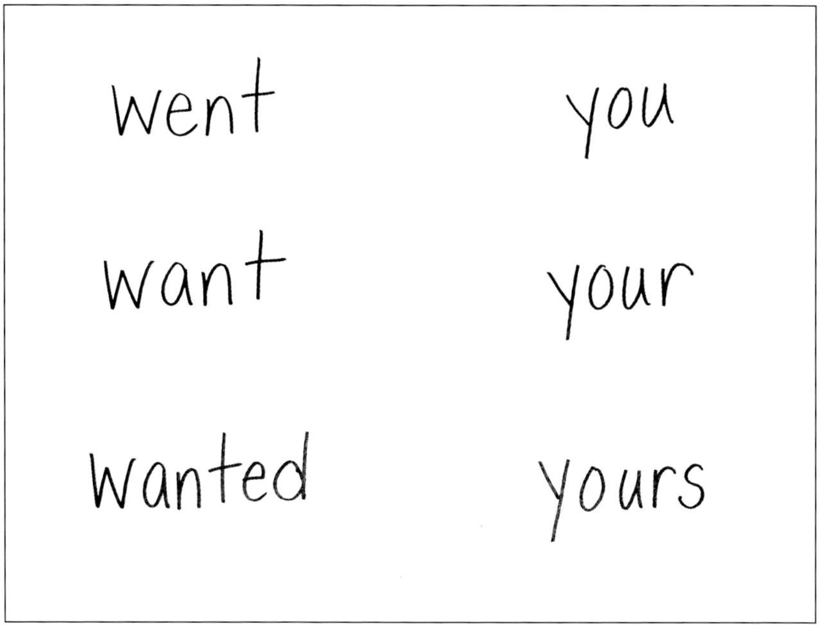

- Do more work with the whiteboard, going from known words or parts to unknown words.
- Suggested word connections: *went, want, wanted; you, your, yours; my, by, try; he, her, here; play, plays, playing; make, bake, baked; day, play, away.*

Word Bags

- Give children the new word cards *out, play, your, you* to read and have them add the cards to their word bags. If time allows, have them make them with magnetic letters.
- Have the children read through their word cards quickly.

Classroom Connection

- Give children the fold sheet to draw and write about two things they like to eat. Have children use the Take-Home book *Baking* as a resource.
- Have children read the Take-Home Book *Baking*.

Home/School Connection

- Give children the Take-Home Book *Baking* to read to family members.
- Have children take the fold sheets home to read to their families. They may draw and write about more foods that they like.

Assessing Reading and Writing Behaviors

Observe to find evidence that children can:

- look at phonogram patterns, letters, and other parts of words to connect them.
- use meaning, language structure, and visual information to solve problems while reading.
- monitor and self-correct reading.
- search actively for information.
- understand that Bunny really wants to go outside and that she has reasons for all the things she does.
- Make connections between this story and other Bunny stories.

Supporting English Language Learners

To support English language learners, you can:

- **use** clear language when demonstrating using known word parts to read new words.
- **use** the language of the text in a conversational way. Have children repeat the language to be sure they understand the structure. Be sure children understand that Bunny is talking to her mom.
- **name** all the objects that Bunny needs.
- **help** children in understanding and pronouncing the past tense verb, *got*.
- **discuss** the difference between *get* and *got*. Explain that when Mom is talking she says *get* because she is saying it right now. When Bunny has the object, the text says *got* because Bunny already did it.
- **use** the pictures to support children in discussing the story. Support them in making connections to other Bunny stories. "Do you remember *My Family*?"
- **expand** children's language in a conversational way, rather than correcting.
- **ask** children if they were surprised by the rain. If not, ask how they knew what would happen. If they were surprised, show how the illustrations show that it will start raining.

Professional Development Links

When Readers Struggle: Teaching that Works
Chapter 10: Learning About Print: Early Reading Behaviors. Use this chapter to understand systems of strategic actions.

Word Matters: Teaching Phonics and Spelling in the Reading/Writing Classroom
Chapter 8 (pp. 80–82). Use this chapter to review how word solvers use what they know about words to figure out new words.

SYSTEM **Orange**

NEW BOOK ***Painting***

GENRE **Fiction**

YOU WILL NEED

- Take-Home Book, *Out to Play*
- *My Writing Book*

From the CD:

- *My ABC Book* ✓
- Verbal Path ✓
- Letters Made in Similar Ways document
- Lotto cards
- word cards for Lotto
- Recording Form for *Out to Play*
- fold sheet
- Parent Letter

NEW BOOK
Painting, Level A

REREADING
Out to Play, Level C
Baking, Level A

Goals

- Self-monitor and self-correct consistently.
- Use what you know about a word to solve an unknown word.
- Read high-frequency words quickly.
- Use known words, first letters, and word parts to self-monitor and self-correct while reading.
- Use meaning, language structure, and visual information to solve problems while reading.
- Write high-frequency words quickly.
- Reread writing to know what to write next.
- Say words slowly, identify sounds, and write letters that represent them.
- Start a sentence with an uppercase letter and write end punctuation.
- Understand and discuss the idea that the boy is painting a whole picture, but he paints one thing at a time.

Analysis of New Book Characteristics

Painting, Level A

GENRE/FORM
- Fiction

TEXT STRUCTURE
- Boy painting a picture, adding something new on each page spread
- Cumulative, ending with a summary picture

CONTENT
- Familiar items for most children

THEMES AND IDEAS
- Family
- Home
- Pets
- Art

LANGUAGE AND LITERARY FEATURES
- NA

SENTENCE COMPLEXITY
- One five-word simple sentence on each page of print
- Present tense
- Repeating pattern on each page with no variation

VOCABULARY
- Names of items in the picture: *tree, flower, house, car, dog, cat, family*
- Content words: *paint, picture*

WORDS
- High-frequency words: *I, can, a, the*
- One-syllable words, two two-syllable words, and one three-syllable word
- See the Word Analysis Charts in the *Program Guide* for specific words in each category.

ILLUSTRATIONS
- Drawings on every right page
- Close match between pictures and text

BOOK AND PRINT FEATURES
- Large font
- Ample space between words
- One line on each page of print
- Print on the left on a blank page; illustrations on the right page, except for last page
- Periods and exclamation point

▸ Rereading Books and Assessment

- *Out to Play*, Level C
- *Baking*, Level A

PROMPTING GUIDE 1
Refer to *Prompting Guide 1* as needed.

- Listen to one child read *Out to Play* as you code the reading behavior on the Recording Form, have a brief comprehension conversation, and select a teaching point that will be most helpful to the reader. Score and analyze the Reading Record following the lesson.
- Have the other children reread *Baking* and then *Out to Play.*
- Prompt readers to search for and use meaning, e.g., "Think about what would make sense," or "Try that again, and think of what would make sense."

Take a Reading Record

▸ Phonics/Word Work

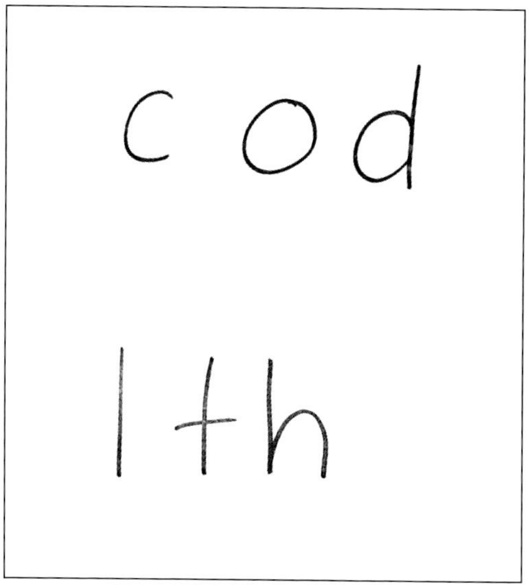

- **PRINCIPLE** Using efficient and consistent motions to form letters

"You can say words that help you learn to make a letter."

- In Lesson 67, you helped children practice using language to help them make letters that they needed to make more efficiently. Review their writing books and your lesson notes to select a few letters to model and have them practice in the air and in *My Writing Book.* Insist on starting the letter in the right way. The following is a list of letters that start in the same way. For example, the following letters start with pull back—*c, o, a, d, g, q*—and the following start with pull down—*l, t, h, b, p, k, i, j.*
- See Letters Made in Similar Ways and the Verbal Path (*Lesson Resources CD*) for a reference.

▸ Writing About Reading

Dictated Writing

- **MY WRITING BOOK**
- **PROMPTING GUIDE 1**

Refer to *Prompting Guide 1* as needed.

- If time allows, you may want to begin by having each child read recent pages from *My Writing Book.* Occasionally ask the child to locate a word in a sentence read.
- Dictate the following sentences:

  I want to go out to play said Bunny.
  Get your hat said Mom.

- You can expect the children to write high-frequency words such as *I, to, go* quickly. Write words like *want, said,* and *Bunny* for children to copy. Also write *out* and *your* on the whiteboard. The children should be able to say the rest of the words slowly and write them. Use sound boxes to support writing *play, get, hat,* and *mom,* if needed.
- Have children reread and illustrate the sentences. When they finish writing, you may want to have them find one or two high-frequency words.

▸ New Book

Painting
Level A

Introducing the Text

- Introduce children to the book by showing the cover. Suggested language: "What do you notice about this little boy? Yes, he is getting ready to paint. In the book, he is painting a picture. On each page, he tells one thing he can paint in his picture. Let's look at what he can paint."
- "Turn to pages 2 and 3. What does the boy say he can paint? Yes, he says he can paint a tree. Find the word can. Run your finger under it, and say *can*."
- "Now turn some of the pages, and look at some of the things the boy can paint."
- "Now turn back to the beginning, and read *Painting*."

PROMPTING GUIDE 1
Refer to *Prompting Guide 1* as needed.

Reading the Text

- As the children read, you can expect a high level of independence and consistent self-monitoring. If they make errors, say something like "Something wasn't quite right" so they can work it out.

Discussing and Revisiting the Text

Invite children to talk about some things they might like to paint. Some key understandings children may express are:

- The boy is painting a lot of things. [Extend by asking for examples. Have children show the pages with their examples.]
- All the things that the boy is painting go together. [Extend by asking children to talk more about that.]

PROMPTING GUIDE 1
Refer to *Prompting Guide 1* as needed.

Teaching Points

- Based on your observations, use *Prompting Guide 1* to select a teaching point that will be most helpful to the readers.
- You may want to revisit a page or two to reinforce self-monitoring or self-correction behavior.

▸ Optional Letter/ Word Work

LOTTO

on	play	her
by	your	out
go	going	but
walk	and	you

- Have the children play Lotto with their more complex high-frequency words.
- One child draws a word card and reads the word (without showing it) while the other children find the word on their Lotto cards. If they have the word, they cover it. The first child to cover all the squares on his card is the winner.
- Lotto cards and word cards are on the *Lesson Resources CD.*

Classroom Connection

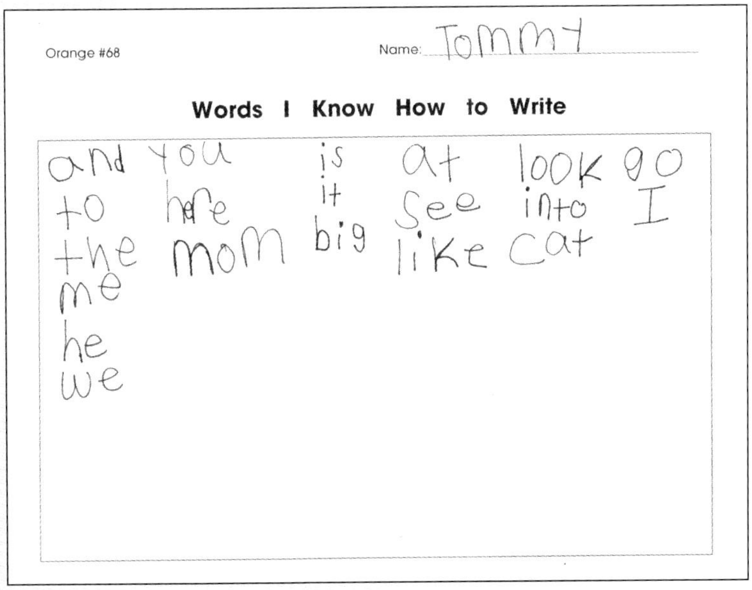
Orange #68 Name: Tommy

Words I Know How to Write

and you is at look go
to here it see into I
the mom big like cat
me
he
we

- Give the children the fold sheet entitled "Words I Know How to Write" to take back to the classroom with the instruction to write all the words they can write. Remind children that you would like them to think of the words they know without looking at words in the classroom.
- Have the children bring this fold sheet back for Lesson 69.
- Give the children the Take-Home Book *Out to Play* to reread.
- Give children *My ABC Book* to read in the classroom.

Home/School Connection

- Have children take the Take-Home Book *Out to Play* home to read to family members.
- Have children take home *My ABC Book* to share with family members.

Assessing Reading and Writing Behaviors

Observe to find evidence that children can:

- use meaning, language structure, and visual information to solve problems while reading.
- self-monitor and self-correct reading.
- search actively for information.
- reread writing to know what to write next.
- say words slowly, identify sounds, and write letters that represent them.
- start a sentence with an uppercase letter and write end punctuation.
- understand that the text shows the process of painting one thing at a time but that the boy really is painting a whole picture.
- make connections to their own lives.

Supporting English Language Learners

To support English language learners, you can:

- **demonstrate** writing new words from words one knows.
- **be sure** children understand all the words being used in Phonics/Letter Word Work.
- **use** the language of the text in a conversational way. Have children repeat the language structure.
- **name** all the objects the boy paints.
- **use** the pictures as support for discussing the story. Ask children what they notice about the last page. Support them in discussing that each item the boy paints is actually in the same large picture.
- **expand** children's language in a conversational way, rather than correcting.
- **ask** children to repeat the dictated sentence with you several times to reinforce the structure.
- **remind** children to say words slowly and listen for the sounds they hear.
- **support** children in using known words to write new words.
- **tell** children that some words cannot be said slowly to record the sounds. They just have to remember how some words look.

Professional Development Links

When Readers Struggle: Teaching that Works
Chapter 10: Learning About Print: Early Reading Behaviors. Use this chapter to understand systems of strategic actions.

Teaching for Comprehending and Fluency: Thinking, Talking, and Writing About Reading, K–8
Chapter 4 (pp. 47–48). Use this chapter to review how to support children's ability to search for and use information.

Classroom Connection

- Give the children the fold sheet with the sentence *I can paint a picture* written at the bottom.
- Have the children take the fold sheet back to the classroom and read the sentence. Then have them draw and color a picture.
- Next, have children label the items in their pictures.
- Have children reread *Painting* in the classroom.

Home/School Connection

- Have children take home their fold sheets to read.
- Give them the Take-Home Book *Painting* to read to family members.

Assessing Reading and Writing Behaviors

Observe to find evidence that children can:

- use meaning, language structure, and visual information to solve problems while reading.
- self-monitor and self-correct reading.
- reflect punctuation and typographical features, such as bold type, in the voice.
- search actively for information.
- understand the central idea of the book, which is the contrast between fast and slow.

Supporting English Language Learners

To support English language learners, you can:

- **demonstrate** using a full stop at a period. Make your voice go down when you see the period. Ask children to repeat after you.
- **model** taking a short breath at the comma. Ask children to repeat after you.
- **demonstrate** using known words/word parts to read/write new words.
- **be sure** children understand the directions of Follow the Path.
- **use** the language of the text in a conversational way. Have children repeat the language to be sure they understand the structure, *This is a....*
- **name** all the animals and their actions.
- **use** the pictures to support children in discussing which animals go fast and which one doesn't.
- **ask** children if they were surprised by the ending.
- **think** aloud about what this book reminds you of and invite children to do the same.
- **expand** children's language in a conversational way, rather than correcting.

Professional Development Links

When Readers Struggle: Teaching that Works
Chapter 10: Learning about Print: Early Reading Behaviors. Use this chapter to understand systems of strategic actions.

Guided Reading: Good First Teaching for All Children
Chapter 12 (pp. 150–151). Use this chapter to understand the importance of supporting pausing and phrasing in early reading.

Thinking Within the Text

Solving Words
- Recognize easy high-frequency words and simple regular words easily with support of meaning and language structure
- Locate the first and last letters of words in continuous text
- Notice the beginning letter of a word, connect to a sound, and say the first sound of a word
- Use letter-sound information in coordination with meaning and language structure to solve words
- Say words slowly to identify first sound, connect to letter, and locate the word in a text
- Recognize ten or more high-frequency words within continuous text
- Make connections between words by letters, sounds, or spelling patterns
- Use known words to make connections and solve words

Monitoring and Correcting
- Reread the sentence to problem solve, self-correct, or confirm
- Self-monitor and self-correct reading using initial letters and connections to sounds
- Self-monitor and self-correct using language structure
- Cross-check one kind of information against another to monitor and self-correct reading (for example, meaning with visual information)
- Self-monitor and self-correct using meaning in text and pictures
- Use known words to self-monitor and self-correct

Searching for and Using Information
- Read left to right across more than one line of print and return to the left to read the next line of print
- Search for and use information in print (letters, sounds, known words)
- Search for and use information from pictures
- Process texts with simple dialogue, all assigned to speakers
- Reread to search for/use information from language or meaning
- Remember and use language patterns to help in reading a text

Summarizing
- Remember information to help in understanding the end of a story
- Remember and use details when discussing a story after reading
- Understand and identify a simple sequence of events in a story

Maintaining Fluency
- Reflect language syntax by putting words together in phrases
- Notice and use ending punctuation and reflect it in the voice
- Notice and use quotation marks and reflect dialogue with the voice
- Demonstrate appropriate stress on words in a sentence

Adjusting
- Slow down to problem solve words and resume reading with momentum

Thinking Beyond the Text

Predicting
- Use knowledge of language structure to anticipate the text
- Make predictions using information from pictures
- Predict the ending of a story based on reading the beginning and middle
- Make predictions based on personal experiences and knowledge
- Make predictions based on information gained through reading

Making Connections
- Make and discuss connections between texts and reader's personal experiences
- Make connections between texts that are alike in some way (topic, ending, characters)

Synthesizing
- Identify what the reader already knows relative to information in the text
- Identify new information in text or pictures
- Remember new information for discussion
- Talk about what the reader already knows about a topic or character prior to reading

Inferring
- Talk about characters' feelings and motives
- Show evidence in the print or pictures to support inference

Thinking About the Text

Analyzing

- Notice and point out connections between text and pictures
- Realize stories have a beginning and an end
- Understand how the ideas in a text are related to the title

Critiquing

- Share opinions about the text as a whole (beginning, characters, ending)
- Share opinions about illustrations

Additional Suggestions for Letter/Word Work

Use a chart or easel, whiteboard, magnetic letters, or pencil and paper to develop fluency and flexibility in visual processing, if needed.

- Recognize a few easy high-frequency words (eg., *the, and, like, here, look, see, is, can, in, it*)
- Make several CVC words (*cat, but, can, hot, get*)
- Recognize several CVC words (for example, *get, sun, man, not*)
- Write/make several easy high-frequency words
- Sort letters quickly by a variety of features (uppercase or lowercase; tall or short; with and without sticks, circles, tails, dots, tunnels)
- Match/sort words with rhymes (using pictures)
- Match pictures with letters using beginning or ending sounds
- Say and clap syllables in one-, two-, and three-syllable words (from pictures)
- Locate words rapidly using first letter and related sounds
- Say words slowly and write letters related to sounds
- Read the Alphabet Linking Chart in a variety of ways (for example, all consonants, all vowels, every other letter)